Virginia Woolf and Being-in-the-world

A Heideggerian Study

Emma Simone

EDINBURGH
University Press

Edinburgh University Press is one of the leading university presses in the UK. We publish academic books and journals in our selected subject areas across the humanities and social sciences, combining cutting-edge scholarship with high editorial and production values to produce academic works of lasting importance. For more information visit our website: edinburghuniversitypress.com

© Emma Simone, 2017

Edinburgh University Press Ltd
The Tun – Holyrood Road, 12(2f) Jackson's Entry, Edinburgh EH8 8PJ

Typeset in 11/13 Adobe Sabon by
IDSUK (DataConnection) Ltd

A CIP record for this book is available from the British Library

ISBN 978 1 4744 2167 6 (hardback)
ISBN 978 1 4744 2168 3 (webready PDF)
ISBN 978 1 4744 2169 0 (epub)

The right of Emma Simone to be identified as the author of this work has been asserted in accordance with the Copyright, Designs and Patents Act 1988, and the Copyright and Related Rights Regulations 2003 (SI No. 2498).

Contents

Acknowledgements	iv
Abbreviations	vi
Introduction	1
1 Being-in-the-world	25
2 A Sense of Place	64
3 Being-at-home and Homelessness	102
4 Historical Dasein	140
5 Moments of Being and the Everyday	182
Confluences, Divergences and Future Directions	229
References	237
Index	252

Acknowledgements

This book had its beginnings as a doctoral dissertation, and as such, I wish to thank my supervisors Marea Mitchell and Robert Sinnerbrink from Macquarie University for their invaluable support, knowledge and advice during my candidature. Many thanks also go to my examiners, Mark Hussey, Jane de Gay and Anthony Uhlmann, for their insightful and inspiring comments and suggestions. Jackie Jones, Adela Rauchova and James Dale from Edinburgh University Press have provided encouragement and guidance, as has my copy editor, Sarah M. Hall. I would like to express my appreciation for the valuable feedback that I received from the two anonymous external Readers who reviewed my initial submission on behalf of Edinburgh University Press.

On a personal level, I must acknowledge the friendship and encouragement that I have received from Michelle Hamadache. In addition, I would like to thank my parents, Les and Dain, as well as my sister, Rebecca. Scott Williams has been a source of love, friendship and laughter. Finally, I must thank three very important people in my life, my children, Patrick, Alex, and Claudia; I am both fortunate and grateful to be surrounded by such loveable, fascinating, complex and inspiring individuals.

Excerpts from *Night and Day, Mrs Dalloway, Between the Acts*, and 'Jane Austen' from the *Common Reader* by Virginia Woolf were reprinted by permission of The Society of Authors as the Literary Representative of the Estate of Virginia Woolf. Excerpt from *Mrs Dalloway* by Virginia Woolf. Copyright 1925 by Houghton Mifflin Harcourt Publishing Company, and renewed 1953 by Leonard Woolf. Reprinted by permission of Houghton Mifflin Harcourt Publishing Company. All rights reserved. Excerpt from *Between the Acts* by Virginia Woolf. Copyright 1941 by Houghton Mifflin Harcourt

Publishing Company. Copyright © renewed 1969 by Leonard Woolf. Reprinted by permission of Houghton Mifflin Harcourt Publishing Company. All rights reserved. Excerpt from 'Jane Austen' from *The Common Reader* by Virginia Woolf. Copyright 1925 by Houghton Mifflin Harcourt Publishing Company, and renewed 1953 by Leonard Woolf. Reprinted by permission of Houghton Mifflin Harcourt Publishing Company. All rights reserved.

Epigraph copyright (1992) from *Acts of Literature* by Jacques Derrida, edited by Derek Attridge. Reproduced by permission of Taylor & Francis Group, LLC, a division of Informa plc.

Some of the material in Chapter 4 was previously published in the *Virginia Woolf Miscellany*, Vol. 89.

Abbreviations

Works by Virginia Woolf

BA	(2000), *Between the Acts*, ed. S. McNichol, London: Penguin.
D1–5	(1977–84), *The Diary of Virginia Woolf*, ed. A. O. Bell, 5 vols, San Diego: Harcourt Brace & Company.
Flush	(1998), *Flush*, ed. K. Flint, Oxford: Oxford University Press.
JR	(2000), *Jacob's Room*, ed. K. Flint, Oxford: Oxford University Press.
Letters 1–6	(1975–80), *The Letters of Virginia Woolf*, ed. N. Nicolson and J. Trautmann, 6 vols, Orlando: Harvest/Harcourt Brace Jovanovich.
MD	(1996), *Mrs Dalloway*, Australia: Penguin.
ND	(1992), *Night and Day*, London: Vintage.
O	(2000), *Orlando*, ed. B. Lyons, London: Penguin.
PA	(1990), *A Passionate Apprentice: The Early Journals, 1897–1909*, ed. M. A. Leaska, San Diego: Harcourt Brace Jovanovich.
RO	(2000), *A Room of One's Own* in *A Room of One's Own; Three Guineas*, ed. M. Schiach, Oxford: Oxford University Press.
'Sketch'	(2002), 'A Sketch of the Past', in V. Woolf, *Moments of Being*, new edition, ed. J. Schulkind, London: Pimlico, pp. 78–160.
TG	(2000), *Three Guineas*, in V. Woolf, *A Room of One's Own; Three Guineas*, ed. M. Schiach, Oxford: Oxford University Press.
TL	(1992), *To The Lighthouse*, London: Vintage.
TW	(2000), *The Waves*, ed. K. Flint, London: Penguin.

TY	(2002), *The Years*, ed. J. Johnson, London: Penguin.
VO	(2001), *The Voyage Out*, ed. L. Sage, Oxford: Oxford University Press.

Works by Martin Heidegger

BT	(2004), *Being and Time*, trans. John Macquarrie and Edward Robinson, Malden, MA: Blackwell.
FC	(1995), *The Fundamental Concepts of Metaphysics: World, Finitude, Solitude*, trans. William McNeill and Nicholas Walker, Bloomington: Indiana University Press.

To my children, Patrick, Alex and Claudia, who continue to call me back to the wonder of the everyday.

No doubt I hesitated between philosophy and literature, giving up neither, perhaps seeking obscurely a place from which the history of this frontier could be thought or even displaced . . .

Jacques Derrida (1992: 34)

Introduction

Referring to the work of the English writer, Virginia Woolf (1882–1941), and the German philosopher, Martin Heidegger (1889–1976), Heidi Storl suggests that a 'discussion of the seemingly unlikely alliance between these two thinkers generates new strategies by which to "look through" much of our daily experience and discover – even if only momentarily – what it is to *be* human' (2008: 303). Despite the marked variances between Woolf and Heidegger in terms of their backgrounds, experiences, vocations, nationalities and political orientations, this book proposes that at the heart of the issue of what it means to be an individual making his or her way in the world, the perspectives of Woolf and Heidegger are founded upon certain shared and profound overarching concerns. Such areas of concern include, but are certainly not limited to, the sustained critique of Cartesian dualism, particularly the resultant binary oppositions of subject and object, and self and Other; an understanding of the individual as a temporal being; the emphasis upon intersubjective relations, insofar as Being-in-the-world is defined by Being-with-Others; and a consistent emphasis upon average everydayness as both determinative and representative of the individual's relationship to and with the world.

The focus of this study is Woolf's understanding and representation of the connection between self and world throughout the various forms of her writings from the perspective of the notion of 'Being-in-the-world', a term coined by Heidegger in his 1927 text, *Being and Time*, which refers to an existential-phenomenological analysis of the connection between human beings and the world from the point of view of lived experience and average everyday involvements within particular physical, societal and historical contexts. It is from such a perspective that references to the term 'world' throughout the following chapters denote 'the web of our social and cultural relations, our relations to artifacts, and our relations to nature' (Thiele 1995: 179). In *Being and*

Time, Heidegger refers to human beings as 'Dasein'; in its everyday German usage, this term possesses an ontological emphasis that is in keeping with Heidegger's focus in *Being and Time*, in that it refers principally to 'the type of Being that is distinctive' of human beings (Mulhall 2003: 14). Stephen Mulhall notes that while other terms that have typically been used to denote human beings have become encumbered with applied meanings that 'could only be prejudicial to Heidegger's enquiry', the appeal of 'Dasein' is that it is a *'tabula rasa*: devoid of misleading implications' (2003: 14). Heidegger places particular emphasis upon the unique position of Dasein in that, in contrast to other entities, 'Being is an *issue* for it' (*BT*: 32); that is, Dasein has an awareness of its own existence.

The subject of this book is Woolf's textual approach to the associations between self and world, where Heidegger's text provides a persistent point of reference, one that reflects and represents not only the similitude of their perspectives, but also the marked divergences of their approaches. It is intended that a reading of Woolf's *oeuvre* from the perspective of Heidegger's philosophy becomes a means of complementing, illuminating, and extending particular aspects of this prolific writer's work.

A shared context – war and modernity

One of the more obvious connections between Woolf and Heidegger is their historical contemporaneity. Although there is no evidence, nor any likelihood, that Woolf ever came into contact with Heidegger's *Being and Time* – which was not translated into English until 1962 – the textual representations of Being-in-the-world created by both these individuals came to be influenced by a shared context that included the forewarnings, eventualities and outcomes of two World Wars. Reflecting a sense of the shared response that permeated the globe in the aftermath of the First World War, George Steiner remarks that

> there is a distinct sense in which *Sein und Zeit* [*Being and Time*], for all its erratic singularity, does belong to the same climate of catastrophe and the same quest for alternative vision as do T. S. Eliot's *The Waste Land* or Hermann Hesse's *Blick ins Chaos*. (1991: 75–6)

The extent to which Woolf's writing career was framed by a context of war – past, present and future – is demonstrated by the fact that her first novel, *The Voyage Out*, was published in the midst of the First World War, while her final novel, *Between the Acts*, was written during the outbreak of the Second World War, and published posthumously in 1941. For Woolf and her contemporaries, the subject of war is an inescapable backdrop to the everyday lived experience. Such a view is expressed in April 1941 in a tribute to Woolf in the *Times Literary Supplement*, published in the weeks following her death:

> Between one great war and another the work of Virginia Woolf has been begun and ended. We cannot look back on it yet, for it is part of us and of our day – of our tormented day, for no moment of which, since 1914, has there been any comforting sense of stability. Every position has been shown to rest on sand, every rock proved to be a congeries of darting particles, nothing that we perceive but is inexorably conditioned by motion and time. Being a poet, with a peculiar sensitivity, Virginia Woolf saw this before we were aware of it. (Anonymous 1941: 175)

It is far from surprising that such a context and its concerns come to be translated into Woolf's writings; for example, novels such as *Jacob's Room* (1922), *Mrs Dalloway* (1925), *The Waves* (1931), *The Years* (1937), and *Between the Acts* (1941) each emphasise the intractable interpenetration of individual and world through their allusions to war. As a committed pacifist, Woolf could neither understand nor condone armed conflict. In her 1938 polemic, *Three Guineas*, Woolf emphasises her sense that the current milieu is dominated by a patriarchal discourse that encourages war, resulting in far-reaching implications for all citizens of the world; it is from such a perspective that Woolf proclaims that: 'A common interest unites us; it is one world, one life' (*TG*: 365).

Yet, it is not simply a world overshadowed by wars that provides a common context for the writings of both Woolf and Heidegger; arguably, an influential and ubiquitous backdrop for these individuals is the age of modernity. Definitions of 'modernity' differ considerably depending on context and emphasis; as such, alongside Zygmunt Bauman, it is acknowledged that this 'concept is fraught with ambiguity, while its referent is opaque at the core and frayed at the edges' (1991: 4). In his discussion of Woolf's writings, Michael Whitworth comments that the 'aesthetic phenomenon of modernism needs to be understood in its relation to the social and historical phenomena of modernity'; Whitworth asserts that such works were 'not conceived in isolation from modernity, but in dialogue with it; sometimes in reaction against modernity, sometimes drawing aspects of modernity into its form and texture' (2010: 107). Such a reactionary approach to modernity is reflected in Michael E. Zimmerman's *Heidegger's Confrontation with Modernity: Technology, Politics, and Art*, where he details the 'rationalist, scientific, commercialist, utilitarian, anthropocentric, secular worldview usually associated with *modernity*' (1990: xiii). Describing Heidegger's critique and dismissal of the tenets of modernity, Zimmerman explains that, alongside many of his fellow German citizens, the philosopher

> hated materialism, scientific reductionism, the decline of community, the evils of urban life, spiritual decay, atomistic individualism, and alienation from the transcendent dimension. Like other reactionaries, he rejected the economic and political values of the Enlightenment and called for a new social order that could arise only by returning to Germany's primal roots. (1990: 4)

While extensive discussions of the significance of the shared contexts of war and modernity from the perspective of Woolf and Heidegger can be relevant and revealing in terms of furthering understandings of both the individuals and their respective writings, a theoretical approach based on contextual confluences does not, in itself, always provide the most convincing outcome or argument. Indeed, there are always multiple processes and tendencies occurring in a given historical, social, cultural, political, economic and ideological context, so that identifying that selected authors, philosophers, or theories are contemporaneous does not always tell us very much. Such an understanding is reflected in Whitworth's observation that 'Woolf was acutely aware of the dangers inherent in generalisation and, in exploring her modernism, we need to acknowledge her differences from, as well as her similarities to, a generalised "modernism"' (2006: 147). As Woolf attests in her 1917 review entitled 'Romance': 'Evidently it is a good thing to avoid, "except for pastime, the discussion of tendencies and movements", and stick as far as we can to the men and the books' (1987: 74).

Indeed, sticking as far as we can to the woman, the man and the books, the elucidation of affinities between Woolf's writings and Heidegger's *Being and Time* gives greatest emphasis to the thematic and conceptual links found within the texts of these two individuals, many of which are clearly influenced or triggered by their shared historical context. As such, the focus of this book is not an explication of Woolf and Heidegger's relationship to modernity; rather, the emphasis is upon the confluences, as well as divergences, of their responses and treatments of particular key issues and areas of concern that are foregrounded or complicated by the age of modernity, against the backdrop of war. Alongside the immeasurable private, communal and national influences that differentiate Woolf and Heidegger as individuals, the experiences of, and the responses to, the prevailing milieu inform and shape, to varying and fluctuating degrees, the shared overarching areas of concern that are represented and reflected in their respective works.

While the purpose throughout this book is to discuss and highlight significant points of confluence in terms of Woolf and Heidegger's understandings and representations of the relationship between self and world, it must be acknowledged that there are also fundamental points of difference in terms of the approaches of each to the notion of Being-in-the-world. Such an admission does not, however, detract from the purpose and legitimacy of this study; indeed, acknowledgement of such disanalogies results in a more comprehensive understanding of the perspectives of both these individuals. Arguably, in terms of Woolf and Heidegger's respective understandings of Being-in-the-world, the principal point of difference pertains to both the personal and textual political orientations and engagements of each.

Woolfian politics

Demonstrated throughout the following chapters is the understanding that Woolf's writings reflect a persistent preoccupation and concern with the explication and critique of the individual's everyday encounters with the dominant social order located in England in the late nineteenth century and the first half of the twentieth century. While Woolf frequently communicates a call – albeit usually muted or deliberately veiled – for social reconfiguration, such a focus upon the political and ideological dimensions of Being-in-the-world differs markedly from Heidegger's ontological emphasis and apolitical stance in the 1920s.

The focus and parameters of this book do not lend themselves to a detailed explication of Woolf's significant and life-long engagements in matters and issues that might be broadly defined as political; nevertheless, some consideration of the political perspectives of both Woolf and Heidegger can only enhance and supplement the understanding and appreciation of their respective textual approaches to Being-in-the-world. Throughout this book, notions of the 'political' and 'ideological' are repeatedly referred to within the context of my discussions of Woolf's personal and textual understandings and representations of Being-in-the-world. In terms of a working definition of the former much-cited and nevertheless frequently undefined term, it is in keeping with that posited by Terry Eagleton, who refers to 'the political' as 'the way we organize our social life together, and the power-relations which this involves' (2002: 169). In terms of 'ideology', this is understood as an

> organizing social force which actively constitutes human subjects at the roots of their lived experience and seeks to equip them with forms of value and belief relevant to their specific social tasks and to the general reproduction of the social order. (Eagleton 1991: 222–3)

Woolf's textual representations of the relationship between self and world have determined the course of the analysis and the areas of emphasis throughout this book; it is from such a basis that the exploration of Woolf's awareness, depiction and critique of the prevailing social order comes to be a dominant and determinative preoccupation throughout this study. In his discussion of the experiences of English men and women during the period between the wars, Leonard Woolf claims that: 'our lives and the lives of everyone have become penetrated, dominated by politics' (1975: 27). Describing his wife's response to such an environment, Leonard Woolf argues that, contrary to the views expressed by 'literary critics or autobiographers who did not know her', Virginia Woolf

> was intensely interested in things, people, and events, and . . . highly sensitive to the atmosphere which surrounded her, whether it was personal, social, or historical. She was therefore the last person who could ignore the political menaces under which we all lived. (1975: 27)

As Woolf writes in 'The Artist and Politics', an essay published in 1936 in the communist newspaper, the *Daily Worker*:

> That the writer is interested in politics needs no saying . . . the novelist turns from the private lives of his characters to their social surroundings and their political opinions. Obviously the writer is in such close touch with human life that any agitation in his subject matter must change his angle of vision. (1981a: 180)

Woolf's acute sense of the representative connections between 'social surroundings' and the social order is foregrounded throughout her 1938 polemic, *Three Guineas*, where she calls on women to think in offices; in omnibuses; while we are standing in the crowd watching Coronations and Lord Mayor's Shows; let us think as we pass the Cenotaph; and in Whitehall; in the gallery of the House of Commons; in the Law Courts; let us think at baptisms and marriages and funerals. Let us never cease from thinking – what is this 'civilization' in which we find ourselves? (*TG*: 243–4)

Melba Cuddy-Keane provides a detailed description of the 'atmosphere' that surrounded Woolf during the span of her writing career, thereby conveying a sense of the vast and varied issues that influenced the political impetus of Woolf's writings, including:

> War and escalating world conflicts, with concomitant counter-movements for peace; the closely related theme of the domination of imperial powers, with, following WWI, concerns (though lesser than ours) about minority and ethnic rights; the position of women – shifting, however, from agitation for the vote and political representation before WWI to issues concerning the family or what has been termed 'welfare feminism' in the interwar years; the burgeoning effects of advertising and propaganda, especially as disseminated through mass media, on a susceptible public – aggravated, in Britain, by additional anxieties about cultural and economic Americanisation; related concerns about the levelling effects of democracy and a consequent focus on the development of working-class and adult education; economic hardship and the depression; censorship and morality; self-rule in India; the royal family and their doings; hygiene and public health – the list could expand at some length. (2010b: 236)

This milieu is characterised by the emergence and dislocation of power-relations across the nation and around the globe; as demonstrated in the following chapters, in the midst of such a confronting and ever-changing national and international context, the focus of Woolf's politically orientated 'angle of vision' is evidenced in the various forms of her writings through her sustained exploration of issues such as war and nationalism, patriarchal discourse, the relationship between education and the social order, and class stratification. Emphasising the importance of both acknowledging and understanding the climate of change and upheaval that defines the political framework of the first half of the twentieth century that surrounded Woolf and her contemporaries, Alex Zwerdling suggests that 'To offer a minimally adequate account of Woolf's social vision demands first of all that her work be seen in the context that produced it, the network of assumptions and traditions she inherited or absorbed' (1986: 36).

When one's gaze is turned to the milieu in which Woolf wrote, it becomes ever clearer that this writer's political values and orientations were not produced in a vacuum. Nevertheless, it was not simply external events and forces that impacted upon Woolf's sustained critique of the social order; Woolf's social circle – including the diverse group of individuals who were associated with the Bloomsbury Group – generated significant influences upon her political understandings and perspectives. Reflecting upon the broad scope of Woolf's theoretical and grass roots knowledge of contemporary political affairs, Zwerdling observes that

> there is no doubt that the more political and historical interests of people like John Maynard Keynes, Beatrice and Sidney Webb, Margaret Llewelyn Davies, Ray Strachey, Ethel Smyth, and, most important, her husband greatly expanded the range of her vision. Their methods were not hers; she was not a social reformer. Yet a writer who teaches for several years at an evening college for working-class men and women, who marries a Fabian socialist and attends Labour Party conferences, who spends time working for the Adult Suffrage movement, who presides at meetings of the Women's Co-operative Guild held in her own house, and who writes significant texts for the feminist and pacifist cause can hardly be accused of political indifference. (1986: 29)

Nevertheless, as Leonard Woolf acknowledges in his 1967 autobiography, critical reception of Woolf's work has tended towards the view that her writings lack engagement with the concerns of the material world. Such a perspective is reflected in David Bradshaw's observation in 2000 that 'it is only relatively recently that the degree to which her novels seem conceived to extend our ethical and political "sympathies" has begun to be recognised' (2006: 191). In the same year, Anna Snaith surmises that 'The image of Virginia Woolf as a writer divorced from the public realm continues to surface ... The idea persists that Woolf's life and writing are somehow apart from reality' (2000: 113). Drawing attention to the progressive acknowledgement and interest in the political dimensions of Woolf's writings, in 2010 Cuddy-Keane comments that

> A substantial body of research has documented the consistency and pervasiveness of Woolf's anti-war and anti-fascist protests; growing attention is being paid to her treatment of illness and social and medical attitudes toward the body; and work has arguably only begun on such topics as her critique of the way public institutions mould their citizens ideologically, or her cultural analysis of the demographic, physical and economic shift from rural to urban life. (2010b: 234)

As critics have rightly suggested, views of Woolf's writings as essentially apolitical are often founded upon her own particular insistence that the writer should not interrupt or dominate his or her works of fiction with intrusive personal didactic assertions (Carroll 1978: 101; Zwerdling 1977: 69–70). In her 1928 essay, 'The Novels of George Meredith', Woolf critically observes that this Victorian novelist

> cannot, even to hear the profoundest secret, suppress his own opinion. And there is nothing that characters in fiction resent more. If, they seem to argue, we have been called into existence merely to express Mr. Meredith's views upon the universe, we would rather not exist at all. Thereupon they die. (1966b: 230)

Such a view is reflected a year later in *A Room of One's Own*, where Woolf declares that throughout *Jane Eyre*, 'anger was tampering with the integrity of Charlotte Brontë the novelist. She left her story, to which her entire devotion was due, to attend to some personal grievance' (*RO*: 95).

In contrast to such authorial intrusions, Zwerdling observes that 'social, historical, and political issues enter the world of Woolf's fiction – not as "issues" but as forces that stamp the fabric of mental and emotional life' (1986: 31). Further to this, Zwerdling remarks that

> Woolf's own methods as a social critic, then, studiously avoid propaganda or direct statement. For her, fiction is a contemplative, not an active, art. She observes, describes, connects, provides the materials for a judgment about society and social issues; it is the reader's work to put the observations together and understand the coherent point of view behind them. (1977: 69)

Reflecting the success of her enterprise, Bradshaw writes that 'we often feel the reach and intensity of Woolf's socio-political vision, but never the push of her hand' (2006: 191).

In terms of Woolf's approach to Being-in-the-world, the following chapters will demonstrate that three social issues are afforded particular emphasis throughout her writings: the situation of women located in patriarchal society; the role and impact of England's class divides; and the associations between nationalism, imperialism and war. Just as a broad range of social issues come to be interwoven throughout Woolf's writings, each of these areas of concern will be approached from a variety of perspectives.

Heidegger as political conservative

Although Woolf and Heidegger are located within the same historical context, clearly the experiences and perspectives of these two individuals were also uniquely shaped by the respective national contexts of post-First World War England and Germany. While both nations suffered extensive and devastating losses, the sense of national desolation experienced by Germany after the Great War was of a tenor that differed in a number of respects from experiences elsewhere. Steiner's 1991 introduction to *Martin Heidegger* provides a valuable overview of the intellectual response in post-First World War Germany, where 'a constellation of books unlike any others produced in the history of Western thought and feeling' was produced; Steiner suggests that writers such as Ernst Bloch, Oswald Spengler, Karl Barth and Franz Rosenzweig 'sought to build a capacious house of words where that of German cultural and imperial hegemony had collapsed' (1991: viii).

Steiner observes that the 'climate of 1918 is such as to compel and permit a more or less enhanced remembrance of the civilities, of the cultural stabilities, of the pre-1914 world' (1991: viii). Such a point of view is reflected in Zimmerman's discussion of the historical and social context of Germany at the turn of the twentieth century, in which, 'Deeply threatened by the advances of modernity and industrial technology, many Germans wanted to defend the traditional ways of life which they believed were essential to German identity. Heidegger shared these concerns' (1990: 3). As discussed in Chapter 4, Heidegger's conservative understanding of tradition, as a necessary cultural horizon and reservoir of present and future possibilities, lies in sharp contrast to Woolf's condemnation of what she views as the propensity of tradition to define, justify and control the possibilities and potentialities open to the individual within society.

Reflecting a further divergence in their approaches to Being-in-the-world, while Woolf's anti-imperialist stance is emphasised throughout her writings, Heidegger's approach to the notion of authentic historical repetition is open to an imperialist – as well as post-colonial – reading, in that a society's collective past is understood to be determinative of its future destiny. Arguably, Heidegger's critique of the 'cosmopolitan' character of 1920s Weimar Germany is evident in *Being and Time* through his representation of the notion of 'homelessness', which can be viewed as indicative of his political conservatism and concomitant rejection of the tenets of modernity.

Rüdiger Safranski explains that in response to the 'democracy of the Weimar Republic', Heidegger, like the majority of German academics, 'places himself above the parties and looks down with contempt on the business of politics' (2002: 169). As noted, while traces of Heidegger's political conservatism are evident throughout his text, the impetus of *Being and Time* is to 'identify the essential – "ontological-existential" – structures that determine the being of beings' (Aho 2005: 16). In contrast to Woolf's conscious engagement in a critique of the social order throughout her writings, Heidegger's focus and intent in *Being and Time* is fundamentally apolitical in nature. Reflecting a defining point of difference in terms of Woolf and Heidegger's textual representations of the relationship between self and world, the phenomenological descriptions and analyses of world undertaken by Heidegger do not automatically lead or relate to an ideologically oriented critique of the issues that are of particular significance to Woolf, such as gender, class, social hierarchies and exclusions, and inequalities of power. In her discussion of feminist reception of Heidegger's philosophy, Patricia Huntington observes:

> One might wonder how Heidegger could be useful to feminist theory, given that he was not primarily a political thinker. Nor was he *explicitly* concerned with social ontology, contemporary issues of sexual identity, moral epistemology, or social ethics. He was above all else a profound thinker on the human condition as such . . . To the extent that fostering a healthier human condition holds implications for social ontology, ethics, philosophy of liberation, and spiritual freedom, Heidegger's deliberately suprapolitical corpus allows feminist theorists to engage and learn from his thought. (2001: 1–2)

Since the aim of *Being and Time* is a formal analysis of the ontological structures of temporal existence, this text is not concerned with the politics of the prevailing social order.

Nevertheless, while Safranski acknowledges the absence of political engagement in *Being and Time*, he does posit the sombre warning that: 'So far Heidegger has found his moments of intensity mainly in philosophy. Before long he will also find them in politics' (2002: 170). Clearly referring to Heidegger's future involvement in the Nazi Party, Safranski's statement demonstrates that Heidegger's 1927 text comes into existence prior to this dark period in the philosopher's personal and national history. As Steiner affirms, 'written during the early 1920s', *Being and Time* 'fully predates National Socialism'

(1991: xxiv). Describing the circumstances of Heidegger's official involvement in this regime, Leslie Paul Thiele explains that

> In May 1933, Heidegger accepted the post of rector of Freiburg University and became one of the small number of university professors to join the Nazi Party. Heidegger claims . . . and his claim is largely supported by his former students and colleagues, that until he accepted the position of rector he had no involvement and little interest in political affairs. (1995: 133)

Insofar as Heidegger's 'political sympathies for Nazism were not reflected in his philosophy' (Safranski 2002: 227) in *Being and Time*, throughout this book limited attention is afforded to his associations with National Socialism.

Approaching the writings of Woolf and Heidegger

Throughout this book, understandings of Woolf's representation of the connection between self and world is founded upon the study of all forms of her writings, including letters, diary entries, articles, essays, reviews, short stories and novels. Such a broad scope reflects an intention to investigate Woolf's biographical, fictional and non-fictional writings, in the sense that the combination of these diverse forms and perspectives creates a comprehensive view of Woolf's approach to Being-in-the-world. In terms of Woolf's novels, final published versions, rather than draft manuscripts, have been the object of study; as far as the other forms of Woolf's writings are concerned, her prolific output means that it is inevitable that certain relevant texts will not be examined within this book; nevertheless, it is hoped that the included examples of Woolf's writings will inspire further readings and explorations of her texts.

The purpose of this book is to survey the recurrent understandings of, and approaches to, Being-in-the-world throughout Woolf's *oeuvre*, rather than to provide a definitive reading of any one text; as such, each of the following chapters is focused upon the explication of particular issues and aspects of Being-in-the-world, as opposed to the in-depth study of a single text. For instance, discussions of Woolf's 1939 memoir, 'A Sketch of the Past', are found in each chapter, reflecting the variety of ways in which Woolf's sense of Being-in-the-world comes to be represented in a single text. Such an approach clearly differs from a methodology that is posited upon a chronological study of Woolf's *oeuvre*, which potentially imposes 'a linear development on her art that the novels themselves do not support' (Hussey 1986: xi). As emphasised in Chapter 4, such notions of linear progression are called into question and dismissed by both Woolf and Heidegger.

As stated, the examination of Heideggerian philosophy in this book has been limited almost exclusively to *Being and Time*, even though a number of the philosopher's earlier and later texts are clearly relevant from the perspective of Woolf's textual representations of Being-in-the-world. The principal explanation is pragmatic in nature: undertaking a study of Woolf's extensive *oeuvre* alongside a number of Heidegger's dense and complex texts lies far beyond the scope of a single-volume work. Exceptions include extensive references to Heidegger's treatment of the mood of boredom in his 1929/30 lecture course, *The Fundamental Concepts of Metaphysics: World, Finitude, Solitude*, in the final chapter of this study. The rationale for the inclusion of this particular text is reflected in Paul Gibbs's assertion that 'The contribution of Heidegger's work on boredom might be seen as an extension of *Being and Time* in its phenomenological approach to the everydayness of our lived experience' (2011: 604). Other references to Heidegger's earlier and later works, such as the 1951 essay 'Building Dwelling Thinking', are made with the intention of drawing attention to both the foundations and extensions of Heidegger's treatment of particular issues relating to Being-in-the-world that are located in *Being and Time*.

Throughout this book, the themes and preoccupations that are representative of Woolf's textual approach to the relationship between self and world have guided and determined those areas of *Being and Time* that receive greatest emphasis; as a result, it must be acknowledged that certain aspects of Heidegger's work that may typically be considered central to his philosophy receive relatively limited discussion, particularly when compared to seemingly peripheral issues. The fundamental point to reiterate is that it is Woolf's writing, rather than Heidegger's philosophy and the structure of his text, which governs the structure and focus of this book.

Critical context

That Woolf possessed no formal training in philosophy is unsurprising given her sustained critique of women's exclusion from formal education; as Ann Banfield remarks: 'In the British tradition and at no time more markedly than in Woolf's formative years, philosophy was a discipline largely confined to those who had passed through either Cambridge or Oxford' (2000a: 27). In *A Room of One's Own*, Woolf draws attention to her ensuing reticence in terms of philosophical proclamations, stating that 'philosophic words, if one has not been educated at a university, are apt to play one false' (*RO*: 143). Despite her lack of formal education, Woolf privately studied classic Greek and Latin literature, including Plato, during her adolescent years under the guidance of Walter Pater's sister, Clara, and the 'Cambridge-trained classicist', Janet Case (Lee 1996: 143).

In terms of influences that have been purported to have informed Woolf's understanding of philosophical matters and perspectives, a number of studies have undertaken to emphasise the sway of Bertrand Russell and G. E. Moore upon Woolf's writings, including S. P. Rosenbaum's 'The Philosophical Realism of Virginia Woolf' (1971), Jaakko Hintikka's 'Virginia Woolf and Our Knowledge of the External World' (1979), and Banfield's more recent monograph, *The Phantom Table: Woolf, Fry, Russell, and the Epistemology of Modernism* (2000a). As both Russell and Moore were associated with the Bloomsbury Group, the understanding that Woolf was familiar with both the men and their work is beyond dispute. And while markers such as shared nationality, historical context, and social ties might point to the potential for a close convergence between Woolf and the work of Moore or Russell, I am unable to locate any convincing or sustained correspondence between Woolf's literary 'philosophy' and that of either of these philosophers. Indeed, I am in agreement with those critics who refute claims of significant philosophical affinities, such as Hussey, who observes that the 'Moorean universe, endorsed by such as Russell and Keynes, is continually questioned by the novels' of Woolf (1986: 99); as James Hafley bluntly asserts, 'Although a superficial consideration of Moore's doctrine . . . does suggest Virginia Woolf's "moments of being," the smallest amount of reflection makes evident a complete lack of correspondence between the two' (1963: 4–5).

Referring to *The Phantom Table*, Christy L. Burns states that Banfield's assertion of Woolf's 'thick connection to the philosophy of Bertrand Russell', not only 'refutes the accepted construct of Virginia Woolf's aesthetic as one marked by rebellion against rationality and logic', but also 'contradicts the established image of Woolf as a feminist who resisted high British imperialism's insistence on the superiority of Western reason and control' (2002: 471, 472). While acknowledging the valuable contribution that Banfield's detailed study makes to Woolfian scholarship, as the following chapters demonstrate, the view that Woolf's writings are in some measure representative of the analytic philosophy of Russell or Moore runs contrary to the central argument of this study, which contends that Woolf's *oeuvre* consistently demonstrates a phenomenological approach to Being-in-the-world.

In terms of recent scholarly criticism, the study of modernist works from a phenomenological perspective has attracted increased interest. Such a response is evidenced by the 2006 Oxford conference entitled 'Phenomenology and Modernism', which resulted in Carole Bourne-Taylor and Ariane Mildenberg's edited collection, *Phenomenology, Modernism and Beyond* (2010). In her review of this work, Cleo Hanaway draws attention to 'Notable modernism and phenomenology studies from the last five years' (2011: 338–9), including Jennifer Anna Gosetti-Ferencei's *The Ecstatic Quotidian* (2007), Ulrika Maude and Matthew Feldman's edited collection *Beckett and Phenomenology* (2009), Cheryl Herr's 'Walking in Dublin' (2006) and 'Being in Joyce's World' (2009), and AnnKatrin Jonsson's *Relations* (2006). Reflecting an emphasis that is also central to the concerns of this book, Jonsson begins her monograph with the assertion that a 'phenomenological manner of thinking' can be located 'in Anglo-American modernism, a thinking that, like phenomenology, involved a new way of perceiving the relationship between subject and world' (2006: 13).

In 'G.E. Moore's Table and Chair in *To the Lighthouse*', Erwin R. Steinberg makes the highly controversial claim that

> Over the years critics have argued that Virginia Woolf's fiction echoes the philosophy of, variously, Henri Bergson, Plato, G.E. Moore, John McTaggart, Bertrand Russell, Friedrich Nietzsche, Sigmund Freud, and C.G. Jung. Since many of these men professed widely differing philosophies, the only conclusion that can be drawn from all of these mutually contradictory claims and counterclaims is that, in her novels, Virginia Woolf does not espouse, adhere to, instantiate, or even reflect the ideas of any particular philosopher or philosophy. (1988: 161)

As the following chapters will demonstrate, the notion that Woolf's writings are without philosophical insight or foundation is one that is strongly refuted; as Mark Hussey asserts: 'I have *always* thought of Woolf "among the philosophers"; indeed, I think of Woolf *as* a philosopher' (2013: 88). Reflecting such a perspective, in March 2013, leading Woolfian scholars met in Paris at the international conference entitled 'Virginia Woolf Among the Philosophers' to discuss this issue from a variety of critical perspectives.

Providing an overview of the conference proceedings, Chantal Delourme reflects upon its 'plurality of approaches', as well as the opportunity it affords participants to 'step back and reappraise the conversations between literary texts and philosophical discourses that have always been present in the critical and philosophical reception of Virginia Woolf's work' (2013: 1). Demonstrating the diversity of such 'conversations', conference participant Scott McCracken discusses the affinities between Woolf and the philosophy of Walter Benjamin (2013); Isabelle Alfandary draws parallels between Woolf and Friedrich Nietzsche's work (2013); J. Hillis Miller suggests that 'Edmund Husserl, Henry James, Maurice Blanchot, Jacques Derrida, and Wolfgang Iser' each 'had ideas similar' to those of Woolf (2013: 118); S. P. Rosenbaum (2013) and Ann Banfield (2013) both build upon earlier assertions about the influence of G. E. Moore on Woolf's writing; Christine Froula (2013) refers to the philosophy of Michel de Montaigne in relation to Woolf's work; Rachel Bowlby (2013) brings Bertrand Russell, G. E. Moore, Charles Baudelaire and Sigmund Freud into contact with Woolf; Edna Rosenthal relates 'Woolf's aesthetics' to 'the Aristotelian critical tradition' (2013: 277); Naomi Toth (2013) reads *To the Lighthouse* from the perspective of Edmund Husserl and Maurice Merleau-Ponty's phenomenology; Jane Goldman (2013) discusses Woolf's textual representation of canines with reference to the philosophy of Jacques Derrida; and Marie-Dominique Garnier suggests that 'Woolf's writing literally . . . forms a "philosophical" alliance with a number of major concepts in Deleuze and Guattari' (2013: 504). It is of particular note that Mark Hussey is the only conference participant to make reference to the presence of affinities between Woolf and Heidegger's philosophy; nevertheless, Hussey makes no explicit reference to *Being and Time* in his presentation.

Despite the profusion of critical responses to Woolf's writings, the textual relationship between Woolf and Heidegger has received limited attention within both Woolfian and Heideggerian scholarship.[1] While certain theorists acknowledge the presence of marked confluences in the respective works of these individuals, there appears to be a reticence by some critics in terms of developing and furthering the study of these connections. Such a response is reflected in Banfield's discussion of 'temporality in modernism' and its relation to Woolf's *To the Lighthouse*; while acknowledging Heidegger's significant and contemporaneous study of the notion of 'time', Banfield nevertheless decides against further reflection upon his work due to the understanding that *Being and Time* 'was not a direct influence on any of the modernists writing in English' (2000b: 43). Although Paul Ricoeur briefly draws attention to a parallel between the work of Woolf and Heidegger with respect to Clarissa Dalloway's approach to Being-towards-death in *Mrs Dalloway*, he nevertheless includes the proviso: 'if we may dare to apply to her this major existential category of *Being and Time*' (1986: 110).

While connections between the writings of Woolf and Heidegger have been thoughtfully touched upon by a relatively limited number of critics, the relationship between Heidegger's *Being and Time* and Woolf's *oeuvre* is an area that has yet to be studied in any sustained manner. As Hussey observes in his 1986 monograph, *The Singing of the Real World: the Philosophy of Virginia Woolf's Fiction*:

> As far as I know, only Graham Parkes . . . and Lucio P. Ruotolo in his *Six Existential Heroes: The Politics of Faith* . . . have drawn attention to the remarkable similarities in the contours of Woolf and Heidegger's thinking about being. As they do, I would stress that there is absolutely no question of 'influence' raised here. (1986: 159, n9)

Within his study, Hussey draws attention to a number of parallels between Woolf's writings and Heidegger's philosophy in *Being and Time*; in particular, Hussey reflects upon Heidegger's evocation of the Greek conception of philosophy commencing in '*Thaumazein*' (xv) – understood as the mood of 'wonder' – stating that 'Wonder at simply being at all is the starting point of Woolf's exploration of the human situation' (1986: xv, 100). Further to this, through a series of endnotes, Hussey observes that manifestations of the Heideggerian issues of 'nothingness', 'anxiety' (162, n3), the '*they-self*' (161, n1), and 'authenticity' (161, n6) can be located throughout Woolf's writings.

In terms of the acknowledgement and utilisation of published literature that touches upon the connections between Woolf's writings and *Being and Time*, the relevant findings of such scholarship are incorporated throughout the chapters of this book. Nevertheless, in order to situate this book within the critical context, a concise overview of critical responses will be provided. In 'Imagining Reality in *To the Lighthouse*', Graham Parkes fleetingly posits the view that Woolf's writings might be read from the perspective of 'the Continental European traditions of existentialism and phenomenology': in particular, the philosophies of Heidegger and Nietzsche (1982: 43,

44, n13). Reflecting a central notion that runs throughout this study, Parkes claims that

> since there appears to have been no influence operating between Woolf and the existential thinkers, the surprising congruence of many of their ideas suggests that they may be approaching from different disciplines and directions some of the same truths about human existence. (1982: 43)

In his 1973 monograph, *Six Existential Heroes: The Politics of Faith*, Lucio P. Ruotolo draws attention to the convergence of the sense of 'nothingness' that is recorded by Woolf in a 1929 diary entry, and the fact that only months earlier:

> Martin Heidegger, appointed to the chair of philosophy at Freiburg, delivered his inaugural lecture on the primacy of such an experience. Heidegger's assertion that man must face nothing in order to be something, and Virginia Woolf's literary treatment of the dilemma she acknowledged in her own life, characterize the ontological reformation that with Schelling and Kierkegaard had begun to transform Western culture. (1973: 13)

Ruotolo cites *The Voyage Out, The Years, The Waves* and *Mrs Dalloway* as literary examples of Woolf's engagement with this Heideggerian notion (1973: 13, 18, 30). Referring to *Mrs Dalloway*, Ruotolo suggests that this novel, 'like Heidegger's now classic study, explores nothingness within the context of Being and time' (1973: 18). Drawing upon Woolf's 1924 essay, 'Mr. Bennett and Mrs. Brown', Ruotolo states that 'Woolf, like Heidegger, asks, What is Being? Both novelist and philosopher charge their contemporaries with uncritically accepting society's concept of reality' (1973: 14). Ruotolo also notes certain parallels between Woolf and Heidegger's representations of intersubjective relations in Woolf's essay (1973: 16). In *The Interrupted Moment: A View of Virginia Woolf's Novels*, Ruotolo again highlights the parallels between Heidegger's philosophy and Woolf's interest in the 'experience of nothingness' (1986: 145) during the period in which she was engaged in the writing of *The Waves*.

In 'Nature and Community: A Study of Cyclical Reality in *The Waves*', Madeline Moore suggests that

> Undoubtedly Woolf's 'moments of being' have much in common with Heidegger's beliefs. In Heideggerian terms, the experience of anguish and wonder reveals us to ourselves as 'existents' when we traverse certain experiences like anguish which put us in the presence of nothingness from which Being erupts. (1980: 221)

Suzette A. Henke also describes the affinities between Woolf's treatment of nothingness and wonder in *The Waves* and Heidegger's philosophy in 'Virginia Woolf's *The Waves*: A Phenomenological Reading' (1989: 467); further to this, Henke reflects upon Woolf's representation of the Heideggerian notions of authenticity and Being-with-Others in this novel (1989: 462, 464). A decade later, in a chapter entitled 'Virginia Woolf's *To the Lighthouse*: (En)Gendering Epiphany', Henke refers briefly to Woolf's representations of death and 'care-taking' in her 1927 novel as Heideggerian in nature (1999: 269, 271).

In '"We All Put Up With You Virginia": Irreceivable Wisdom about War', Roger Poole details his understanding – albeit at times contentious – of the parallels that might be drawn between Woolf and Heidegger's philosophy from the perspective of notions such as 'the They', 'Thrownness', 'Idle Talk', 'Curiosity', and 'Falling' (1991: 88). In *The Subject of Modernism: Narrative Alterations in the Fiction of Eliot, Conrad, Woolf, and Joyce,* Tony E. Jackson refers to Woolf's depiction of nothingness in the final chapter of *The Waves* as 'a moment of Heideggerian vision'; Jackson observes that Woolf's representation of death in this chapter is indicative of Heidegger's notion of Being-towards-death (1994: 157, 159–60). In her 2001 monograph, *The Philosophy of Virginia Woolf: A Philosophical Reading of the Mature Novels*, A. O. Frank highlights various points of convergence in terms of Woolf's writings and Heidegger's philosophy; nevertheless, a sustained discussion of the relationship between the two individuals is not the intention of her study.

More recently, in *Modernism, Feminism, and the Culture of Boredom* (2012), Allison Pease discusses affinities between Woolf's representation of boredom in *The Voyage Out* and Heidegger's philosophy. Sara Crangle's essay, 'The Time Being: On Woolf and Boredom', refers to Heidegger's understanding of 'boredom' and its relation to Woolf's personal and literary representations of this notion (2008). Also published in 2008 is Storl's 'Heidegger in Woolf's Clothing', which posits the understanding that Woolf and Heidegger's disruption of the Cartesian subject and object dualism may be understood as symptomatic of their shared understanding of the individual's primordial state of Being-in-the-world. In his 2011 monograph, *Hellenism and Loss in the Work of Virginia Woolf,* Theodore Koulouris briefly draws parallels between Woolf's approach to the 'act of "writing"' and Heidegger's philosophy of Being; while Jason Wakefield's 'Mrs. Dalloway's Existential Temporality' (2013) reflects upon the affinities between Woolf's novel and Heidegger's understanding of the 'temporality of being.' In the second chapter of his 2013 dissertation, 'Metaphor and Metanoia: Linguistic Transfer and Cognitive Transformation in British and Irish Modernism', Andrew C. Wenaus discusses Woolf's *To the Lighthouse* 'amidst an assemblage of Martin Heidegger's early speculations on the temporality of being' (2013: 90).

As a result of the relative sparsity of studies that explicitly draw connections between Woolf's writing and Heidegger's *Being and Time*, my own research has principally relied upon those scholars whose interest in either Woolf or Heidegger has been directed towards the particular areas of concern that are discussed in this work. From the perspective of Woolfian scholarship, Hermione Lee's extensive and unparalleled study of the biographical details of Woolf's life and their relationship to, and impact upon, her writings has provided a significant source of reference. Susan M. Squier's studies concerning the political dimensions of Woolf's depictions of the city of London are particularly relevant to discussions in the second chapter of this book, as is Youngjoo Son's 2006 monograph, *Here and Now: The Politics of Social Space in D. H. Lawrence and Virginia Woolf*. The work of Jane de Gay has also proved useful, most particularly in terms of her pronouncements concerning Woolf's complex stance towards organised religion (2009). In Chapter 3, various discussions by the political philosopher, Iris Marion Young, provide a significant and cogent backdrop to discussions of the 'lived body' and 'Being-at-home'.

Research by Melba Cuddy-Keane provides valuable insights into the scope and form of Woolf's political engagements (2010b), as well as her 'historical practice' (1997), as reflected in the reading of Woolf's critique of traditional historical discourse in Chapter 4. In terms of analysis of Woolf's questioning and disruption of historicism within that chapter, Angeliki Spiropoulou's 2010 study, *Virginia Woolf, Modernity and History: Constellations with Walter Benjamin* was an informative source. Both the fourth and final chapters incorporate the findings of Teresa Prudente's 2009 monograph, *A Specially Tender Piece of Eternity: Virginia Woolf and the Experience of Time*, from the perspective of Woolf's approach to the notion of temporality throughout her writings. The final chapter of this study draws upon Morris Beja's 1971 study, *Epiphany in the Modern Novel*, in addition to the insightful research pertaining to Woolf's 'moments of Being' contained in Lorraine Sim's 2010 study, *Virginia Woolf: The Patterns of Ordinary Experience*.

Alongside my own readings and interpretations of Heidegger's *Being and Time*, as well as the thought-provoking insights of

Dr Robert Sinnerbrink from the Macquarie University Department of Philosophy, the research and perspectives of a number of Heideggerian scholars working in the fields of philosophy, politics and human geography have proved invaluable. Thiele's commentary and analysis of issues such as homelessness, the everyday, moods and boredom has greatly influenced and informed the book's approach to Heidegger's philosophy. Jeff Malpas's explication of Heidegger's relationship to place in *Place and Experience: A Philosophical Topography* (1999) and *Heidegger's Topology: Being, Place, World* (2006) proved to be particularly relevant and useful, alongside Edward S. Casey's extensive discussion of Heidegger's sense of place in *Being and Time* in *Getting Back into Place: Towards a Renewed Understanding of the Place-World* (1993). Charles R. Bambach's 1995 study, *Heidegger, Dilthey, and the Crisis of Historicism*, provides a useful theoretical background in terms of the relationship between the German post-First World War milieu and Heidegger's critique of traditional historical discourse.

Content and structure

The chapters of this book are organised under a series of headings that signify those elements of Being-in-the-world that are particularly pertinent and representative of Woolf's focus of concern throughout her *oeuvre*. The chapters have been ordered to complement and build upon each other so as to form a trajectory that leads the reader through Woolf's understandings and representations of Being-in-the-world in a systematic manner. In Chapter 1 a comprehensive overview of the Heideggerian understanding of Being-in-the-world is presented, placing particular emphasis upon the ways in which this notion relates to Woolf's writings. Providing a foundation and context for the discussions that are to follow in the remaining chapters, key Heideggerian concepts relating to Being-in-the-world are defined and discussed, including 'Being-with-Others'; the average everyday mode of 'theyness'; and 'authentic' and 'inauthentic' modes of Being. Emphasised throughout this chapter are the ways in which Woolf and Heidegger's understandings of the relationship between self and world lie in sharp contrast to the Cartesian dualism that separates subject and object, and self and Other.

In the second chapter, the significance of the notion of 'place' throughout Woolf's *oeuvre* is explored. Sharing affinities with the Heideggerian perspective, Woolf's writings both demonstrate and reinforce the significance of place as an essential aspect of the individual's state of Being-in-the-world. For both Woolf and Heidegger, place becomes the means by which individuals form connections not only with the Other, but also with the past. Throughout her *oeuvre*, Woolf privileges an existential understanding of place; setting is rarely represented as an inert backdrop or a geographic co-ordinate on a map. Woolf demonstrates that the individual's everyday involvements are always already inextricably connected to particular physical contexts. Diverging from the focus of Heidegger's analysis in *Being and Time*, for Woolf, place is understood as both a literal and figurative representation of the prevailing social order. With respect to her accounts of everyday life in the city of London in the first half of the twentieth century, Woolf emphasises the ways in which public places and spaces encourage or prohibit the entry of particular individuals based upon attributes such as class and gender: it is from such a perspective that Woolf's concern is repeatedly directed to the ways in which women located in English society come to be situated as 'outsiders-within.'

In Chapter 3, the previous focus upon place is narrowed to that of 'home', an element of Being-in-the-world that is granted particular significance throughout Woolf's writings. Having reflected upon the understanding of women as outsiders-within in the previous chapter, Heideggerian understandings of 'not-Being-at-home', 'thrownness', and 'theyness' are drawn upon in order to explore Woolf's representations of women in the private space as 'homeless at home.' From her autobiographical accounts, to her essays and her fiction, Woolf emphasises the ways in which the physical spaces of the home – including its objects, and architectural features such as doors and rooms – are representative of a social order that privileges class distinctions, the strict adherence to the prescriptions of patriarchal discourse, and the dualisms of public and private, and insider and outsider. Nevertheless, Woolf's textual representations of homelessness are not confined to the subject of women within the private sphere; reflecting a recurrent preoccupation throughout her writings, Woolf explores the sense of homelessness and deep unease experienced by social 'outsiders' such as Septimus Smith in *Mrs Dalloway*, and Louis and Rhoda in *The Waves*, each of whom unveil, question and reject society's call for conformity and compliance. In contrast to these outsiders who are not-at-home in the world, for both Woolf and Heidegger, it is the individual who unquestioningly immerses him or herself in the sway of the prevailing constructs and prescriptions of 'theyness' who is most likely to feel 'at-home' in the world.

Having discussed Woolf's representations of certain spatially defined aspects of Being-in-the-world in the previous two chapters, Chapter 4 details Woolf's treatment of the relationship between self and world from the perspective of 'time', a subject that is a predominant area of concern in Heidegger's seminal text. Specifically, attention is drawn to both Woolf and Heidegger's critiques of the metaphysical perspective that defines time as linear, successive and dominated by a homogeneous present. In contrast to such understandings, for Woolf and Heidegger, time is defined by the heterogeneous unity of past, present and future. It is from this perspective that the individual is viewed as a temporal – and therefore historical – being: the basis of his or her present and future possibilities is founded upon both the personal and collective past. Throughout her *oeuvre*, Woolf reflects upon the individual's average everyday unquestioning immersion in the concerns and preoccupations of the present at the expense of an acknowledgement of his or her inherent temporality. Woolf emphasises the role of traditional historical discourse as a means of strengthening and justifying the political and ideological framework of patriarchal society, through the exclusion and marginalisation of the average everyday lives of ordinary individuals, particularly women and the lower classes, at the expense of accounts of 'great men' and 'grand events', such as war and imperialism.

The final chapter of this study examines what are understood to be the most convincing affinities in terms of Woolf and Heidegger's understandings of Being-in-the-world. Drawing attention to Woolf and Heidegger's respective notions of 'moments of Being' and 'moments of vision', the ways in which such moments, always ephemeral in nature, are triggered by particular moods that are experienced by the individual are discussed. Disrupting the individual's everyday inauthentic immersion in the preoccupations and prescriptions of the present, such moments provide the potential for the disclosure of the typically concealed extraordinary nature of the ordinary. Divided into two sections, this chapter begins with a discussion of the significance and history of the literary epiphany, and draws attention to the influence of precursors such as Thomas Hardy, Joseph Conrad and William Wordsworth upon Woolf's writings. In the second section, attention is directed to a number of Heideggerian notions – including 'anxiety', 'nothingness', 'boredom', 'wonder' and the 'numinous' – in terms of their relations to the Woolfian 'moment'. Acknowledged and demonstrated throughout this chapter is Woolf's emphasis upon the significance of art as both an origin and site of the epiphanal moment.

While the reading of Woolf's work from the perspective of Heidegger's *Being and Time* discloses a mostly unexamined understanding of this writer's approach to the relationship between self and world, as the following chapters will also demonstrate and explore, Heidegger's understanding of the notion of Being-in-the-world takes on new, and clearly never-intended, directions and connotations when viewed through the lens of Woolf's writings. Indeed, it is suggested that there are marked spaces and absences in Heidegger's text that Woolf's writings fill; most particularly, the explication of particular concrete everyday involvements that are representative of the individual's connection to the world, as well as the exploration of certain significant 'factical' elements of Being-in-the-world, such as gender and embodiment. Further to this, as suggested in Chapter 5, in contrast to Heidegger's esoteric text, Woolf's writings ultimately come closer to communicating to the 'common reader' the meaning of 'Being-in-the-world.'

Notes

1. Such a claim is reiterated by Andrew C. Wenaus in his 2013 dissertation, 'Metaphor and Metanoia: Linguistic Transfer and Cognitive Transformation in British and Irish Modernism', in which he claims that 'While Woolf scholars have intimated Heideggerian readings of her fiction, there is yet to appear an extended analysis in this mode' (2013: 40).

Chapter 1

Being-in-the-world

With a brain working and a body working one could keep step with the crowd and never be found out for the hollow machine, lacking the essential thing, that one was conscious of being. (*ND*: 245–6)

Evident throughout the various forms of Woolf's writings – from her novels and short stories, through to her essays, reviews, memoirs, letters and diary entries – is a consistent and dominant preoccupation with the relationship between the individual and the world. Reflected in these works is Woolf's understanding that while the 'world' consists of the physical environment and its tangible objects, as well as those individuals with whom we co-exist, this notion also comes to be defined by the individual's everyday involvements and engagements; that is, 'our *experience* of the world' (Hussey 1986: xiii). As this chapter will demonstrate, for Woolf, definitive elements of this 'experience' are those expectations, prescriptions and hierarchical structures of the prevailing milieu and social order that not only regulate and direct the everyday lives of members of society, but also define the individual's view of the world.

Woolf's understanding of the world as an inclusive and fluid phenomenon is poetically elucidated in the fourth section of her 1931 novel, *The Waves*. As the six central characters, now in their early twenties, prepare to go their separate ways after spending an evening together, Louis reflects upon the 'common feeling' that embraces those within this group, and warns:

> 'Do not move, do not let the swing door cut to pieces the thing that we have made, that globes itself here, among these lights, these peelings, this litter of bread crumbs and people passing. Do not move, do not go. Hold it for ever.'

> 'Let us hold it for one moment,' said Jinny; 'love, hatred, by whatever name we call it, this globe whose walls are made of Percival, of youth and beauty, and something so deep sunk within us that we shall perhaps never make this moment out of one man again.'
> 'Forests and far countries on the other side of the world,' said Rhoda, 'are in it; seas and jungles; the howlings of jackals and moonlight falling upon some high peak where the eagle soars.'
> 'Happiness is in it,' said Neville, 'and the quiet of ordinary things. A table, a chair, a book with a paper-knife stuck between the pages. And the petal falling from the rose, and the light flickering as we sit silent, or, perhaps, bethinking us of some trifle, suddenly speak.'
> 'Week-days are in it,' said Susan, 'Monday, Tuesday, Wednesday; the horses going up to the fields, and the horses returning; the rooks rising and falling, and catching the elm-trees in their net, whether it is April, whether it is November.'
> 'What is to come is in it,' said Bernard. (*TW*: 109)

As the responses of these young men and women demonstrate, the context of each individual's life is multifarious, incorporating and accommodating one's ties to other individuals; the seasons; the past, present and future; flora and fauna; emotions and moods; and the intangible and only-imaginable, each of which are inextricably related so as to create a heterogeneous whole that might be broadly defined as the 'world'. Emphasised in this passage is the sense that, for each of these characters, their relationship to each other and the world-at-large is all-encompassing, indivisible, immeasurable and bordering on the incomprehensible.

The musings of these characters also reflect Woolf's view that the quotidian, rather than grand events, defines and forms the ties between self and world. As will be emphasised throughout this book, for both Woolf and Heidegger, it is the individual's 'average everyday' mode of Being that provides the foundation and context for understanding and uncovering the individual's relationship to the world. As Heidegger explains in *Being and Time*:

> The theme of our analytic is to be Being-in-the-world, and accordingly the very world itself; and these are to be considered within the horizon of average everydayness – the kind of Being which is *closest* to Dasein. We must make a study of everyday Being-in-the-world. (*BT*: 94)

Arguably, Woolf's writings explore, from a literary perspective, the phenomenology of everyday Being-in-the-world that is represented throughout Heidegger's text.

Despite such affinities, in terms of Woolf and Heidegger's representations of the 'everyday', it is important to acknowledge what might initially appear to be a significant disanalogy in terms of their respective textual approaches to Being-in-the-world. While Heidegger's understanding of average everydayness is principally concerned with the ways in which the individual's practical and instrumental comportments with things, such as tools and equipment, defines for the most part how he or she exists in the world, such a perspective seems to differ significantly from Woolf's reliance upon more poetic, aesthetic and seemingly non-instrumental modes of world-disclosure in her writings. Indeed, Woolf's writings reflect little or no explicit interest in the Heideggerian understanding that

> there is an involvement in hammering; with hammering, there is an involvement in making something fast; with making something fast, there is an involvement in protection against bad weather; and this protection 'is' for the sake of [um-willen] providing shelter for Dasein – that is to say, for the sake of a possibility of Dasein's Being. (*BT*: 116)

Nevertheless, it must be emphasised that Woolf's approach to Being-in-the-world, while couched in literary and aesthetic form, is very much concerned with the individual's practical engagement with the world, in that her understandings of average everydayness are anchored in politically and ideologically marked contexts that each individual must inevitably encounter and contend with.

As the title of this chapter reflects, its focus is upon an explication of the Heideggerian term, 'Being-in-the-world', and the relationship of this notion to Woolf's textual representations of the connections between self and world. Beginning with a discussion of the ways that both Woolf and Heidegger's approaches to Being-in-the-world represent a disruption and rejection of the Cartesian subject and world dualism, it is from this perspective that Woolf's use of 'weather' and 'atmosphere' are examined as motifs for the primordial and inextricable connection between self and world. This is followed by an analysis of Heidegger's treatment of intersubjectivity, understood as 'Being-with': indeed, for both writer and philosopher, a fundamental aspect of Being-in-the-world involves Being-with-Others. Attention is drawn to the problematic nature of forming and maintaining connections with the Other as a recurrent concept in Woolf's writings. This leads to a discussion of Heidegger's notion of 'theyness', which refers to the individual's unthinking and inauthentic average everyday immersion in the constructs, expectations and preoccupations of the present. For Heidegger, 'curiosity', 'ambiguity' and 'idle talk' are understood as manifestations of the 'they', and this chapter reflects upon the ways in which these notions are given literary expression in Woolf's texts. Demonstrating Woolf's concern with the impact of the social order upon the life of the individual, attention is focused upon the parallels between her textual representations of the 'societal machine' – which comes to be manifested in areas as diverse as education, religion and the medical profession – and theyness. So far as these key Heideggerian concepts are concerned, this chapter provides a foundation for those that are to follow, where Woolf's treatment of each of these areas will be analysed in greater detail.

The subject and world dualism

Thiele suggests that Being-in-the-world might be understood as 'an irreducible amalgam composed of three elements: the world, human being, and the relation of Being-in' (1997: 496). In *Being and Time,* Heidegger explains that this notion of 'Being-in' equates to the individual's engagement, experience and relationship with the world, rather than any form of containment – such as when a bird is placed inside a cage. Heidegger emphasises that the individual is 'never "proximally" an entity which is, so to speak, free from Being-in' (*BT*: 84), in the sense that one's connection to the world is a fundamental and inextricable element of what it means to be human.

Such a view might be contrasted with the Cartesian understanding of the relationship between the self and the world. Through his distinction of the '"*ego cogito*" from the "*res corporea*"' (*BT*: 123), the pronouncements of the French philosopher, René Descartes, concerning the subject as a knowing, thinking, autonomous observer of the world, proved to be far-reaching in terms of its scope of influence. This distinction between the subject and object 'relegates the other, the "not-self," to the realm of objectivity, to be articulated and controlled according to the dictates of the ego and its rationality' (Pheby 1988: 92). As emphasised throughout this book, such demarcations provide the foundation for many of the discourses, ideologies, and hierarchies upon which the English social order in the first half of the twentieth century is based; indeed, as Thiele remarks, 'Descartes's philosophy most clearly marks the beginning of modernity' (1995: 25). Through her writings, Woolf's preoccupation with the interdependent relationship between the individual and world, and self and Other, becomes a means of both revealing and calling into question such dualisms and structures of authority and control. For Heidegger and Woolf, the metaphysical dualism of subject and world is replaced with a heterogeneous unity, in the sense that Being-in is representative of the individual's fundamental involvement in the world. It is from such a perspective that, in contrast to the point of view forwarded by Descartes, 'Heidegger's protagonists are actors rather than spectators' (Mulhall 2003: 39).

In her essay, 'Heidegger in Woolf's Clothing', Storl reflects upon Woolf and Heidegger's shared response to the Cartesian legacy; referring to Woolf's *To the Lighthouse* and Heidegger's *Being and Time*, Storl writes:

> Both writers were reacting to the commitments and costs of modernity: the separation of subject and object that enabled the rise of scientific materialism and various forms of philosophical realism, yet at the same time caused the formation of an ever-deepening normative void. (2008: 303)

Through their respective writings, Woolf and Heidegger each seek to provide an alternative to this dualism. In Woolf's novel, such an intention is highlighted through her depiction of the response of the artist, Lily Briscoe, to the work of the philosophical realist, Mr Ramsay. When Lily asks Andrew Ramsay to describe his father's work, she is told that it is concerned with '"Subject and object and the nature of reality."' Reacting to Lily's bewildered response, Andrew prompts her to '"Think of a kitchen table then . . . when you're not there"' (*TL*: 21). It is from such a perspective that Lily

> always saw, when she thought of Mr. Ramsay's work, a scrubbed kitchen table. It lodged now in the fork of a pear tree, for they had reached the orchard. And with a painful effort of concentration, she focused her mind, not upon the silver-bossed bark of the tree, or upon its fish-shaped leaves, but upon a phantom kitchen table . . . which stuck there, its four legs in air. (*TL*: 21)

Lily's image of a kitchen table situated in a pear tree is representative of Woolf's critique of the absolute, and ultimately incongruous, separation of subject and object; located outside its average everyday context of the kitchen, the table's intended use as a place to sit, eat a meal, and Be-with-Others is denied. Reflecting Heidegger's emphasis upon involvement and engagement as defining features of the individual's relationship to the world, Storl suggests that this passage demonstrates the understanding that

> Though one can artificially subtract an object (Woolf's 'phantom kitchen table') from its surroundings, such an abstraction is contrary to the *being* of the object thus abstracted as well as contrary to the *being* of the one doing the abstraction . . . Things exist, or more accurately, have being only insofar as they participate in our way of being. (2008: 308)

Along similar lines, Frank draws attention to the difficulty Lily experiences when she attempts to extract the 'phantom kitchen table' from its everyday lived context of involvement; the image of the table located in a tree emphasises 'the absurd alienation and the impoverishing, distancing effect of the discursive, de-worlding attitude' of philosophers such as Mr Ramsay. As Frank asserts, ultimately

> The condition whereby Lily and the table are inside the network of significations and associations that the world constitutes is not fortuitous or secondary but is a basic ontological condition . . . In this form it more closely resembles Heidegger's notion of being-in-the-world. (2001: 35)

Two years earlier, in Woolf's 1925 novel, *Mrs Dalloway*, the metaphysical dualism of subject and world is replaced by the protagonist's sense of involvement in the world. As Clarissa Dalloway purposefully makes her way through the city on the morning of her society party, she possesses the certainty that

> somehow in the streets of London, on the ebb and flow of things, here, there, she survived, Peter survived, lived in each other, she being part, she was positive, of the trees at home; of the house there, ugly, rambling all to bits and pieces as it was; part of people she had never met; being laid out like a mist between the people she knew best, who lifted her on their branches as she had seen the trees lift the mist, but it spread ever so far, her life, herself. (*MD*: 7)

Contrary to the Cartesian understanding that Clarissa's connection with the external world is based upon the objective and detached contemplation of a centred and autonomous subject, this character views herself as essentially decentred, integrated and diffused in relation to all that surrounds her. Justyna Kostkowska details the ways in which Woolf's novel represents the interconnectedness of the individual and nature, suggesting that Woolf 'subverts the Cartesian mind–body dualism, and the idea of human intellectual and evolutionary superiority' (2004: 197). Kostkowska argues that the repression of nature and the non-human is representative of the oppression of the individual that results from the social order's approach to issues such as imperialism, medicine, patriarchy and religion; in contrast, Clarissa finds herself boundlessly entwined in the Being not only of other individuals, but also various physical locations and objects.

Such a sense of Being-in-the-world shares affinities with Heidegger's explanation of the individual's relationship with the world in the second section of *Being and Time*, where he explains:

> When Dasein directs itself towards something and grasps it, it does not somehow first get out of an inner sphere in which it has been proximally encapsulated, but its primary kind of Being is such that it is always 'outside' alongside entities which it encounters and which belong to a world already discovered. Nor is any inner sphere abandoned when Dasein dwells alongside the entity to be known, and determines its character; but even in this 'Being-outside' alongside the object, Dasein is still 'inside', if we understand this in the correct sense; that is to say, it is itself 'inside' as a Being-in-the-world which knows. And furthermore, the perceiving of what is known is not a process of returning with one's booty to the 'cabinet' of consciousness after one has gone out and grasped it; even in perceiving, retaining, and preserving, the Dasein which knows *remains outside*, and it does so *as Dasein*. (BT: 89)

Demonstrating the understanding that 'Being-in' does not equate to any form of containment that might be defined by the separation of inside and outside, or self and Other, Heidegger displaces the metaphysical subject and object dualism through his assertion that the individual's primordial connection with, and knowledge of, the world is made possible by the engagement and involvement that is definitive of Being-in-the-world. Such an understanding is given further emphasis in the second half of *Mrs Dalloway*, as Clarissa travels through the streets of London atop an omnibus, feeling herself to be 'everywhere; not "here, here, here"; and she tapped the back of the seat; but everywhere. She waved her hand, going up Shaftesbury Avenue. She was all that' (*MD*: 154). Just as Heidegger explains that the individual's primordial relationship with all that he or she encounters in the world does not lead to an abandonment of his or her 'inner sphere', Clarissa's sense of involvement and connection to the world does not result in a loss of self; rather, such an association comes to define and constitute her mode of Being-in-the-world.

In her 1939 memoir, 'A Sketch of the Past', Woolf describes her personal sense of the ties that bind the self to the world, observing that

> the murmur and rustle of the leaves makes me pause here, and think how many other than human forces are always at work on us. While I write this the light glows; an apple becomes a vivid green; I respond all through me; but how? Then a little owl [chatters] under my window. Again, I respond. ('Sketch': 137–8)

As such observations attest, for Woolf, the writing-process is inspired and influenced by her response to the connectedness and openness that results from her involvement in, and experience of, the world. The significance of the influence of this relationship upon Woolf as an artist is an issue that will be explored throughout this book.

Weather and atmosphere

Just as 'the murmur and rustle of the leaves' inspires in Woolf a conscious awareness of her relationship with the world, throughout her *oeuvre* the motifs of climate, weather, and atmosphere also become means of demonstrating the heterogeneous unity of individual and world. Paula Maggio suggests that for Woolf, 'weather and literature are linked in a manner that parallels the symbiotic connection between the human world and the natural world, a view that allows her to disavow the commonly held belief that the two operated within an independent duality' (2010: 24). In contrast to Heidegger's existential-ontological understanding of Being-in-the-world, in a number of instances, Woolf uses representations of weather and atmosphere to highlight the individual's inherent connection to the physical world and its natural forces. In her 1925 essay, 'On Not Knowing Greek', for instance, Woolf refers to Greek literature, and suggests that such writing is shaped by the climate, in that the 'warmth and sunshine and months of brilliant, fine weather' results in a life that is 'transacted out of doors . . . That is the quality that first strikes us in

Greek literature, the lightning-quick, sneering, out-of-doors manner' (1968: 2).

Watsuji Tetsuro suggests that as a result of 'changes in the weather, we first of all apprehend changes in ourselves . . . In other words, we find ourselves – ourselves as an element in the "mutual relationship" – in "climate"' (1988: 5).[1] Such a perspective is apparent in *The Waves*, where Susan's practical, physical and emotional connection to the world is manifested through her experience of the seasons:

> 'But who am I, who lean on this gate and watch my setter nose in a circle? I think sometimes (I am not twenty yet) I am not a woman, but the light that falls on this gate, on this ground. I am the seasons, I think sometimes, January, May, November; the mud, the mist, the dawn . . . I shall lie like a field bearing crops in rotation; in the summer heat will dance over me; in the winter I shall be cracked with the cold. But heat and cold will follow each other naturally without my willing or unwilling . . . I shall be lifted higher than any of you on the backs of the seasons.' (*TW*: 73, 99)

Passionately privileging a life on the land over that of the city, Susan is more aware and receptive than any of the other characters in *The Waves* to the connection between the individual and the natural world. Embracing the ultimate contingency of her existence, Susan's coupling to the world comes to be defined by the rotation of the seasons.

Despite such direct representations of the ties between the individual and the natural world, Woolf's references to weather, climate and atmosphere are typically positioned as tropes that indicate not only the connections between self and world that define Being-in-the-world, but also the impact that such connectedness has upon the everyday life of the individual. This is particularly evident in *The Waves*, where weather and atmosphere determine the novel's structure, so that each of the nine sections begins with an interlude describing the sun's gradual movement from morning to night.[2] As the novel progresses, it is clear that the sun is a motif for the lives of this group of friends as they move from childhood into the uncertain years of early adulthood, and finally into their later years. As the novel begins, the sun slowly rises, signalling not only the dawning of a new day, but also the awakening consciousness of the young characters, as their encounters with the world begin.

The novel's fourth and fifth interludes detail the commonality of individuals, nature and objects, as each come to be affected by the sun that now lies higher in the sky, so that '*Whatever the light touched became dowered with a fanatical existence*' (TW: 82). It is during these sections that the six friends meet Percival for the last time, and learn soon afterwards of his untimely death in India. In the remaining interludes, as the sun descends, it maintains its role as a symbol of the interconnectedness of Being-in-the-world so that, as '*The afternoon sun warmed the fields . . . whatever moved in it was rolled round in gold*' (TW: 139). In the final section of the novel, as the sun disappears from view, darkness represents the inescapable inevitability of life's end. Throughout this novel, both the sun's light and the darkness of the night demonstrate Woolf's sense of the inherent and inescapable unity of self and world.

Three years prior to the publication of *The Waves*, Woolf uses atmosphere and weather extensively in her mock-biography *Orlando*, as a means of indicating not only the passage of time, but also representing and critiquing the political and social 'climates' of each of the ages that the protagonist encounters in her centuries-long life. As the novel begins, the biographer facetiously pardons the young male Orlando's promiscuity with the assertion that

> The age was the Elizabethan; their morals were not ours; nor their poets; nor their climate . . . Everything was different. The weather itself, the heat and cold of summer and winter, was, we may believe, of another temper altogether . . . Thus, if Orlando followed the leading of the climate, of the poets, of the age itself, and plucked his flower in the window-seat even with the snow on the ground and the Queen vigilant in the corridor, we can scarcely bring ourselves to blame him. (O: 19–20)

While it is clear that the biographer's description of the relationship between the individual and climate reflects a degree of poetic licence, it confirms Tetsuro's assertion that one can 'discover climatic phenomena in all expressions of human activity, such as literature, art, religion, and manners and customs' (1988: 7–8).

As the novel continues, such a view is emphasised through Woolf's account of the Great Frost, a natural event that actually took place in England in 1608. Recounting this climatic anomaly, the biographer draws attention to the marked class divides in England during that time, attesting that, 'while the country people suffered the extremity of want, and the trade of the country was at a standstill,

London enjoyed a carnival of the utmost brilliancy' (O: 24), as the city took advantage of the frozen River Thames. Demonstrating the ubiquitous nature of this extreme weather, through its effects upon not only men and women, but also birds, sheep and cattle, porpoises, eels, boats and ships, Woolf dissolves the subject and object dualism, highlighting the interconnectedness of the 'human and non-human' (Kostkowska 2004: 184). This understanding is reinforced upon the onset of the thaw, where 'All was riot and confusion', so that noblemen, young watermen, and post-boys, as well as 'furniture, valuables, possessions of all sorts' (O: 44, 45) are each denied immunity from the immense force that this change in the weather creates.

Throughout *Orlando*, Woolf uses meteorology as a satirical means of both signalling and commenting upon the social context, or 'spirit of the age' (O: 162), which comes to define each of the various centuries of Orlando's life. Marking the transition from the eighteenth to the nineteenth century by the formation of a cloud that gathers behind the dome of St Paul's Cathedral, Woolf writes:

> As the ninth, tenth, and eleventh strokes struck, a huge blackness sprawled over the whole of London. With the twelfth stroke of midnight, the darkness was complete. A turbulent welter of cloud covered the city. All was darkness; all was doubt; all was confusion. The Eighteenth century was over; the Nineteenth century had begun ... A change seemed to have come over the climate of England. (O: 156, 157)

In this passage, weather represents the influence of the emerging zeitgeist upon all individuals, regardless of their place or standing in society. Noting the pervasive everyday ramifications of this shift, where fashions, home decoration, diet, music, and even relations between men and women alter, Orlando's biographer asserts that this change was to 'have extraordinary consequences upon those who lived beneath its shadow.' The onset of incessant rain that heralds the start of this new century creates a dampness that infiltrates the environment, the home, and the 'hearts' and 'minds' of all individuals, so that 'Everywhere the effects were felt.' Describing this dampness as 'the most insidious of all enemies ... damp is silent, imperceptible, ubiquitous' (O: 157, 158), such an atmosphere becomes a motif for the political and ideological spirit that this repressive age represents.

In her 1932 essay 'Great Men's Houses', Woolf uses atmosphere rather than weather as a means of commenting upon the prevailing social order, as she records her largely negative impressions of London. Gazing down at the city from a hilltop perspective, Woolf writes:

> One sees London as a whole – London crowded and ribbed and compact, with its dominant domes, its guardian cathedrals; its chimneys and spires; its cranes and gasometers; and the perpetual smoke which no spring or autumn ever blows away. London has lain there time out of mind scarring that stretch of earth deeper and deeper, making it more uneasy, lumped and tumultuous, branding it for ever with an indelible scar. There it lies in layers, in strata, bristling and billowing with rolls of smoke always caught on its pinnacles. (2006b: 39)

Throughout this bleak description of London, the city is defined by the foul and enduring residue of industrialisation. Morphing into an unstoppable force, London has become a harsh captor of the piece of earth that it dominates and mutilates. The scarring of the land is clearly the result of human intention and action, yet tangible human presence is eerily absent. The industrially produced smoke is an all-pervasive and ominous presence, casting a veil upon its environment. Such airborne pollution provides a material measure of the sense that Being-in-the-world consists of Being-with-Others: all people of London, regardless of gender, class or origin, share the common experience of breathing this contaminated air. In this essay, the overwhelming presence of pollution offers a record and critique, not only of London's economy, but also the concomitant quality of life experienced by those living in this city.

A less severe, though nevertheless dark account of London is reflected in *The Waves*; as Bernard travels by train towards the city, he muses: '"How fair, how strange . . . glittering, many-pointed and many-domed London lies before me under mist. Guarded by gasometers, by factory chimneys, she lies sleeping as we approach' (*TW*: 83). Like Woolf's description of London in 'Great Men's Houses', in this passage, atmosphere is representative of the physical symptoms of London's capitalist economy: enveloped in mist, and guarded by the built forms of industry, London appears both concealed and concealing.

In her 1937 novel *The Years*, Woolf again uses weather to comment upon the effects of capitalism and industrialisation upon the everyday London environment and its inhabitants. The fourth chapter commences with a detailed description of a destructive wind that is tearing its way through London:

> It was scraping, scourging. It was so cruel ... it was like the curve of a scythe which cuts, not corn, usefully; but destroys, revelling in sheer sterility ... Triumphing in its wantonness it emptied the streets. (*TY*: 107)

Woolf makes explicit the connection between this cruel wind and the detrimental effects of the capitalist market through her reference to the Isle of Dogs, a site of docks, industry and slum-like working-class dwellings: 'Had it [this wind] any breeding place it was in the Isle of Dogs among tin cans lying beside a workhouse drab on the banks of a polluted city' (*TY*: 107). Demonstrating the far-reaching force of this wind, Woolf describes its violence as it reaches the Pargiter home, where 'It pressed on the house; gripped it tight, then let it fall apart', causing windows to bang, and sending 'glass crashing' (*TY*: 113, 115, 117).

Within this novel Woolf also uses rain as a means of demonstrating her understanding that all individuals, regardless of education, class or gender, are inevitably united by their primordial borderless state of Being-in-the-world:

> It was raining ... Down on the roofs it fell – here in Westminster, there in the Ladbroke Grove; on the wide sea a million points pricked the blue monster like an innumerable shower-bath. Over the vast domes, the soaring spires of slumbering University cities, over the leaded libraries, and the museums, now shrouded in brown holland, the gentle rain slid down, till, reaching the mouths of those fantastic laughers, the many-clawed gargoyles, it splayed out in a thousand odd indentations. A drunken man slipping in a narrow passage outside the public house, cursed it. Women in childbirth heard the doctor say to the midwife, 'It's raining.' And the walloping Oxford bells, turning over and over like slow porpoises in a sea of oil, contemplatively intoned their musical incantation. The fine rain, the gentle rain, poured equally over the mitred and the bareheaded with an impartiality which suggested that the god of rain, if there were a god, was thinking Let it not be restricted to the very wise, the very great, but let all breathing kind, the munchers and chewers, the ignorant, the unhappy, those who toil in the furnace making innumerable copies of the same pot, those who bore red hot minds through contorted letters, and also Mrs Jones in the alley, share my bounty. (*TY*: 34–5)

As this passage suggests, weather creates a sense of unity and commonality that disregards physical, social and ideological boundaries. It is from such a perspective that weather also becomes a means of highlighting the sense that an inseparable element of Being-in-the-world involves Being-with-Others.[3]

Intersubjectivity and authenticity

The understanding that the individual's state of Being-in-the-world is influenced, formed and defined by his or her relations with the Other, is a leading preoccupation that runs throughout each of the various forms of Woolf's writings; as such, this issue will be examined in detail from a variety of perspectives in the following chapters. The significance of the individual's inextricable state of Being-with-Others is highlighted by Woolf in 'A Sketch of the Past' through her representation of atmosphere. Now fifty-seven years of age, Woolf reflects upon the significant influences that have generated the form and shape of her life, most particularly her mother, whom she lost at the age of thirteen. As Woolf writes,

> of course she was central. I suspect the word 'central' gets closest to the general feeling I had of living so completely in her atmosphere that one never got far enough away from her to see her as a person. ('Sketch': 94)

Stressing the fluid and pervasive influence that her relations with others have had upon her life, Woolf notes that

> among the innumerable things left out in my sketch I have left out the most important – those instincts, affections, passions, attachments – there is no single word for them, for they changed month by month – which bound me, I suppose, from the first moment of consciousness to other people. ('Sketch': 91–2)

In her 1924 essay, 'Mr. Bennett and Mrs. Brown', Woolf uses the motif of atmosphere as a means of remarking upon the potential for an individual to form connections with the Other. Discussing the importance of 'character-creating' in the art of writing, Woolf draws attention to a fellow train-traveller, Mrs Brown, stating that, so far as this individual's circumstances were concerned, 'details could wait. The important thing was to realize her character, to steep oneself in her atmosphere' (1966a: 319, 324). Drawing upon Woolf's pronouncements in this essay, Ruotolo makes brief mention of direct parallels with Heidegger's understanding of Being-with-Others (1973: 16).

In *Being and Time*, Heidegger asserts that Being-with-Others must be considered Dasein's primordial state in the sense that 'the world is always the one that I share with Others. The world of Dasein is a *with-world* [*Mitwelt*]. Being-in is *Being-with* Others' (*BT*: 155).[4] Further to this, Heidegger emphasises that knowledge of the Other has the potential to generate greater insights into one's own particular context and mode of Being-in-the-world. Such a notion is expressed and elucidated by Woolf in 'Mr. Bennett and Mrs. Brown', where she asserts that

> in or about December, 1910, human character changed . . . All human relations . . . shifted – those between masters and servants, husbands and wives, parents and children. And when human relations change there is at the same time a change in religion, conduct, politics, and literature. (1966a: 320, 321)

In her account, Woolf suggests that the individual's relationship to and with the Other both reveals and reinforces the constructs, ideologies and values of a particular society: as societal expectations and prescriptions shift, so do intersubjective relations, and vice versa.

Continuing her argument that knowledge of the Other allows for greater knowledge of the self, Woolf discusses the capacity of 'great novels' to create characters that allow the reader access to 'all sorts of things through its eyes – of religion, of love, of war, of peace, of family life, of balls in country towns, of sunsets, moonrises, the immortality of the soul' (1966a: 325). Reflecting upon the marked difference between Edwardian and Georgian approaches to character-creation, Woolf asserts that Edwardian novelists such as H. G. Wells, John Galsworthy and Arnold Bennett fail to turn due attention to the characters in their writings, laying instead 'an enormous stress upon the fabric of things' (1966a: 332). While social-historical and material circumstances are essential aspects of Being-in-the-world, ultimately, as Heidegger insists in *Being and Time*, it is the everyday lived experience of the individual that provides the foundation for an understanding of his or her relationship to the world. It is from such a perspective that Woolf finds the literature of these Edwardians lacking. As she imagines how such novelists would approach the representation of an individual such as the fairly nondescript Mrs Brown, Woolf reports that 'They have looked very powerfully, searchingly, and sympathetically out of the window; at factories, at

Utopias, even at the decoration and upholstery of the carriage; but never at her, never at life, never at human nature' (1966a: 330). In this sense, by overlooking the individual, such novelists have failed to turn their attention to the question of Being itself.

Heidegger claims that the individual's relationship with the Other is fundamentally based on '*solicitude*' (*BT*: 157). While notions of care and concern towards the Other are clearly implicated in such a term, as Heidegger explains, the degree to which such attributes are present in terms of the individual's average everyday dealings can vary and shift considerably:

> Dasein maintains itself proximally and for the most part in the deficient modes of solicitude. Being for, against, or without one another, passing one another by, not 'mattering' to one another – these are possible ways of solicitude. And it is precisely these last-named deficient and Indifferent modes that characterize everyday, average Being-with-one-another. (*BT*: 158)

Heidegger maintains that while it is possible for the individual to experience a sense of empathy for the Other, such a state is 'not a primordial existential phenomenon', so that in our everyday encounters with the Other, it is often the case that 'a genuine "understanding" gets suppressed' (*BT*: 163). For Woolf, the problematic nature of the individual's ability to form connections with the Other is a dominant concern throughout her writings.

The propensity for separation between individuals within the modern context is highlighted in Woolf's 1927 essay, 'The Narrow Bridge of Art', where she describes

> a walk through the streets of any large town. The long avenue of brick is cut up into boxes, each of which is inhabited by a different human being who has put locks on his doors and bolts on his windows to ensure some privacy, yet is linked to his fellows by wires which pass overhead, by waves of sound which pour through the roof and speak aloud to him of battles and murders and strikes and revolutions all over the world. And if we go in and talk to him we shall find that he is a wary, secretive, suspicious animal, extremely self-conscious, extremely careful not to give himself away. Indeed, there is nothing in modern life which forces him to do it. (1960: 15–16)

As this passage attests, the modern condition is defined by separation in the midst of close proximity. Walls, doors, locks and bolts act to secure and ensure the severance of bodily contact with the Other. Nevertheless, a fundamentally anonymous, pervasive and outwardly consensual contact ensues as wires connect the media to the individual, who is fed the same news, advertisements, opinions and worldviews as every other individual. Woolf highlights the sense that such artificial, highly orchestrated connections between separate individuals ultimately fuels a suspicion and distrust of the Other, whom one seldom comes to know from a first-hand perspective.

Such a sense of modern disconnection is imparted by Woolf five years earlier in *Jacob's Room*, as the narrator discusses the individual's typical approach to the Other within the context of public transport:

> The proximity of the omnibuses gave the outside passengers an opportunity to stare into each other's faces. Yet few took advantage of it. Each had his own business to think of. Each had his past shut in him like the leaves of a book known to him by heart; and his friends could only read the title, James Spalding, or Charles Budgeon, and the passengers going the opposite way could read nothing at all. (*JR*: 85)

In both her essay and novel, Woolf draws upon some of the most common features of modern living – the layout of one's home, the media, public transport – in order to stress the typical average everyday quality of separation between the self and the Other.

While the problematic nature of the formation of connections between the self and Other in a collective sense is a concern throughout Woolf's writings, so too are the difficulties experienced by the individual seeking a personal level of intimacy with other individuals. In *To the Lighthouse*, for instance, the problematic nature of intersubjective relations is highlighted and explored by Woolf as the character, Lily Briscoe, eloquently describes her thwarted desire to co-exist in a unified state with Mrs Ramsay:

> she imagined how in the chambers of the mind and heart of the woman who was, physically, touching her, were stood, like the treasures in the tombs of kings, tablets bearing sacred inscriptions, which if one could spell them out would teach one everything, but they would never be offered openly, never made public. What art was there, known to love or cunning, by which one pressed through into those secret chambers? What device for becoming, like waters poured into one jar, inextricably the same, one with the object one adored? Could the body achieve it, or the mind, subtly mingling in the intricate passages of the brain? or the heart? Could loving, as people called it, make her and Mrs. Ramsay one? for it was not knowledge but unity that she desired, not inscriptions on tablets, nothing that could be written in any language known to men, but intimacy itself, which is knowledge, she had thought, leaning her head on Mrs. Ramsay's knee. (*TL*: 47)

Ultimately, despite Lily's fervent hopes and desires, no connection ensues: 'Nothing happened. Nothing! Nothing!' (*TL*: 47).

Lily's experience of Mrs Ramsay as fundamentally unknowable comes to be represented in her artistic process; unable to complete the painting of Mrs Ramsay that was begun before her untimely death, it is only when this woman is no longer physically present that Lily is able to capture that sense of the Other that had previously eluded her. Indeed, Lily experiences a moment of revelation as she finally completes her painting ten years after Mrs Ramsay's death: 'It was done; it was finished. Yes, she thought, laying down her brush in extreme fatigue, I have had my vision' (*TL*: 198). As Woolf explains in 'A Sketch of the Past', Mrs Ramsay provides a fictional representation of her own mother, Julia Stephen; stressing the unknowable quality of this maternal figure, Woolf suggests that

> if one could give a sense of my mother's personality one would have to be an artist. It would be as difficult to do that, as it should be done, as to paint a Cézanne . . . [I]f I turn to my mother, how difficult it is to single her out as she really was; to imagine what she was thinking, to put a single sentence into her mouth! ('Sketch': 96, 98)

In his discussion of *The Years,* Hafley suggests that 'one of the major ideas of the novel' is 'that people *can* know one another, but refuse to do so' (1963: 137). Woolf's 1937 novel follows the lives of the Pargiter family from 1880 until the early 1930s. As is too commonly the case, between these family members, rifts develop, misunderstandings fester, and long periods pass where little or no contact is made. Although familial and emotional ties continue to draw the lives of each of the individuals together, their ability to truly connect and understand one another remains a struggle. Such a sense of this difficulty is evinced through the reflections of the character Peggy Parigiter, as she and her elderly Aunt Eleanor travel by cab to a family gathering:

> Where does she begin, and where do I end? She thought [. . .] On they drove. They were two living people, driving across London; two sparks of life enclosed in two separate bodies; and those sparks of life enclosed in two separate bodies are at this moment, she thought, driving past a picture palace. But what is this moment; and what are we? The puzzle was too difficult for her to solve it. She sighed. (*TY*: 245)

Although Peggy finds herself on the cusp of some form of intersubjective insight, she turns away before it is reached, deciding that 'She would far rather have stayed at home or gone to the pictures' (*TY*: 244).

Unlike Peggy, who wishes to shy away from connections with the Other, throughout *The Waves*, Bernard expresses his sense of frustration and discontent regarding the seemingly insurmountable chasm that exists between him and those with whom he wishes to be closest. This is emphasised in Bernard's lamentation at the end of the novel: 'Our friends – how distant, how mute, how seldom visited and little known. And I, too, am dim to my friends and unknown; a phantom, sometimes seen, often not' (*TW*: 211). As Bernard calls to mind his overwhelming sense of loss upon hearing of the death of Percival many years earlier, he painfully recalls that his search for solace through the company of friends only resulted in a feeling of disconnectedness:

> Thus I visited each of my friends in turn, trying, with fumbling fingers to prise open their locked caskets. I went from one to the other holding my sorrow – no, not my sorrow but the incomprehensible nature of this our life – for their inspection. Some people go to priests; others to poetry; I to my friends, I to my own heart, I to seek among phrases and fragments something unbroken – I to whom there is not beauty enough in moon or tree; to whom the touch of one person with another is all, yet who cannot grasp even that, who am so imperfect, so weak, so unspeakably lonely. (*TW*: 205)

Despite the sense of detachment that characterises so many of his interactions and relations with the Other, Bernard comes to realise that ultimately, however complicated, opaque, and indefinable those relationships are, both his sense of self and state of Being-in-the-world are premised upon, and formed through, the primordial condition of Being-with:

> when I meet an unknown person, and try to break off, here at this table, what I call 'my life', it is not one life that I look back upon; I am not one person; I am many people; I do not altogether know who I am – Jinny, Susan, Neville, Rhoda, or Louis: or how to distinguish my life from theirs. (*TW*: 212)

Commenting upon this passage, Henke briefly draws attention to the parallels between Woolf's representation of the six friends and Heidegger's understanding of Being-with-Others: 'For a moment, the walls of the individual ego grow porous, and the self is fused with a larger whole' (1989: 464).

The difficulty of grasping and maintaining a connection with the Other is explicitly foregrounded by Woolf as Bernard laments the sense that the everyday sway of 'hate and rivalry', 'different desires', 'necessity, and 'Some miserable affair of keeping an appointment, of buying a hat' (*TW*: 84), ultimately lead to separation. Bernard's musings emphasise Heidegger's claim that in the average everyday mode of Being-with, one's attachments to other individuals come to be compromised and concealed. This understanding is foregrounded in Woolf's 1927 essay, 'Street Haunting: A London Adventure', where she juxtaposes the desire to connect with the Other, with the everyday reality of the intersubjective disconnectedness that arises from 'aloofness, hiding oneself away, or putting on a disguise' (*BT*: 161). Spending the afternoon wandering through the streets of London under the pretence of buying a pencil, the essay's protagonist encounters a variety of individuals, including a dwarf purchasing a pair of new shoes, two blind brothers, and a quarrelling husband and wife at a stationer's shop; as she makes her way home at twilight, this street haunter muses:

> Into each of these lives one could penetrate a little way, far enough to give oneself the illusion that one is not tethered to a single mind, but can put on briefly for a few minutes the bodies and minds of others. One could become a washerwoman, a publican, a street singer. And what greater delight and wonder can there be than to leave the straight lines of personality and deviate into those footpaths that lead beneath brambles and thick tree trunks into the heart of the forest where live those wild beasts, our fellow men? (1942e: 28)

As Woolf explains earlier in this piece, it is through such excursions into the lives of the Other that

> The shell-like covering which our souls have excreted to house themselves, to make for themselves a shape distinct from others, is broken, and there is left of all these wrinkles and roughnesses a central oyster of perceptiveness, an enormous eye. (1942e: 20)

Nevertheless, having highlighted the potential pleasures of Being-with the Other, as well as the heightened insight and awareness that ensues when the individual allows his or her defences to be shattered, Woolf draws her essay to a close with a description of the individual's inherent everyday propensity to thwart and deny the possibility of such connections:

> Still as we approach our own doorstep again, it is comforting to feel the old possessions, the old prejudices, fold us round; and the self, which

has been blown about at so many street corners, which has battered like a moth at the flame of so many inaccessible lanterns, sheltered and enclosed ... And here – let us examine it tenderly, let us touch it with reverence – is the only spoil we have retrieved from all the treasures of the city, a lead pencil. (1942e: 29)

Reflected in the protagonist's ironic observation that a pencil is 'the only spoil' from her wanderings, is an acknowledgement of the deficient nature of our everyday approach to Being-with. Such a perspective, whereby connections with the Other are essentially closed-off, is viewed by Heidegger as an inauthentic mode of Being.

While the protagonist in 'Street Haunting' believes that separation from the Other is attainable in a state of solitude, Heidegger asserts that one is always already in a state of Being-with, regardless of the physical presence or absence of the Other. As Heidegger declares, 'Even Dasein's Being-alone is Being-with in the world', so that, 'Even if the particular factical Dasein does *not* turn to Others, and supposes that it has no need of them or manages to get along without them, it *is* in the way of Being-with' (*BT*: 156–7, 160).

The question of social isolation implicated in Heidegger's assertion is an issue that is explored throughout *The Waves*. For Woolf's social 'outsiders', Rhoda and Louis, alienation and disconnection ultimately define their sense of Being-in-the-world. The devastating sense of isolation experienced by those seemingly unable to form connections with the Other is illuminated as Rhoda describes her impressions upon meeting her long-time friends after a prolonged absence:

> 'I fear, I hate, I love, I envy and despise you, but I never join you happily ... I perceived, from your coats and umbrellas, even at a distance, how you stand embedded in a substance made of repeated moments run together; are committed, have an attitude, with children, authority, fame, love, society; where I have nothing. I have no face ... Yet there are moments when the walls of the mind grow thin; when nothing is unabsorbed, and I could fancy that we might blow so vast a bubble that the sun might set and rise in it and we might take the blue of midday and the black of midnight and be cast off and escape from here and now.' (*TW*: 170–2)

Throughout this passage, Woolf depicts not only Rhoda's sense of disengagement from socially sanctioned ways of living, but also this character's heartfelt yearning to bond with those around her through a vision of a different world order that would allow for union rather than separation.

Ultimately unable to experience or grasp a sense of acceptance or belonging in relation to the Other, life becomes so intolerable for Rhoda that she finally believes that her only means of transcending the inextricable state of Being-with is through the disavowal of Being itself:

> 'Oh, life, how I have dreaded you,' said Rhoda, 'oh, human beings, how I have hated you! How you have nudged, how you have interrupted, how hideous you have looked in Oxford Street, how squalid sitting opposite each other staring in the Tube! Now as I climb this mountain, from the top of which I shall see Africa, my mind is printed with brown-paper parcels and your faces. I have been stained by you and corrupted. You smelt so unpleasant too, lining up outside doors to buy tickets. All were dressed in indeterminate shades of grey and brown, never even a blue feather pinned to a hat. None had the courage to be one thing rather than another. What dissolution of the soul you demanded in order to get through one day, what lies, bowings, scrapings, fluency and servility!' (*TW*: 156)

Aware of the ubiquitous power of the social and ideological constructs that insidiously command conformity by the individual, Rhoda rejects the social life that she has repeatedly and unsuccessfully tried to emulate. Yet, far from an act of liberation from such forces, Rhoda's suicide provides confirmation of her ultimate immersion in the common order.

Discussing the inauthentic propensity of the individual to measure the value of his or her life against that of the Other, Heidegger asserts that

> In one's concern with what one has taken hold of, whether with, for, or against, the Others, there is constant care as to the way one differs from them, whether that difference is merely one that is to be evened out, whether one's own Dasein has lagged behind the Others and wants to catch up in relationship to them, or whether one's Dasein already has some priority over them and sets out to keep them suppressed . . . If we may express this existentially, such Being-with-one-another has the character of *distantiality* [*Abständigkeit*] . . .
>
> But this distantiality which belongs to Being-with, is such that Dasein, as everyday Being-with-one-another, stands in *subjection* [*Botmässigkeit*] to Others. It itself *is* not; its Being has been taken away by the Others. Dasein's everyday possibilities of Being are for the Others to dispose of as they please. (*BT*: 163–4)

From such a perspective, Rhoda's inability to summon 'the courage to be one thing rather than another', results in a state of subjection as the sway of the Other becomes determinative of her eventual state of non-Being.

Average everydayness and the 'they'

As Heidegger emphasises in the previous passage, the average everyday tendency of the individual to judge and measure him- or herself in relation to the Other results in a distancing or concealment of one's authentic self. Such an understanding of the sway that the Other has upon the individual's experience of Being-in-the-world is indicated by Woolf in 'A Sketch of the Past', where she describes those 'invisible presences' that impact upon the art of life-writing:

> This influence, by which I mean the consciousness of other groups impinging upon ourselves; public opinion; what other people say and think; all those magnets which attract us this way to be like that, or repel us the other and make us different from that; has never been analysed in any of those Lives which I so much enjoy reading, or very superficially.
>
> Yet it is by such invisible presences that the 'subject of this memoir' is tugged this way and that every day of his life; it is they that keep him in position. Consider what immense forces society brings to play upon each of us, how that society changes from decade to decade; and also from class to class; well, if we cannot analyse these invisible presences, we know very little of the subject of the memoir; and again how futile life-writing becomes. I see myself as a fish in a stream; deflected; held in place; but cannot describe the stream. ('Sketch': 92)

Woolf's sense of the invisibility of such influences is in keeping with Heidegger's understanding that the forces of the social order usually go unnoticed, principally as a result of the individual's propensity to unquestioningly immerse him or herself in the affairs and preoccupations of everydayness. As will be explored, it is the ubiquity of these invisible presences throughout Woolf's writings, and their influence upon the individual's everyday engagement with the world, that is of particular concern and focus.

In *Being and Time* Heidegger refers to the term *das Man*, or the 'they', as representative of the societal and cultural norms, expectations and ideologies that define the average everyday lives of individuals, so that theyness comes to be equated with everydayness. As discussed in the Introduction, it is important to emphasise that, in contrast to Woolf's focus, Heidegger's interest in the effects of such influences upon the individual is ontological rather than political in nature. Describing the characteristics that typify the individual who is immersed in 'theyness', Heidegger asserts that

> We take pleasure and enjoy ourselves as *they* [*man*] take pleasure; we read, see, and judge about literature and art as *they* see and judge; likewise we shrink back from the 'great mass' as *they* shrink back; we find 'shocking' what *they* find shocking. The 'they', which is nothing definite, and which all are, though not as the sum, prescribes the kind of Being of everydayness. (BT: 164)

For Heidegger, conformity and the abandonment of self-determination are representative of this inauthentic mode of Being-in-the-world.

Such a view of the individual's relationship to theyness is underscored in Woolf's final novel, *Between the Acts*; as the pageant's audience reassembles after an intermission, Woolf provides the reader with snatches of 'The inner voice, the other voice' of a number of anonymous audience members:

> 'When we wake' (some were thinking) 'the day breaks us with its hard mallet blows.' 'The office' (some were thinking) 'compels disparity. Scattered, shattered, hither thither summoned by the bell. "Ping-ping-ping" – that's the phone. "Forward!" "Serving!" – that's the shop.' So we answer to the infernal, agelong and eternal order issued from on high. And obey. (BA: 73)

What is particularly telling in this passage is the sense that although each of these individuals possesses some degree of awareness that unseen forces beyond their control determine his or her everyday actions and activities, such an understanding ultimately remains unspoken, and as such, unchallenged.

Woolf's personal experience of the propensity of the they to sway, overwhelm and convert the individual is emphasised in 'A Sketch of the Past', where she describes her early experiences of being coerced by her eldest half-brother, George Duckworth, to engage in the machinations of London society:

> I felt, at twenty, that George no less than Herbert Fisher was going through the hoops; doing the required acts. In a thousand ways he made me feel that he believed in society. A belief which is so commonly accepted, as his was by all his friends, had depth, swiftness, inevitability. It impresses even the outsider by the sweep of its current. Sometimes when I hear God Save the King I too feel a current belief but almost directly I consider my own splits asunder and one side of me criticises the other. George never questioned his belief in the old tune that society played. He rose and took his hat off and stood. Not only did he never question his behaviour; he applauded it, enforced it. ('Sketch': 155)

Throughout this passage, Woolf both acknowledges and undermines the force of society's 'current' and its impact upon the individual. Unlike her brother, whose immersion in the social order is so complete that its constructs remain unseen and unexamined, Woolf's rejection of such socially-defined expectations affords her a sense of distance and clarity that allows for questioning to begin. As Woolf explains, 'There was a spectator in me who, even while I squirmed and obeyed, remained observant, note taking for some future revision' ('Sketch': 155). Arguably, it is such a propensity and capacity for observation that provides the impetus for Woolf's literary capacity to represent the often unseen and unexamined aspects of everyday life.

A sense of the immense influence of the social order upon the individual is reflected in fictional form in *The Waves*, as Bernard laments the habitual and prescribed mode of everyday life:

> We are all swept on by the torrent of things grown so familiar that they cast no shade; we make no comparisons; think scarcely ever of I or of you; and in this unconsciousness attain the utmost freedom from friction and part the weeds that grow over the mouths of sunken channels. We have to leap like fish, high in the air, in order to catch the train from Waterloo. And however high we leap we fall back again into the stream . . . I am wedged into my place in the puzzle. (*TW*: 166)

Not unlike George Duckworth's unquestioned existence, Bernard's ruminations highlight the individual's typical inability to perceive, let alone understand, the dominant forces that surround and direct him or her. Nevertheless, Bernard's assertions in themselves reflect a conscious awareness that contradicts the all-encompassing nature of such claims. In keeping with Woolf's observations concerning her brother's way of life, Bernard's response demonstrates that it is possible to experience moments of vision in which the constructs and constraints of the everyday come to be revealed.

Nevertheless, while Bernard asserts that, through a degree of effort and a certain amount of 'friction', one might 'leap' out of the stream in order to escape and behold society's sway, such escapes are only ever temporary as, inevitably, one must 'fall back again into the stream', and return to the folds of the everyday. Such a sense of the unavoidable nature of theyness is in keeping with Heidegger's assertion that the shared societal norms and expectations that one encounters are a structural feature of everyday Being-in-the-world, rather than a self-chosen mode of inauthenticity that one can simply discard through an act of choice. Ultimately, in order to exist in the world, some level of adherence to such structures is inevitable: it is the degree and type of adherence that differentiates and defines individual approaches to Being-in-the-world. As Nancy J. Holland asserts, 'Authenticity is, to a certain extent at least, dependent on the particular possible configurations of the they-self available within a specific social world' (2001: 134).

In his discussion of the six friends in *The Waves,* Hafley observes that, despite their differences, 'None of them – although Jinny comes close to being an exception – is content with a day-to-day living regulated by the social standards and patterns that can so easily drown out their questions' (1963: 107). Such a perspective is evident in the novel when, after dining with his five friends, Bernard calls on each to assume and maintain an authentic mode of Being, even as he acknowledges the propensity of society to overcome and subsume the will of the individual:

> We are not slaves bound to suffer incessantly unrecorded petty blows on our bent backs. We are not sheep either, following a master. We are creators. We too have made something that will join the innumerable congregations of past time. We too, as we put on our hats and push open the door, stride not into chaos, but into a world that our own force can subjugate and make part of the illumined and everlasting road. (*TW*: 110)

The language used in this passage, which includes words such as 'slaves', 'bent backs', 'sheep', and 'master', indicates Bernard's awareness of the everyday repression experienced by the individual under the yoke of theyness.

As Rhoda prepares for her suicide later in the novel, her burning resentment towards the propensity of theyness to strip the individual of his or her authentic identity and agency is brought into sharp relief:

> 'But I yielded. Sneers and yawns were covered with my hand. I did not go out into the street and break a bottle in the gutter as a sign of rage. Trembling with ardour, I pretended that I was not surprised. What you did, I did. If Susan and Jinny pulled up their stockings like that, I pulled mine up like that also. So terrible was life that I held up shade after shade. Look at life through this, look at life through that.' (*TW*: 156–7)

For this character, theyness colours and transforms the individual's vision of the world so that one's sense of reality is replaced by an outlook of conformity and uniformity. In *Being and Time*, Heidegger emphasises such dissolution of individuality through his suggestion that

> In utilizing public means of transport and in making use of information services such as the newspaper, every Other is like the next. This Being-with-one-another dissolves one's own Dasein completely into the kind of Being of 'the Others', in such a way, indeed, that the Others, as distinguishable and explicit, vanish more and more. In this inconspicuousness and unascertainabilty the real dictatorship of the 'they' is unfolded. (*BT*: 164)

Inauthenticity as the forgetting of Being

For both Heidegger and Woolf, the 'social-self' is understood to be the everyday default position assumed by the individual. As a result, an authentic state of Being-in-the-world requires a conscious choice by the individual to look beyond the concerns, demands and constructs of everyday life in order to surmount, albeit temporarily, his or her immersion in the constructs of theyness. In *Being and Time*, Heidegger describes the shift that occurs when an individual chooses to pursue an authentic mode of Being-of-the-world, rather than average everyday theyness:

> Proximally Dasein is 'they', and for the most part it remains so. If Dasein discovers the world in its own way [eigens] and brings it close, if it discloses to itself its own authentic Being, then this discovery of the 'world'

and this disclosure of Dasein are always accomplished as a clearing-away of concealments and obscurities, as a breaking up of the disguises with which Dasein bars its own way. (*BT*: 167)

In *Mrs Dalloway*, the protagonist, Clarissa Dalloway, provides a sense of the fluidity of each individual's mode of Being-in-the-world, insofar as authenticity and inauthenticity necessarily co-exist within each of us. Throughout the novel, Clarissa repeatedly grasps, and then loses, a conscious awareness that a large part of her life is ordered and dominated by societal prescriptions and conventions. While Clarissa feels the 'intoxication of the moment' as she entertains the Prime Minister at her society party, she also finds that such 'triumphs . . . had a hollowness; at arm's length they were, not in the heart; and it might be that she was growing old, but they satisfied her no longer as they used' (*MD*: 177). Along similar lines, as Clarissa walks through London earlier that day, she experiences

> the oddest sense of being herself invisible; unseen; unknown; there being no more marrying, no more having of children now, but only this astonishing and rather solemn progress with the rest of them, up Bond Street, this being Mrs Dalloway; not even Clarissa any more; this being Mrs Richard Dalloway. (*MD*: 8–9)

Such meditations reflect Clarissa's awareness – however limited and fleeting – of her everyday anonymity, as well as the compromised nature of her agency and autonomy. Although a willing participant in the social order, Clarissa nevertheless experiences a disturbing sense of unease upon the realisation that society views her as a politician's wife and member of a certain social class, rather than as an individual in her own right, with her own name and identity.

In *Night and Day*, Ralph Denham is representative of the difficulties faced by the individual who is conscious that his life does not have to automatically follow the directions that have been pre-ordained by the prevailing expectations and conventions of society. Aware that his personal aspirations are not of a type that would be sanctioned or supported by the social order, Ralph consciously decides to follow a path of conformity that can only be realised at the expense of his authentic sense of self. As he envisions a future career in politics, 'it needed all Ralph's strength of will, together with the pressure of circumstances, to keep his feet moving in the path which led that way' (*ND*: 117). Reflecting the influence of the they upon the choices that each individual makes, the novel's narrator describes the struggle that Ralph experiences in his efforts to deny his authentic self:

> like all beliefs not genuinely held, this one depended very much upon the amount of acceptance it received from other people, and in private, when the pressure of public opinion was removed, Ralph let himself swing very rapidly away from his actual circumstances upon strange voyages which, indeed, he would have been ashamed to describe. (*ND*: 117)

As the novel progresses, Ralph's friendship with Mary Datchet – a young woman who, through her involvement in the suffragette movement, unflinchingly seeks to reveal and call into question society's demand for compliance and conformity – inspires this young man to question his rigid views and alliances, so that as the novel progresses, Ralph's authentic sense of self begins slowly to emerge.

In 'A Sketch of the Past', Woolf reflects upon her personal experience of the ways in which the individual is compelled to engage with the world in a performative manner in order to conform to the prescriptions of the social order. Discussing the expectations thrust upon herself and her siblings at the time of her mother's death, Woolf writes:

> We were made to act parts that we did not feel; to fumble for words that we did not know. It obscured, it dulled. It made one hypocritical and immeshed in the conventions of sorrow. Many foolish and sentimental ideas came into being. Yet there was a struggle, for soon we revived, and there was a conflict between what we ought to be and what we were. ('Sketch': 105)

As her account attests, even as a young girl, Woolf is conscious that her outward response to her mother's death is inauthentic; yet the process of inculcation is so absolute that Woolf and her siblings believe that to behave in any other manner – to have moments of happiness and laughter in the wake of such a tragedy – would be unacceptable and unforgivable.

In the fourth section of *Being and Time,* Heidegger discusses the notion of 'Being-one's-self', declaring that: 'As they-self, the particular Dasein has been *dispersed* into the 'they', and must first find itself' (*BT*: 167). The sense that the individual loses his or her authentic sense of self through the immersion in the concerns, involvements and prescriptions of the everyday is given literary expression in

Between the Acts during the annual historical pageant. Throughout Woolf's final novel, the often-repeated refrain, '*dispersed are we*', becomes a motif for the principal message of the pageant's creator, Miss La Trobe, who seeks to disrupt the audience's immersion in the concerns and preoccupations of the everyday, and draw attention to their historical complicity in the world events that are unfolding in June 1939.

Curiosity, ambiguity and idle talk

According to Heidegger, the individual's typical state of dispersal can be attributed to his or her immersion in preoccupations such as 'curiosity', 'ambiguity' and 'idle talk', as each of these everyday modes of relating to the world distracts and distances the individual from an authentic mode of Being-in-the-world. As Heidegger explains, curiosity

> concerns itself with seeing, not in order to understand what is seen (that is, to come into a Being towards it) but *just* in order to see. It seeks novelty only in order to leap from it anew to another novelty. (*BT*: 216)

As a result, 'curiosity is concerned with the constant possibility of *distraction*' (*BT*: 216).

In the fourth section of *The Waves*, Bernard reflects upon the ways in which such inevitable and recurring preoccupations deter the individual not only from conducting authentic relations with the Other, but also from attaining an awareness of his or her own inauthenticity. As Bernard walks through London, he is conscious that his attempts to contemplate life and its meanings are 'interrupted, torn, pricked and plucked at by sensations, spontaneous and irrelevant, of curiosity, greed, desire, irresponsible as in sleep. (I covet that bag – etc.)' (*TW*: 85). As Heidegger attests, curiosity, ambiguity and the idle talk of gossip serve 'not so much to keep Being-in-the-world open for us in an articulated understanding, as rather to close it off, and cover up the entities within-the-world' (*BT*: 213).

Bernard describes the people who surround him on the city streets of London as 'these engrossed flocks; these starers and trippers; these errand-boys and furtive and fugitive girls who, ignoring their doom, look in at shop-windows'. In contrast to those immersed in such preoccupations, Woolf describes Bernard's desire to forego a shallow relationship to Being, and instead 'advance like one carried beneath the surface of a stream' (*TW*: 85). Woolf's representation of theyness as a current of water that directs the individual is reflected again later in the novel, as Bernard likens average everydayness to being 'swept on by the torrent of things grown so familiar that they cast no shadow. We float, we float' (*TW*: 198). The notion of floating reinforces the aforementioned propensity of the everyday self to maintain a superficial position in relation to Being, in the sense that he or she can rarely 'visit the profound depths' (*TW*: 85).[5]

Not unlike curiosity, Heidegger describes ambiguity as a further means by which the individual comes to be dispersed in the concerns of the everyday. As Heidegger remarks:

> When, in our everyday Being-with-one-another, we encounter the sort of thing which is accessible to everyone, and about which anyone can say anything, it soon becomes impossible to decide what is disclosed in a genuine understanding, and what is not. (*BT*: 217)

In *Mrs Dalloway*, the character, Peter Walsh, levels such a charge at the politician, Richard Dalloway, whom he believes is the source of Clarissa's tendency towards inauthenticity. Peter claims that Richard possesses 'a great deal of the public-spirited, British Empire, tariff-reform, governing-class spirit' (*MD*: 77), insofar as he both adheres to, and replicates, the prevailing dominant order. As he considers Clarissa, Peter laments his sense that: 'With a mind of her own, she must always be quoting Richard – as if one couldn't know to a tittle what Richard thought by reading the *Morning Post* of a morning!' (*MD*: 77). Peter's understanding of the newspaper as a prescriptive societal tool is in keeping with Heidegger's own reference, cited earlier in this chapter, to the newspaper as a public means of inhibiting and dissolving one's own authentic mode of Being (*BT*: 164). It is the pervasive and insidious quality of the newspaper in *Mrs Dalloway*, and the wireless in Woolf's essay, 'The Narrow Bridge of Art', which grants these media forms such immense influence and authority in terms of naturalising and homogenising particular perspectives, opinions, and approaches to Being-in-the-world.

In addition to Heidegger's stance regarding curiosity and ambiguity, in *Being and Time* the philosopher also refers to idle talk as a manifestation of theyness:

> Things are so because one says so. Idle talk is constituted by such gossiping and passing the word along – a process by which its initial lack of grounds to stand on [Bodenständigkeit] becomes aggravated to complete

> groundlessness [Bodenlosigkeit]. And indeed this idle talk is not confined to vocal gossip, but even spreads to what we write, where it takes the form of 'scribbling'. (*BT*: 212)

In much the same vein as Heidegger's assertion of the groundlessness and triviality of idle talk, in *Jacob's Room*, Woolf asks the reader to consider the social role of letters:

> Life would split asunder without them. 'Come to tea, come to dinner, what's the truth of the story? have you heard the news? life in the capital is gay; the Russian dancers [. . .]' These are our stays and props. These lace our days together and make of life a perfect globe. And yet, and yet [. . .] when we go to dinner, when pressing finger-tips we hope to meet somewhere soon, a doubt insinuates itself; is this the way to spend our days? the rare, the limited, so soon dealt out to us – drinking tea? dining out? And the notes accumulate. And the telephones ring. And everywhere we go wires and tubes surround us to carry the voices that try to penetrate before the last card is dealt and the days are over. 'Try to penetrate,' for as we lift the cup, shake the hand, express the hope, something whispers, Is this all? Can I never know, share, be certain? Am I doomed all my days to write letters, send voices, which fall upon the tea-table, fade upon the passage, making appointments, while life dwindles, to come and dine? Yet letters are venerable; and the telephone valiant, for the journey is a lonely one, and if bound together by notes and telephones we went in company, perhaps – who knows? – we might talk by the way. (*JR*: 125–6)

Aspiring to a greater collective sense of connection with the Other, the narrator of this passage is positioned from a perspective of authentic awareness, in that he or she can see beyond and beneath the social proclivities that govern everyday social relations and rituals. The repeated reference to the finitude of one's life is in keeping with Heidegger's assertion that the authentic individual acknowledges and understands that the choices that he or she makes matter in light of his or her inevitable state of Being-towards-death. It is from such a perspective that the narrator questions whether one should really live the day-to-day life in such a superficial manner. Throughout this passage, the narrator emphasises that authentic, meaningful communication and connection with the Other is neither the purpose, nor the outcome, of such everyday correspondence; similarly, Heidegger attests that 'when Dasein maintains itself in idle talk, it is – as Being-in-the-world – cut off from its primary and primordially genuine relationships-of-Being towards the world, towards

Dasein-with, and towards its very Being-in' (*BT*: 214).⁶ Drawing attention to Bernard's disavowal of idle talk in the final section of *The Waves*, Henke suggests that such a stance reflects his 'attempt to transcend everyday being-in-the-world and return to authentic discourse'; thus, he 'wants to get back to the primordial ground of being that has been "covered up" by Dasein's public mode of existence' (Henke 1989: 462).

The societal machine

Throughout her *oeuvre*, Woolf uses the motif of the societal 'machine' as a means of drawing attention to the constructs and ideological systems that distance the individual from his or her 'genuine relationships-of-Being towards the world'. In 'A Sketch of the Past', for instance, as Woolf describes the milieu at the turn of the twentieth century, she notes that 'Society in those days was a perfectly competent, perfectly complacent, ruthless machine. A girl had no chance against its fangs. No other desires – say to paint, or to write – could be taken seriously' ('Sketch': 158). As a young woman living in the family home during this time, Woolf experienced firsthand the effects of the societal machine in the form of a patriarchal discourse that denied women a formal tertiary education or a choice of profession.

Such a perspective is emphasised throughout Woolf's 1938 essay, *Three Guineas*, where she draws attention to the complicity of the public schools and universities as significant cogs in the societal machine. Arguably, such a view bears certain parallels with that of the Marxist thinker, Louis Althusser, who argues in 1970 that education, understood as an Ideological State Apparatus, functions 'massively and predominantly by *ideology*' and 'secondarily by repression, even if ultimately, but only ultimately, this is very attenuated and concealed, even symbolic' (Althusser 2011: 208). Such a sense of the repressive role and effect of education upon its students is evinced in *The Waves*, where Rhoda finds the conformity and uniformity that is expected and demanded by her English boarding school intolerable: 'we sit herded together . . . here I am nobody. I have no face. This great company, all dressed in brown serge, has robbed me of my identity' (*TW*: 23–4).

In *The Waves*, Bernard refers directly to society as a machine after he learns of the unexpected death of his friend, Percival. As an awareness of his own finitude overcomes him, Bernard finds himself standing temporarily outside 'the usual order' (*TW*: 117). Although granted a view of the world from an altered perspective, Bernard almost immediately finds himself becoming subsumed back into the everyday preoccupations of the they:

> Yet already signals begin, beckonings, attempts to lure me back. Curiosity is knocked out only for a short time. One cannot live outside the machine for more perhaps than half an hour . . . The sequence returns; one thing leads to another – the usual order. (*TW*: 117)

Reflecting the understanding that the individual's everyday default position is one of theyness, and that authenticity is only achieved through some degree of struggle, Bernard describes his sense of weariness: '"I am yawning. I am glutted with sensations. I am exhausted with the strain and the long, long time – twenty-five minutes, half an hour – that I have held myself alone outside the machine"' (*TW*: 119).

In her 1923 diary, Woolf records her desire that her fourth novel, *Mrs Dalloway*, would allow her to 'criticise the social system, & to show it at work, at its most intense' (*D2*: 248). Such an intention is demonstrated through Woolf's treatment of both the medical profession and religion, which are represented as significant cogs within the societal machine. Throughout her lifetime, Woolf repeatedly had her own faith in the medical profession compromised due to the questionable treatments she endured as a result of recurring bouts of mental illness. Woolf's damning view of the medical profession is openly expressed in *Mrs Dalloway*, where she equates the perspective of the psychiatrist, Sir William Bradshaw, with the socially sanctioned management, control and suppression of the lives of the mentally ill. Sir William's strict and chilling prescription that one must maintain a sense of 'proportion' (*MD*: 100) represents a disavowal of individuality in favour of the strict adherence to established and dominant norms and ideologies, regardless of the personal cost to the individual. As the novel's omniscient narrator observes:

> Sir William said he never spoke of 'madness'; he called it not having a sense of proportion . . . Proportion, divine proportion, Sir William's goddess . . . Worshipping proportion, Sir William not only prospered himself, but made England prosper, secluded her lunatics, forbade childbirth, penalised despair, made it impossible for the unfit to propagate their views until they, too, shared his sense of proportion. (*MD*: 97, 100)

Woolf is even more scathing in her treatment of religion in this novel; declaring that 'proportion has a sister, less smiling, more formidable', Woolf asserts that

> Conversion is her name and she feasts on the wills of the weakly, loving to impress, to impose, adoring her own features stamped on the face of the populace. At Hyde Park Corner on a tub she stands preaching; shrouds herself in white and walks penitentially disguised as brotherly love through factories and parliaments; offers help, but desires power; smites out of her way roughly the dissentient, or dissatisfied; bestows her blessing on those who, looking upward, catch submissively from her eyes the light of their own. (*MD*: 100–1)

In keeping with the understanding of theyness, Woolf highlights the propensity of religion to demand and create a conformity that requires unthinking submission at the expense of personal will. Religion's call for compliance and acquiescence is also stressed in *The Waves*, where a young Louis embraces religion while at boarding school in a conscious attempt to acquire a sense of belonging and acceptance:

> 'Now we march, two by two,' said Louis, 'orderly, processional, into chapel. I like the dimness that falls as we enter the sacred building. I like the orderly progress. We file in; we seat ourselves. We put off our distinctions as we enter . . . I become a figure in the procession, a spoke in the huge wheel that turning, at last erects me, here and now.' (*TW*: 24–5)[7]

Louis's response is in sharp contrast to that of his friend, Neville, as he too listens to the sermon given by Dr Crane:

> 'The brute menaces my liberty,' said Neville, 'when he prays. Unwarmed by imagination, his words fall cold on my head like paving-stones, while the gilt cross heaves on his waistcoat. The words of authority are corrupted by those who speak them. I gibe and mock at this sad religion, at these tremulous, grief-stricken figures advancing, cadaverous and wounded, down a white road shadowed by fig trees where boys sprawl in the dust.' (*TW*: 25)

Unlike Louis, who desperately desires to become inculcated into the stream of the social order, Neville rejects those prescriptions that threaten, control or deny his sense of self. As a homosexual situated in England in the first half of the twentieth century, Neville is also a social outsider; nevertheless, in contrast to Louis, Neville refutes the word of authority, having no desire to compromise or ingratiate himself for the sake of convention (*TW*: 52).

Neville's rejection of theyness is evident throughout the novel, from his opinion of the 'shop-girls' whose 'titter, their gossip, offends', to the 'pomp and the indifference and the emphasis, always on the wrong place, of people holding forth under chandeliers in full evening dress, wearing stars and decorations' (*TW*: 64, 136–7). In contrast to those individuals who do not question their everyday mode of Being, Neville describes an alternative, authentic sense of Being-in-the-world, one that is defined by, and achieved through, unconcealment and heterogeneous unity. As Neville proclaims:

> to myself I am immeasurable; a net whose fibres pass imperceptibly beneath the world. My net is almost indistinguishable from that which it surrounds. It lifts whales – huge leviathans and white jellies, what is amorphous and wandering; I detect, I perceive. Beneath my eyes opens – a book; I see to the bottom; the heart – I see to the depths. (*TW*: 164)

Conclusion – truth and reality

Not unlike Neville's grasp and perception of that which lies beneath and beyond the average everyday mode of Being-in-the-world, while holidaying in Italy in 1908, the 26-year-old Woolf records her desire to use writing as a means by which she might 'discover real things beneath the show' (*PA*: 384). Hafley suggests that such a wish to question and uncover is in keeping with Georgian approaches to literature evident at the turn of the century; indeed, unlike the Edwardian novelists who were concerned with facts,

> the Georgians, asking question after question, tried to probe beneath the surface of society and of human character, down to where they felt that the real truth lay hidden . . . The function of the artist, then, was not to reproduce 'actual facts' faithfully – indeed, he must give them the lie – but to assert the validity of the 'deeper world' and 'under-life' as the basis of a living reality. (Hafley 1963: 12–13)

As will be explored in detail in the final chapter, Heidegger emphasises that in the midst of the concerns of the everyday, the individual is typically unable to recognise, locate or uncover such a sense of truth, or 'living reality':

> Proximally and for the most part Dasein is lost in its 'world' . . . Its absorption in the 'they' signifies that it is dominated by the way things are publicly interpreted. That which has been uncovered and disclosed stands in a mode in which it has been disguised and closed off by idle talk, curiosity, and ambiguity. Being towards entities has not been extinguished, but it has been uprooted. (*BT*: 264)

In her fragmentary 1921 short story, 'Monday or Tuesday', Woolf defines truth as a site in which presence and absence, and concealment and unconcealment co-exist:

> the heron passes over the church beneath the sky. White and distant, absorbed in itself, endlessly the sky covers and uncovers, moves and remains. A lake? Blot the shores of it out! A mountain? Oh, perfect – the sun gold on its slopes. Down that falls. Ferns then, or white feathers, for ever and ever –
> Desiring truth, awaiting it, laboriously distilling a few words, for ever desiring . . . for ever desiring . . . for ever desiring truth . . .
> Flaunted, leaf-light, drifting at corners, blown across the wheels, silver-splashed, home or not home, gathered, scattered, squandered in separate scales, swept up, down, torn, sunk, assembled – and truth? . . .
> Lazy and indifferent the heron returns; the sky veils her stars; then bares them. (Woolf 2003b: 25–6)

In this story, Woolf signifies truth and reality as fluid and heterogeneous rather than centred and homogeneous. Indeed, for both Woolf and Heidegger, truth is defined by its propensity to incorporate and embrace concealment and unconcealment: as one truth is revealed, other truths are covered over in a continual process of flux so that presence and absence necessarily co-exist. Ultimately, such a delimitation of the metaphysical understanding of truth as absolute allows for 'alterity, otherness, a multiplicity and dispersal of centres, origins, presences' (Bennett and Royle 1999: 240). Reflecting a foundation for such a motivation, as early as 1908 Woolf records the desire that her writing might 'achieve a symmetry by means of infinite discords . . . & achieve in the end, some kind of whole made of shivering fragments' (*PA*: 393).

As her short story reflects, Woolf's understanding of the role of the writer is defined by a process of 'laboriously distilling a few words' in the pursuit of a reality that typically remains concealed by the preoccupations of the everyday. Arguably, Woolf's desire for a new understanding of reality is indicative of her political concern and engagement with the world in which she and her characters exist. Throughout the various forms of her writing, Woolf exposes the ideologies, dualisms and norms that govern, direct and control the individual's average everyday life. In contrast, Heidegger's treatment of truth can be understood as a reaction to what he perceives to be modernity's abandonment of the question of Being.

Despite such differences in terms of emphasis, Woolf and Heidegger share an understanding that Being-in-the-world is defined by a heterogeneous unity, insofar as the strict dichotomies of subject and world, and self and Other, come to be dismantled and rejected. This is in contrast to the metaphysical perspective, where truth is synonymous with *logos*, that is, a homogeneous and autonomous centre of presence and meaning. And while such a definition is critiqued by both Woolf and Heidegger, neither disallows the importance of truth or meaning; rather, they redefine it. Reflecting a central characteristic of Being-in-the-world, reality and truth come to be understood as multi-faceted, fluid and inclusive.

Notes

1. It is of note that Tetsuro credits his reading of *Sein und Zeit* in Berlin in 1927 as an inspiration for his reflections upon 'the problem of climate' (1988: v) in his monograph.
2. Not unlike *The Waves,* each chapter of *The Years* begins with descriptions of the weather and seasons as a means of representing the circumstances and events that are to be experienced by the extended Pargiter family.
3. From a personal perspective, such a sense of Being-with-Others is reflected in Woolf's 'A Sketch of the Past', through her discussion of the influence of war upon English attitudes to weather: 'I continue (22nd September 1940) on this wet day – we think of weather now as it affects invasions, as it affects raids, not as weather that we like or dislike privately' (2002d: 132).
4. It should be noted that Heidegger is far from alone in his assertion that individual existence always presupposes co-existence in a shared world with the Other.

5. Such a perspective is reflected in the mode of Being of the character Hugh Whitbread in *Mrs Dalloway*, a man who 'had been afloat on the cream of English society for fifty-five years', and 'did not go deeply. He brushed surfaces' (*MD*: 103).
6. In her discussion of Heidegger's notion of 'idle talk', Nancy J. Holland states:

    > This is the medium through which scripts are infused from the social environment into specific configurations of family life, from the media fascination with abnormally slender female bodies, for instance, into a family where emotional and physical control is valued above all else. (2001: 135)

7. De Gay draws attention to Louis's faith in Dr Crane's pronouncements as symptomatic of his desire to find 'a sense of rootedness and "continuity"'; as de Gay observes:

    > If Louis is a parody of T.S. Eliot, as has often been suggested, then here is a cruel suggestion that Eliot's adoption of Anglicanism was a part of a coping strategy to help assuage his insecurity at being born in America. (de Gay 2009: 18, 19)

Chapter 2

A Sense of Place

[T]o know her, or any one, one must seek out the people who completed them; even the places. (*MD*: 154–5)

As emphasised in the previous chapter, it is the average everyday lived experience of Being-in-the-world that is a central concern and preoccupation throughout Woolf's writings. Despite the incalculable variety of everyday experiences that any individual may encounter during his or her lifetime, each is always and inevitably located in a particular place, whether it be the home, the street, a city, the countryside, the workplace or an armchair. Place provides the setting and context for all experience.[1] The inherent connection between the individual, experience and place, and how each depends upon the other for definition and actuality, is a view that is repeatedly reinforced throughout Woolf's *oeuvre*. Woolf's representations of place demonstrate her understanding that such locations provide the individual with the potential means to carry out his or her intentions, form and gather memories, and feel safe and welcome; alternatively, and even simultaneously, Woolf's writings signify place as the site of threat, unease, and thwarted hopes and desires. Place facilitates our connections with the Other and sense of inclusion, as well as our moments of solitude, isolation and exclusion. From conception to death, place is a primordial and integral element of what it means to be human. Emphasised and demonstrated throughout this chapter is the understanding that, for Woolf, place provides a tangible representation of the hierarchies and ideologies that underlie the formations of English society in the late nineteenth century and first half of the twentieth century.

From the outset of this chapter, it must be acknowledged that the issues of place and spatiality within *Being and Time* have been largely overlooked or strongly criticised by critics, due mainly to Heidegger's preoccupation with the issues of time and temporality; indeed, as Heidegger emphasises: 'The temporality of Being-in-the-world' is 'the foundation for that spatiality which is specific for Dasein' (*BT*: 384). Despite such assertions, as his later work testifies, the notion that space and place are derived from time is a view that Heidegger himself comes to abandon. Works such as Jeff Malpas's monograph, *Heidegger's Topology: Being, Place, World* (2008), and Edward Casey's *The Fate of Place: A Philosophical History* (1997) reflect a turn towards Heidegger's *Being and Time* as a significant contribution to understandings of place.

In his study of Heidegger's treatment of place in *Being and Time*, Malpas rightly asserts that one needs to be aware that this topic 'emerges, not so much in Heidegger's use of the specific language of place', but rather 'through his employment of terms such as "*Dasein*" . . . "*Welt*" (world), "*Umwelt*" (environment, environing world), and "*Situation*" or "*Lage*" (both of which can be translated as "situation")' (Malpas 2008: 32). Through his repeated insistence upon the significance of Dasein's practical everyday engagement with the world, Heidegger demonstrates that it is the individual's interactions and involvements with his or her environment, as opposed to any quantifiable measurement of space, which defines that individual's relationship to place. As Heidegger asserts, Dasein 'is "in" the world in the sense that it deals with entities encountered within-the-world, and does so concernfully and with familiarity. So if spatiality belongs to it in any way, that is possible only because of this Being-in' (*BT*: 138).

This chapter will detail Woolf's personal involvements with place, particularly the city of London, and the ways that her own experiences come to be translated into her writings; demonstrating Woolf's understanding of place as the site of the individual's everyday interactions, activities and involvements, not only the manners in which place influences and shapes such experiences are detailed, but also the ways in which the average everyday lives of the individual impact upon formations of place. From such a perspective, Woolf's interest in the connection between place and socio-economic disparities within English society will be examined, most particularly through a study of her representation of the 'street', which becomes a motif not only for class divides, but also for the potential transcendence of difference. The relationship between place and time will be discussed, with the suggestion that Woolf's emphasis upon the temporal nature of place has implications for understandings of the individual's inherent temporality.

One of the more significant characteristics of place that this chapter will explicate is its capacity to reflect, facilitate and impede the primordial state of Being-with-Others. Central to this concern is the notion of 'de-severance', a Heideggerian term that refers to the degree of connection and involvement that an individual has with the Other or a particular place, regardless of measurable physical distance (*BT*: 139–44). Instances of de-severance in Woolf's writings reflect an existential approach to place: the individual's relationship with place comes to be defined by involvement. For Woolf, the ways that different individuals experience public and communal places not only reflect one's average everyday mode of Being-in-the-world; such interactions also reveal much about the prevailing social order and its capacity to determine which members of society are granted access to, or excluded from, particular sites. From the perspective of a writer situated between the two World Wars, Woolf both observes and calls into question the prevailing inside and outside dualism that she believes provides the foundation for the discourses of nationalism, imperialism, patriarchy and war, each of which impacts upon understandings and manifestations of place.

Ultimately, the thread that connects each of these perspectives and issues is Woolf's understanding that place both reflects and defines each individual's location in the world; not in terms of a geometric co-ordinate; rather, as a manifestation of one's mode of Being-in-the-world. As Woolf's writings attest, every place in which we find ourselves is representative of innumerable forces that typically go unseen or unrecognised, thereby representing more than simply a mark on a map.

Woolf's London

The biographical details of Woolf's often intense connections to place are prominent throughout her essays, diaries, memoirs and letters. It is Woolf's own attachments to and experiences of place that provide the foundation for the representations of many of the settings incorporated into her writings. In terms of large-scale manifestations of place, those sites that were of particular significance and influence during Woolf's lifetime were the city of London and the English countryside. Aside from the five years she spent living in suburban Richmond, from childhood through to the last years of her life, Woolf maintained both city and rural abodes, dividing her time between the two according to her obligations, engagements, and the fluctuating desire for the stimulation of the city or the quiet and solitude of the country. Woolf's feelings for both locales shifted constantly as a result of the demands that her work, mental health and innumerable social obligations placed upon her.

Purchased by the Woolfs in 1919, Monk's House, in the village of Rodmell, East Sussex, was an essential retreat for Woolf after the often overwhelming social engagements and obligations experienced while in London.[2] On various occasions, Woolf records her everyday experience of life in London as both stressful and unsettling: 'I felt as if the telephone were strung to my arm & anybody could jerk me who liked. A sense of interruption bothered me' (D3: 238). Nevertheless, while Woolf's fiction is littered with negative impressions of the city, just as her diaries describe London as 'stony hearted, & callous' (D2: 298), 'too tight, too hot, & distracted' (D5: 90), and characterised by 'extreme jadedness' (D5: 302), for this writer, London is also the site of culture, society, excitement, as well as 'More pack & thrill' (D5: 329) than her countryside abodes. Despite Woolf's repeated criticism of London throughout her fictional and non-fictional writings, her fascination for this city is unswerving; for Woolf, this place is not simply a site that has the capacity to overwhelm, depress and frustrate; this city also stimulates, invigorates and inspires.[3]

Having spent the greater part of her life in London, this city remained a centre of meaning for Woolf even during those periods when she resided elsewhere. The influence of this place upon not only Woolf's creativity, but also the quality of her life, is highlighted in a diary entry recorded in 1923, during a period of enforced exile from the city that resulted from a particularly severe episode of mental illness:

> I ... now sit down baffled & depressed to face a life spent, mute & mitigated, in the suburbs, just as I had it in mind that I could at last go full speed ahead. For the capacities in me will never after 40, accumulate again. And I mind missing life far more than he [Leonard] does, for it isn't life to him in the sense that it is life to me. Oh to be able to slip in & out of things easily, to be in them, not on the verge of them – I resent this effort & waste ... Always to catch trains, always to waste time, to sit

here & wait for Leonard to come in . . . when, alternatively, I might go & hear a tune, or have a look at a picture, or find out something at the British Museum, or go adventuring among human beings. Sometimes I should merely walk down Cheapside. But now I'm tied, imprisoned, inhibited . . . For ever to be suburban . . . Moreover for my work now, I want freer intercourse, wider intercourse. (*D2*: 250–1)

As this passage demonstrates, in contrast to suburban Richmond, for Woolf London provides the impetus for life itself, from creative inspiration, to Being-with-Others, and mental and physical freedom.[4] Even after her slow recovery, Woolf was strongly encouraged by her husband, Leonard, to avoid London, due to his fear that the stimulation of this city might result in his wife's relapse. In fact, it was not until early 1924, and only as a result of Woolf's repeated insistence, that the couple were to return to London. On the day of signing her ten-year lease for a property in Tavistock Square, Woolf writes ecstatically of her sense that 'music, talk, friendship, city views, books, publishing, something central & inexplicable, all this is now within my reach' (*D2*: 283).

An existential view of place

In her 1931 essay, 'Portrait of a Londoner', Woolf describes this city as not only 'a gorgeous spectacle, a mart, a court, a hive of industry, but as a place where people meet and talk, laugh, marry, and die, paint, write and act, rule and legislate' (2006d: 76). Emphasised in this account is Woolf's sense that the individual's relationship to place is defined by everyday involvements, an understanding that reverberates throughout her writings. It is in this sense that Woolf, like Heidegger, views place principally from an existential perspective, that is, one that is founded upon the average everyday ways in which both the individual and the collective utilise and involve themselves in and with the sites that they encounter.

For both Woolf and Heidegger, the relationship between the individual and place is a reciprocal one: each defines and shapes the other through an inseparable connection that is formed by and through average everyday involvements. In particular, it is the repetitious activities of the quotidian that have the greatest impact, not only upon the individual's connection to place, but also upon the physical characteristics of place itself. Such a view is evinced in

Woolf's 1922 memoir, 'Old Bloomsbury', where she reflects upon her London childhood home at 22 Hyde Park Gate:

> The place seemed tangled and matted with emotion. I could write the history of every mark and scratch in my room ... The walls and the rooms had in sober truth been built to our shape. We had permeated the whole vast fabric – it has since been made into an hotel – with our family history. (2002b: 45)

Woolf's recollections emphasise the ways that this place comes to be a tangible representation of the involvements and experiences of the lived life, insofar as its built structure is both formed and informed by the physical and emotional lives of this large and diverse family. Such an understanding of the tangible connection between place and individual is also underscored in Heidegger's 1927 lecture course *The Basic Problems of Phenomenology*, where he refers to Rainer Maria Rilke's 1910 novel, *The Notebooks of Malte Laurids Brigge*. In the novel, Rilke's protagonist provides an extended description of a group of partially demolished houses:

> most unforgettable were the walls themselves. The tenacious life of these rooms refused to let itself be trampled down. It was still there; it clung to the nails that had remained; it stood on the handsbreadth remnant of the floor. (Heidegger 1982: 172)

Responding to this passage, Heidegger writes:

> Notice here in how elemental a way the world, being-in-the-world – Rilke calls it life – leaps towards us from the things ... Let us recall Rilke's description in which he shows how the inhabitants of the demolished house, those fellow humans, are encountered with its wall. The fellow humans with whom we have to do daily are also there, even without any explicit existentiell relation of one Dasein to others. (1982: 173, 289)

The understanding that place comes to be defined by such human connections and everyday experiences is also highlighted in the interlude of *To the Lighthouse*, a novel that is largely based upon Woolf's childhood experiences at Talland House in St Ives, Cornwall. In this novel, after the unexpected death of the matriarch, Mrs Ramsay, the family's summer residence is abandoned, and concern for its upkeep is suspended for many years. The absence of those who once lived within this busy family home changes not only the appearance of this place, but also its meaning; whereas this house was once the site of all the joys and complexities of family life, upon the subsequent passing of three of the family members, the significance of this place is transformed to become a painful reminder of people and events that can never be reclaimed or relived. Deserted, the house itself becomes cadaver-like as it slowly decays and rots, becoming infested with rats, moths, mould, flies and weeds. The process of this home's regeneration only begins upon the remaining family members' return.

Not unlike her depiction of the Ramsay's summer house, in her 1932 essay, 'Great Men's Houses', Woolf's description of the now-bare rooms that were once inhabited by John Keats highlights the impact of the absence of human presence upon manifestations of place:

> And perhaps it is because the rooms are so empty and furnished rather with light and shadow than with chairs and tables that one does not think of people, here where so many people have lived. The imagination does not evoke scenes. It does not strike one that there must have been eating and drinking here; people must have come in and out; they must have put down bags, left parcels; they must have scrubbed and cleaned and done battle with dirt and disorder and carried cans of water from the basement to the bedrooms. All the traffic of life is silenced. (2006b: 37–8)

In this passage, Woolf places greatest emphasis upon the commonplace events of everyday life, such as shopping and housework, and the ways that such daily acts and rituals turn a nondescript space into a place. When those everyday routines cease, through the absence of the individual, the significance of a place inevitably shifts.

In contrast to Woolf's representations of the individual's everyday involvements within the context of the private space of the home, in *A Room of One's Own*, Woolf explores the relationship between the quotidian, the individual and the suburban street:

> In my little street ... domesticity prevailed. The house painter was descending his ladder; the nursemaid was wheeling the perambulator carefully in and out back to nursery tea; the coal-heaver was folding his empty sacks on top of each other; the woman who keeps the greengrocer's shop was adding up the day's takings with her hands in red mittens. (*RO*: 51)

The configuration of this street demonstrates the basic average everyday requirements of an individual located in English urban society, such as a home to provide security and shelter; a store to supply food; and a mode of employment in order that one might afford to live. Woolf's depiction of this street also neatly highlights the gendered nature of working-class employment in the first half of the twentieth century.

As her essay progresses, Woolf turns her attention to the city street, recording the varied modes of everyday life experienced in a place as radically diverse as London:

> The fascination of the London street is that no two people are ever alike; each seems bound on some private affair of his own. There were the business-like, with their little bags; there were the drifters rattling sticks upon area railings; there were affable characters to whom the streets serve for clubroom, hailing men in carts and giving information without being asked for it. Also there were funerals to which men, thus suddenly reminded of the passing of their own bodies, lifted their hats. And then a very distinguished gentleman came slowly down a doorstep and paused to avoid collision with a bustling lady who had, by some means or other, acquired a splendid fur coat and a bunch of Parma violets. They all seemed separate, self-absorbed, on business of their own. (*RO*: 124–5)

Despite their shared location on this busy city street, each of the characters described in Woolf's essay is unique in terms of their physical characteristics, financial status, purpose and intentions.

While Woolf's overt claim appears to be that the city street is representative of the inherent separateness of individuals, the low modality of her statements, where each person only 'seems bound on some private affair of his own' and 'seemed' to be 'separate, self-absorbed, on business of their own' undermines such a view. Woolf's descriptions of the various interactions and involvements that take place on this street provide evidence of her sense of the inextricable connectedness that defines Being-with-Others: funeral processions remind passers-by of their shared mortality; a gentleman must change his course to make way for a 'bustling lady'; certain 'characters' seek discourse with the strangers with whom they share the street. Emphasised in Woolf's description is the understanding that the city street, to at least some degree, is a place that provides the individual with the opportunity to connect with the Other, all the while maintaining his or her sense of self.

Place and socio-economic disparities

Throughout her novels and essays, Woolf's representation of the city street becomes a means of both emphasising and calling into question the ingrained class stratifications that are a defining element of the London social order. In her 1932 essay, 'Oxford Street Tide', Woolf highlights the everyday struggles of working-class Londoners through her description of this bustling, noisy place, which is defined by its consumerism and crowds. Woolf's representation of Oxford Street demonstrates her impression that this locale possesses a brutal honesty that refuses to mask the everyday hardships that many members of society have no choice but to experience. Drawing attention to the man who must make a sale in order to have a bed for the night; the woman whose husband's meagre earnings do not allow her to dress like her neighbours; and the woman who is both thief and prostitute, Woolf asserts that

> A thousand such voices are always crying aloud in Oxford Street. All are tense, all are real, all are urged out of their speakers by the pressure of making a living, finding a bed, somehow keeping afloat on the bounding, careless, remorseless tide of the street. And even a moralist, who is, one must suppose, since he can spend the afternoon dreaming, a man with a balance in the bank – even a moralist must allow that this gaudy, bustling, vulgar street reminds us that life is a struggle. (2006c: 26–7)

Referring to Woolf's essay, Squier observes that 'By stripping us of the defining and limiting possessions of the private home, the city street permits imaginative passage into many lives' (1983: 494). Such a perspective is evident in *A Room of One's Own*, as Woolf contemplates the unrecorded and therefore little-known everyday lives of women, which have been carried out unseen behind the closed doors of the private space throughout history. Pondering how the achievements and struggles of these women might be illuminated, Woolf finds herself wandering 'in thought through the streets of London' (*RO*: 117), demonstrating her understanding that it is the street, as a public and communal site, which provides the opportunity for a glimpse of the everyday goings-on of women of all classes; indeed, it is in this locale that one might view not only the 'respectably booted and furred', but also the 'violet-seller and match-sellers and old crones stationed under doorways', and 'drifting girls whose faces, like waves in sun and cloud, signal the coming of men and women and the flickering lights of shop windows' (*RO*: 116, 117).[5]

In Woolf's writings, the street is consistently representative of the social status of her characters, thereby granting the reader a deeper insight into the lives of such individuals. Hana Wirth-Nesher suggests that in *Mrs Dalloway*: 'The particular route of each pedestrian is a telling indicator of character: Clarissa walks down Bond Street, the most elegant shopping street of the city, pausing nostalgically in front of shops patronized by generations of family members' (1996: 184–6). The notion of the street as a measure and means of characterisation is particularly evident in Woolf's depiction of the sisters, Sara and Maggie Pargiter, in her 1937 novel *The Years*. Highlighting the permeability and fluidity of class distinctions, while their parents are alive, these two young women reside in a well-appointed home in a middle-class suburb of London, complete with a manservant and housemaid; after their parents' death, Sara and Maggie find themselves living on a 'shabby street', in a room that 'was rather poverty-stricken' (*TY*: 119, 121). As Tamar Katz remarks, the migration of characters to different areas of London as the novel progresses becomes a tangible expression of their 'different locations on the economic and cultural spectrum . . . The Pargiters accordingly journey across the city repeatedly' (2010: 12).

Sara and Maggie's fall from a comfortable middle-class existence dispels the notion that poverty is simply the result of life choices, rather than circumstance and social inequality. The propensity of the former view is underscored when North Pargiter visits his cousin, Sara, towards the end of the novel; unlike her sister, who has since married, Sara lives alone in a lodging-house in what North describes as a 'dirty', 'sordid', 'low-down street' of London. Disgusted by the surroundings, North asks his cousin, 'Why d'you always choose slums –' (*TY*: 227, 230). Despite the fact that Sara is clearly without the financial means to afford better accommodation, North maintains the naive view that his cousin could and should be better situated.

In her 1933 mock-biography, *Flush*, Woolf highlights society's lack of knowledge or understanding of the reality of poverty when Elizabeth Barrett is forced to visit nearby slums in order to recover her stolen dog. Riding by cab through this sordid area that lies only a 'stone's-throw' (*Flush*: 51) from her own home, Elizabeth is faced with the realisation that

> This, then, was what lay on the other side of Wimpole Street – these faces, these houses. She had seen more while she sat in the cab at the public-house than she had seen during the five years that she had lain in the back bedroom at Wimpole Street. (*Flush*: 64)

Woolf emphasises the blinkered vision of the upper classes, who fail to acknowledge or explore the world and circumstances that lie outside their immediate experiences. Acknowledging her own 'social blindness' in 'The Niece of an Earl', Woolf describes writers' 'ignorance of the working classes', asserting that 'the English novelist in particular . . . cannot escape from the box in which he has been bred' (1986c: 216–17).

Providing explicit and unsettling details of the extreme squalor in *Flush*, Woolf describes 'ruined sheds in which human beings lived herded together above herds of cows', and 'a jerry-built tenement house' where the 'rain dripped through the roof and the wind blew through the walls'. Located in the midst of such an environment, a child is forced to dip 'a can into a bright-green stream' that was used for both drinking and washing because 'the landlord only allowed water to be turned on twice a week' (*Flush*: 52).[6] Depicted as a dark, menacing, dangerous site, this scene of abject poverty lies in sharp contrast to affluent Wimpole Street, where Elizabeth Barrett and her family reside; as the biographer ironically attests:

> when the world seems tumbling to ruin, and civilization rocks on its foundations, one has only to go to Wimpole Street; to pace that avenue; to survey those houses; to consider their uniformity; to marvel at the window curtains and their consistency; to admire the brass knockers and their regularity . . . one has only to go to Wimpole Street and drink deep of the peace breathed by authority. (*Flush*: 13–14)

Despite such a contrast, Elizabeth's visit to this site of desolation does not become a means of justifying the division of the classes; rather, as a result of her experience, Elizabeth grasps a greater awareness of the commonality of all individuals through the recognition that it is circumstance and inequality, rather than inherent differences, that lay the foundations for such social disparities. As Elizabeth remarks, 'Here lived women like herself; while she lay on her sofa, reading, writing, they lived thus' (*Flush*: 64).

Like the slums described in *Flush*, there is little physical distance between the homeless people situated in Woolf's 1927 essay, 'Street Haunting', and the more affluent members of society:

> Often enough these derelicts choose to lie not a stone's throw from theatres, within hearing of barrel organs, almost, as night draws on, within touch of the sequined cloaks and bright legs of diners and dancers. They lie close to those shop windows where commerce offers to a world of

old women laid on doorsteps, of blind men, of hobbling dwarfs, sofas which are supported by the gilt necks of proud swans; tables inlaid with baskets of many coloured fruit; sideboards paved with green marble the better to support the weight of boars' heads. (Woolf 1942e: 23)

While Woolf emphasises the stark inequality that divides the classes located within London's capitalist society, her use of the designation 'us' for the upper classes, and 'they' for the lower classes in this essay would appear to reinforce rather than question the prevailing class stratification: 'They do not grudge us, we are musing, our prosperity' (1942e: 23). As the narrator wanders through the sordid streets between Holborn and Soho, she gazes at the individuals whom she describes as 'the humped, the twisted, the deformed', questioning, 'In what crevices and crannies, one might ask, did they lodge, this maimed company of the halt and the blind?' (1942e: 23, 22).

In keeping with her depiction of the slums in *Flush,* the streets inhabited by these poverty-stricken individuals are deemed unsanitary, remote and frightening; what is most unsettling for the reader is the fact that those dwelling in these areas are, in effect, often dehumanised through Woolf's descriptions of their locality. While acknowledging Woolf's blatantly harsh treatment of the Other, there is merit in Squier's assertion that 'Street Haunting' 'makes use of an urban situation to initiate a consideration of the origins of social stratification and the impact of gender, class, and material possessions upon one's sense of self' (1985: 49). Such a view of Woolf's writing shares affinities with those presented by Alison Light in her monograph, *Mrs Woolf and the Servants*; drawing attention to 'The offensive passages in Virginia's writing about the poor or the suburban, about "the Jew" or "negroes"', Light suggests that Woolf was nevertheless 'highly unusual in examining many of her reactions and feelings, probing her sore spots, especially in her diaries'. Putting Woolf's work into its historical and social context, Light rightly reminds contemporary readers that 'Between the wars the English were not incidentally class-conscious; it was how their society was structured' (2007: xviii).[7]

The temporality of place

During the turbulent period spanning the two World Wars, throughout English society the desire to maintain the strict hierarchies of class was based to some extent upon a perceived need to preserve this significant benchmark of the social order amid the uncertainty created by external forces; as Neil Rattigan suggests, at this point 'the rigid division of British society along class lines was its key defining structure, both socially and culturally' (2001: 15). The individual was faced not only with the devastating effects of the First World War, but also with the ominous dread of impending war. It is within such a context that Woolf's final novel, *Between the Acts*, takes place. Set in 1939, when Britain's involvement in the Second World War is only months away, the story represents a point in time when its characters are faced with the knowledge that their everyday way of life is under imminent threat.

Such a sense of the impending violence and devastation of war is highlighted as Giles gazes at the landscape surrounding the family home, envisaging that 'At any moment guns would rake that land into furrows; planes splinter Bolney Minster into smithereens and blast the Folly' (*BA*: 34). Having been the residence of the Oliver family for over 120 years, Pointz Hall is a symbol of permanence and continuity for the three generations of the family who currently make it their home: 'Butterfly catching, for generation after generation, began there; for Bartholomew and Lucy; for Giles; for George it had begun only the day before yesterday' (*BA*: 36). Under the threat of war, however, it is possible that young George will belong to the last generation of Olivers to be born in this house. It is of note that the land surrounding Pointz Hall is the subject of discussion that opens this novel; addressing his guests, Bartholomew Oliver describes the history of the site that was chosen for the cesspool:

> From an aeroplane, he said, you could still see, plainly marked, the scars made by the Britons; by the Romans; by the Elizabethan manor house; and by the plough, when they ploughed the hill to grow wheat in the Napoleonic wars. (*BA*: 5)

Menaced by the risk of future annihilation, this historically rich plot of land signifies the temporal interpenetration and co-existence of the past, present and future.

The connection between place and history is a notion that is briefly explored in Heidegger's *Being and Time,* which, as the title suggests, is concerned with the relationship between time and the individual's state of Being-in-the-world. Under the subheading,

'Dasein's Historicality, and World-History', Heidegger claims that, 'even Nature is historical', explaining that 'Nature is historical as a countryside, as an area that has been colonized or exploited, as a battlefield, or as the site of a cult' (*BT*: 440). As Bambach explains, Heidegger's reference to nature as historical implies that: 'As phenomena, history and nature are temporal processes or, rather, are experienced temporally by human beings. This original mode of experiencing precedes all explicitly scientific thematization of nature or history as "objects"' (1995: 244).

Heidegger asserts that such historicising of place indicates and expresses the inherent unity of the world and Dasein: both are intrinsically temporal. As discussed in the previous chapter, for Heidegger, authentic time is understood as the interpenetration of past, present and future, rather than a linear sequence that privileges the present. As will be explored in detail in the fourth chapter, such a perspective has significant implications for Heidegger's understanding of the individual, whose mode of Being-in-the-world is defined as temporal.

In *Being and Time*, Heidegger states that 'history belongs to Dasein's Being, and this Being is based on temporality'. The philosopher emphasises that 'what is *primarily* historical is Dasein. That which is *secondarily* historical, however, is what we encounter within-the-world' (*BT*: 431, 433). It is from such a perspective that 'entities' such as buildings or nature are viewed as 'secondarily historical' in relation to human beings, as they

> have a character of 'the past' and of history by reason of the fact that they have belonged as equipment to a world that has been – the world of a Dasein that has been there – and that they have been derived from that world. (*BT*: 432)

Heidegger's understanding of the historical nature of both individual and place, as well as the relationship between the two, is given fictional representation in *Orlando,* a novel that follows the adventures of a protagonist whose life spans several centuries. As the story draws to a close, Orlando is now a 36-year-old woman living in the present time of 1927. Travelling home in her motor-car, Orlando contemplates the notion that one's 'true self' may be understood to be comprised 'of all the selves we have it in us to be' (*O*: 214). Feeling a sense of discombobulation as she attempts to come to some understanding of who she really is, Orlando concedes, 'if there are (at a venture) seventy-six different times all ticking in the mind at once, how many different people are there not – Heaven help us – all having lodgment at one time or another in the human spirit?' (O: 212). Contemplating her long and varied past, and the way that it forms and defines her sense of identity, Orlando's search for her 'true self' becomes ever more elusive; it is not until her return home, as '(she had passed through the lodge gates and was entering the park)', that she suddenly became 'what is called, rightly or wrongly, a single self, a real self' (O: 216).

Mirroring the unity of the built form of her ancestral home – which bears the mark of each of the generations of ancestors that have gone before her (O: 74) – it is only upon Orlando's return to this place of significance that her past and present selves interpenetrate to form a heterogeneous whole. Treating her home like a friend, Orlando muses that she understands the rooms of this place like no other:

> They had known each other for close on four centuries now . . . She knew what age each part of them was and its little secrets – a hidden drawer, a concealed cupboard, or some deficiency perhaps, such as a part made up, or added later. (O: 218)

Like her own 'true self', this place is temporal: its past is inextricably connected to its present and future possibilities.

As a means of illustrating the notion that the past and present are not separate and autonomous, but in fact interpenetrate, in *Being and Time* Heidegger posits the example of a Greek temple, suggesting that

> 'the past' has a remarkable double meaning; the past belongs irretrievably to an earlier time; it belonged to the events of that time; and in spite of that, it can still be present-at-hand 'now' – for instance, the remains of a Greek temple. With the temple, a 'bit of the past' is still 'in the present.' (*BT*: 430)

Such an understanding is representative, at least to a certain degree, of Orlando's relationship to her grand ancestral estate. By the novel's end, Orlando's home has become a museum, so that, by definition, 'It belonged to time now; to history; was past the touch and control of the living' (O: 219). Nevertheless, as she enters the gallery, Orlando finds that within this place the events and people of the past are far from removed or inaccessible:

> The gallery stretched far away to a point where the light almost failed. It was as a tunnel bored deep into the past. As her eyes peered down it, she could see people laughing and talking; the great men she had known; Dryden, Swift, and Pope; and statesmen in colloquy . . . and people eating and drinking at the long tables . . . A coffin was borne into the chapel. A marriage procession came out of it. Armed men with helmets left for the wars. They brought banners back from Flodden and Poitiers and stuck them on the wall. The long gallery filled itself thus. (O: 219–20)

Just as each of Orlando's experiences throughout the centuries have left their mark on her sense of self, so too does Orlando's home carry the trace of all who have walked through its halls. Reflecting the temporal nature of both individual and place, each comes to be defined in the present by their experiences in the past. As de Gay remarks, within this scene in Woolf's novel, 'the past is represented spatially rather than temporally, so that it still exists to be viewed from the present' (2007a: 66). As this passage suggests, it is the images and memories of the average everyday lives of the '*primarily* historical' people who once walked through these rooms, combined with the '*secondarily* historical' (*BT*: 433) architecture itself, which provides the richest source of history.

Place and Being-with-Others

In his autobiographical writings, Leonard Woolf describes the experience of living in the historic homes that he and Virginia shared in Rodmell and Richmond:

> In both one felt a quiet continuity of people living. Unconsciously one was absorbed into this procession of men, women, and children who since 1600 or 1700 sat in the panelled rooms, clattered up and down stairs, and had planted the great Blenheim apple-tree or the ancient fig-tree. One became a part of history and of a civilization by continuing in the line of all their lives. (1975: 15–16)

Emphasised in Leonard Woolf's description is not only the temporal connection that unites the individual with place, but also the ties that are created between the self and the Other.

As explained in the previous chapter, for Heidegger, an essential element of Being-in-the-world is one's relationship to and with the Other. In *Being and Time*, Heidegger demonstrates the ways in which place comes to be representative of the understanding that Being-in-the-world equates to Being-with-Others:

> When, for example, we walk along the edge of a field but 'outside it', the field shows itself as belonging to such-and-such a person, and decently kept up by him; the book we have used was bought at So-and-so's shop and given by such-and-such a person, and so forth. The boat anchored at the shore is assigned in its Being-in-itself to an acquaintance who undertakes voyages with it; but even if it is a 'boat which is strange to us', it still is indicative of Others. (*BT*: 153–4)

From such a perspective, place – whether it is a city, a room, a painting or a bed – becomes the means by which the individual is afforded the ability and opportunity to form connections with the Other. Such associations can take many forms, and may be defined by physical immediacy, or, as Leonard Woolf attests, through a piece of architecture constructed centuries earlier that was once inhabited by those who are now long gone.

Such a view is reflected in Woolf's depiction of the breakfast table in *To the Lighthouse*. Upon her return to the Ramsays' summer house after a ten-year absence, Lily Briscoe finds herself sitting 'at her old place at the breakfast table, but alone' (*TL*: 139). This simple image comes to represent not only present and past time, but also the notion of loss, and the significance of average everyday routines. The breakfast table is a tangible reminder that the deaths of members of the Ramsay family years earlier determine the possibilities of both the present and future: on the most basic of levels, Lily will never again sit at this table and share a meal and conversations with these individuals. Woolf's representation of this scene emphasises her understanding that our primordial state of Being-with-Others is imbued in the places we inhabit: these sites retain the trace of those who have come before, and anticipate those who will appear in the future.

The connection between past, place and our relationships with the Other is highlighted in *Mrs Dalloway*. For Clarissa Dalloway, her childhood companions, Peter and Sally, are inseparably connected to her former family home at Bourton. Clarissa's memories of this place act as a frame for the novel, which opens with her calling to mind scenes from Bourton as she walks through London: Clarissa 'could hear now' (*MD*: 1) the sound of the French windows opening onto a crisp Bourton morning, one that clearly features her former beau, Peter Walsh. Throughout the novel, Peter's return to London compels Clarissa to revisit her feelings for this figure from her past, which are inevitably tied and connected to 'scene after scene at Bourton' (*MD*: 4). Clarissa's recollections demonstrate that an individual's memories of past experiences and interactions with the Other are always located in a particular place; for Clarissa, the recurring memory of her rejection of Peter's marriage proposal would always include the setting of 'the little garden by the fountain' (*MD*: 5); it was in this place, years before, that the present and future lives of Clarissa, Peter and Richard were each set on a particular course. For Clarissa, the past is defined by the interweaving of self and place: '(all day she had been thinking of Bourton, of Peter, of Sally)' (*MD*: 187).

In his discussion of *Mrs Dalloway*, Ricoeur refers to Woolf's technique of using a single setting, such as a park or street, as a means of drawing together those characters who are unknown to each other, such as Clarissa Dalloway and Septimus Smith. Ricoeur suggests that 'A bridge is built between these souls both through the continuity of place and the reverberation of an internal discourse in another person' (1986: 105). Such a perspective is particularly pertinent in a novel such as *Mrs Dalloway*, which is set in London five years after the end of the First World War. That the whole city, in a sense, remains shell-shocked after such immense loss and hardship, is apparent not only through a character such as the returned soldier Septimus Smith, but also through peripheral characters such as 'Lady Bexborough who opened a bazaar, they said, with the telegram in her hand, John, her favourite, killed' (*MD*: 2). London comes to symbolise both the reason and the reward for such loss: it has been defended and retained, along with its traditions and ways of life. Clarissa can walk the city streets, buy flowers and hold a party as a result of such sacrifices. It is in this sense, among others, that the city becomes a conduit for the many and varied connections between its seemingly disparate inhabitants.

In his discussion of Heidegger's treatment of space and intersubjectivity, Malpas states that while the philosopher does not make explicit his understanding that 'social being is *necessarily* spatial being' (2008: 88), such a perspective is consistently demonstrated through Heidegger's emphasis upon the primordial connection between Being-in-the-world and Being-with-Others: 'Being-with is such that the disclosedness of the Dasein-with of Others belongs to it' (*BT*: 160). From the perspective of spatiality, Heidegger's approach to this issue is reflected in his discussion of the environment of 'the work-world', where he explains that 'along with the equipment to be found when one is at work [in Arbeit], those Others for whom the "work" ["Werk"] is destined are "encountered too"' (*BT*: 153). As Malpas asserts, for Heidegger

> It is only through the location of others in space, and so also in relation to the things and places with which I am myself located in that space, that I can grasp others as existing both outside and yet alongside myself, as having a view on the world that is like my own and yet a view that is not my own. (2008: 88)

In her first novel, *The Voyage Out,* Woolf uses the architecture of the Santa Marina hotel as a means of illustrating her own understanding that Being-with-Others is an inextricable element of each individual's fundamental state of Being-in-the-world. With its many rooms, this building would initially appear to demonstrate the potential of place to both literally and metaphorically separate self and Other. Yet, as the following passage indicates, the divisions that appear to create such separation are in fact fragile and permeable constructs:

> the downstairs rooms at the hotel grew dim and were almost deserted, while the little box-like squares above them were brilliantly irradiated. Some forty or fifty people were going to bed. The thump of jugs set down on the floor above could be heard and the chink of china, for there was not as thick a partition between the rooms as one might wish, so Miss Allan, the elderly lady who had been playing bridge, determined, giving the wall a smart rap with her knuckles. It was only matchboard, she decided, run up to make many little rooms of one large one. (*VO*: 113)

As the various occupants of these rooms prepare for bed, the sound of Old Mrs Paley's bell is heard in the corridor (*VO*: 116); as Miss Allan attempts to immerse herself in Wordsworth's poetry, she is interrupted by the sound of boots falling to the floor in the room above, as well as a dress 'swishing' next door (*VO*: 113); Miss Allan's solitude is interrupted as she contemplates and imagines to whom the boots and dress belong. Despite their physical separation, the underlying unity of the hotel occupants is emphasised when, in the early hours of the morning, 'One could almost hear a hundred people breathing deeply' (*VO*: 122). Regardless of whether or not each of these hotel guests wishes to form connections with the Other, the everyday lives of each will inevitably be affected and influenced to varying degrees by the intentions and actions of those around them. The hotel, as place, allows, creates and ultimately forces interactions between people who would otherwise remain unknown to each other.

De-severance and involvement

Throughout Woolf's writings, the individual's fluctuating sense of connection and disconnection in relation to the Other is a recurrent and dominant theme. This is reflected in the final chapter of *The Waves*, as Bernard surveys his life and the threads of connection that bind him to his childhood friends:

> 'Who am I?' I have been talking of Bernard, Neville, Jinny, Susan, Rhoda and Louis. Am I all of them? Am I one and distinct? I do not know. We sat here together. But now Percival is dead, and Rhoda is dead; we are divided; we are not here. Yet I cannot find any obstacle separating us. There is no division between me and them. As I talked I felt 'I am you.' (*TW*: 222)

As Bernard's soliloquy attests, regardless of any physical separation imposed by distance, time, or even death, his bond with these individuals remains irrevocably intact. In *Being and Time*, Heidegger uses the term *Ent-fernung* – translated by John Macquarrie and Edward Robinson as 'de-severance' – to describe the ways in which the self forms a connection with place or the Other, regardless of physical proximity. Like Bernard's relationship with his friends, for Heidegger, the individual's sense of 'nearness' or connection to something or someone is determined by his or her particular sense of involvement rather than any measurable distance.[8] As Heidegger asserts:

> That which is presumably 'closest' is by no means that which is at the smallest distance 'from us' . . . If Dasein, in its concern, brings something close by, this does not signify that it fixes something at a spatial position with a minimal distance from some point of the body. (*BT*: 141, 142)

Reflecting the existential bias of Heidegger's philosophy, Malpas explains that it is our involvement 'in particular activities and tasks, that allows particular things, places, and regions, and thereby also, it would seem, particular persons, to become salient' (2008: 90).

In 'A Sketch of the Past', Woolf records her own experience of existential nearness and distance in relation to place and the Other, as she recalls 'How large for instance was the space beneath the nursery table', where she and her sister Vanessa played as children. As Woolf details, the connection between the two sisters is so intense and inclusive that this small area is transformed into 'a great black space with the table-cloth hanging down in folds on the outskirts in the distance' ('Sketch': 90). Regardless of the measurable dimensions of this table, its perceived size is greatly magnified due to the sisters' complete involvement in each other and their private make-believe world: anything outside the parameter of this table lies outside the girls' concern, and as such, comes to be located at an immense distance. In contrast to Woolf's sense of connectedness to her sister, in *The Years*, the adult brother and sister, North and Peggy Pargiter, experience an uncomfortable sense of detachment even as they stand beside each other at a family gathering: struggling to communicate, the pair eventually 'had to fall back on childish slang, on childish memories, to cover their distance, their hostility' (*TY*: 289).

The issue of separation and distance between self and Other is explored in *Between the Acts,* where the pageant crowd remain detached and removed from both the meaning of the play and their fellow audience members, despite their close physical proximity. Through its dramatic representation of the fall of the great empires of Babylon and Troy, the pageant signals the potential fate of England, which is heralded by the distraught bellowing of cows in a nearby field. Acting as a catalyst that draws the audience members together, the anguished sounds of the surrounding herd 'annihilated the gap; bridged the distance' through their expression of the sense of doom that touches all as war draws ever closer. Despite this, and much to the disappointment and frustration of the director of the play, Miss La Trobe, as the cows become silent and begin 'browsing', so too does the audience grow separate and detached as they 'lowered their heads and read their programmes' (*BA*: 85).

The problematic nature of both attaining and maintaining an existential sense of nearness to the Other is also emphasised in *Flush,* where the canine protagonist must come to terms with the growing intersubjective distance between himself and his mistress after she falls in love with Mr Browning. In contrast to her previous sense of connection to her canine companion, as they sit side by side, Elizabeth Barrett concludes that

> Flush, poor Flush could feel nothing of what she felt. He would know nothing of what she knew. Never had such wastes of dismal distance separated them. He lay there ignored; he might not have been there, he felt. Miss Barrett no longer remembered his existence. (*Flush*: 39)

It is clear that, as the direction of Elizabeth's involvement shifts, so too does her sense of connection to those in her midst.

In her 1919 novel, *Night and Day*, Woolf explores the nature of the relationship between involvement and physical distance through her representations of the character, Katharine Hilbery, a young woman who is defined by an underlying sense of loneliness and detachment from the Other. Walking through the streets of London on her way to meet her fiancé, William Rodney, Katharine looks into the faces of the passers-by and realises 'how much alike they were, and how distant, nobody feeling anything as she felt nothing, and distance, she thought, lay inevitably between the closest, and their intimacy was the worst pretence of all' (*ND*: 256). By her own admission, Katharine's engagement to Rodney is a passionless farce; as the couple sits alone in Rodney's flat that evening, Katharine observes her fiancé as he composes a letter to her cousin Cassandra, with whom he is beginning to form a romantic attachment. Katharine is overcome by the realisation that she and Rodney are strangers: 'The head bent over the paper, thoughtful as usual, had now a composure which seemed somehow to place it at a distance, like a face seen talking to some one else behind glass' (*ND*: 271). Despite their physical proximity, each is unable to connect to the other, as the greater part of their involvement and interest lies outside the confines of this room.

As the relationship between Katharine and Ralph Denham develops, Ralph finds that the only way that he can freely love and worship a woman who is engaged to another man is to consciously attempt to maintain 'the distance which separates the devotee from the image in the shrine' (*ND*: 354). When Ralph learns that Katharine is no longer engaged to Rodney, he must still contend with her continued remoteness, where 'Their physical closeness was to him a bitter enough comment upon the distance between their minds' (*ND*: 456).

When the couple finally acknowledges and declares their love for the other, each 'lapsed gently into silence, travelling the dark paths of thought side by side towards something discerned in the distance which gradually possessed them both' (*ND*: 486–7). For Katharine and Ralph, their relationship is no longer defined by existential separation; rather, distance is transformed into that which lies outside their involvement with each other.

Based upon Woolf's father, Leslie Stephen, Mr Ramsay in *To the Lighthouse* has, as a defining characteristic, difficulty in forming and maintaining connections with the Other. This surly, sympathy-seeking, self-involved philosopher is so preoccupied by the contents of his own mind and the pursuit of professional acclaim that he is seemingly unaware of the feelings, needs and aspirations of those who surround him, including his long-suffering wife. Nevertheless, even for an individual such Mr Ramsay, a connection to the Other, while fleeting, does become a possibility as a result of a greater sense of involvement and concern with and towards those around him. As Mr Ramsay watches his wife read to their young son, the narrator poses the question:

> Who will not secretly rejoice when the hero puts his armour off, and halts by the window and gazes at his wife and son, who very distant at first, gradually come closer and closer, till lips and book and head are clearly before him, though still lovely and unfamiliar from the intensity of his isolation and the waste of ages and the perishing of the stars. (*TL*: 33)

As Lily watches Mr Ramsay, Cam and James sail to the lighthouse at the end of the novel, she muses about the effect of physical and emotional distance upon connections between individuals:

> So much depends . . . upon distance: whether people are near us or far from us; for her feeling for Mr. Ramsay changed as he sailed further and further across the bay. It seemed to be elongated, stretched out; he seemed to become more and more remote. (*TL*: 182)

While Lily's initial response would seem at odds with Heidegger's understanding of the relationship between de-severance and connections between self and Other, Laura Doyle suggests that, in terms of Lily's relationship with Mr Ramsay, 'As far as he might go, the distance always spins out of her feelings for him'; as such, 'it is not the case that distance, whether of time or of space, drains away the power of feeling' (1994: 172). Indeed, after the Ramsay party's departure for the lighthouse, Lily found herself 'curiously divided, as if one part of her were drawn out there – it was a still day, hazy; the Lighthouse looked this morning at an immense distance; the other had fixed itself doggedly, solidly, here on the lawn' (*TL*: 149). Doyle asserts that Lily's responses are representative of distance as 'the net of intimacy, thrown wide. It is the space of imagination, of "nonsense," of the leap "from the pinnacle of a tower into the air" ... into the world of the Other' (1994: 172). It is from such a perspective that, despite their measurable separation, Lily can proclaim her ongoing involvement with Mr Ramsay as he lands at the lighthouse: 'Whatever she had wanted to give him, when he left her that morning, she had given him at last' (*TL*: 197).

Similarly, in *Mrs Dalloway*, Woolf describes the sense of nearness experienced by the characters Peter and Clarissa, even as the two are separated by time and vast geographic distance. As Clarissa remarks in the opening pages of the novel, while she and Peter 'might be parted for hundreds of years', certain days, sights or places would bring 'him back to her' (*MD*: 5). From Peter's perspective, while face-to-face meetings with Clarissa would often result in pain, misunderstanding and an overwhelming sense of division and distance, such interactions also planted the seeds for Peter's deferred feelings of connection to his former lover, so that

> in absence, in the most unlikely places, it would flower out, open, shed its scent, let you touch, taste, look about you, get the whole feel of it and understanding, after years of lying lost. Thus she had come to him; on board ship; in the Himalayas; suggested by the oddest things (so Sally Seton, generous, enthusiastic goose! thought of *him* when she saw blue hydrangeas). She had influenced him more than any person he had ever known. And always in this way coming before him without his wishing it, cool, lady-like, critical; or ravishing, romantic, recalling some field or English harvest. He saw her most often in the country, not in London. (*MD*: 155)

So far as Peter's connection to Clarissa is concerned, there is an inverse relationship between physical distance and nearness to the Other; while their sense of connection is repeatedly clouded by emotions and disagreements while physically close, upon separation the two find that their irrevocable bond is repeatedly revealed. Peter's description also demonstrates the significance of place in terms of one's associations with the Other: it is in the countryside, rather than the city, that Peter is most aware of Clarissa's presence, a distinction that is unsurprising, given that Bourton is the site of Peter's much earlier romantic involvement with Clarissa, prior to her marriage to Richard Dalloway and her subsequent move to London.

Social manifestations of place

Although Clarissa's immediate ties to London are repeatedly interrupted by her memories of Bourton as she walks through the city's streets during the novel's opening scene, she consciously calls herself back to the here and now, conceding: 'But every one remembered; what she loved was this, here, now, in front of her' (*MD*: 7). Making her way up Bond Street, Clarissa enters Mulberry's florist shop in preparation for her party that evening. While making her choice, Clarissa's gaze turns to the window as a motor-car backfires in the street. As the official-looking vehicle stops outside the shop, traffic in the street begins to accumulate, and passers-by gather to stare, wondering to whom the motor-car belongs: 'Was it the Prince of Wales's, the Queen's, the Prime Minister's?' (*MD*: 12).

Among these onlookers is Septimus Smith; as he watches on, the halted traffic, the faces all turned to the one direction, and 'this gradual drawing together of everything to one centre before his eyes, as if some horror had come almost to the surface and was about to burst into flames, terrified him' (*MD*: 13). In contrast, as Clarissa comes out of Mulberry's, she calmly surmises that the car probably belongs to the Queen: 'And for a second she wore a look of extreme dignity standing by the flower shop in the sunlight while the car passed at a foot's pace' (*MD*: 15). As they stand in the same street of London, and view the same event, Septimus's reaction is one of terror in the face of this symbol of authority and conformity; in stark contrast, Clarissa comfortably embraces all that the car and its occupants represent. As Clarissa and Septimus's responses explicitly reflect, it is the particular perspective of the beholder that comes to define a place as welcoming and comforting, or oppressive and threatening.

Throughout her writings, Woolf's juxtaposition of the responses of different characters to the same social space – be it a city, a street, an official building – reveals much about each individual's sense of Being-in-the-world. In her memoir, 'Old Bloomsbury', Woolf personally acknowledges that each individual's interpretation and response to the same environment is subjective when she prefaces her essay with the warning that 'Naturally I see Bloomsbury only from my own angle – not from yours' (2002b: 43). From the perspective of fiction, as Mary Datchet and Ralph Denham make their way by foot towards the rural village of Lincoln in *Night and Day*, both characters see 'nothing of the hedgerows, the swelling ploughland, or the mild blue sky' (*ND*: 207); instead, arguing about social issues, each visualises

> the Houses of Parliament and the Government Offices in Whitehall. They both belonged to the class which is conscious of having lost its birthright in these great structures and is seeking to build another kind of lodging for its own notion of law and government. (*ND*: 207)

In both a concrete and an abstract sense, for Mary and Ralph, these public buildings represent a history of repression and exclusion for working-class individuals. Mary and Ralph's basic need for a sense of inclusion and agency within the social context is demonstrated by their shared desire to create a new type of built form that will house and forward the political struggle of this class. As this passage suggests, not unlike the structure of a city, official architecture reflects the dominant culture, values and ideology that a particular society propagates. Edward Relph argues that it is through such 'official public places that centralised governments and organisations make overt their status and authority' (1976: 35).

For Woolf, places of worship are public sites that are of particular interest and concern throughout her writings; as will be discussed in greater detail in the final chapter, Woolf repeatedly calls into question the sway of organised religion upon both the individual and society. For Woolf, the physical structure of places of worship are representative of the authority, power and patriarchal bias that she equates with religion. Such a point of view is expressed in *Three Guineas*, where Woolf describes her impressions of what she understands to be London's male-dominated public scene:

> At first sight it is enormously impressive. Within quite a small space are crowded together St Paul's, the Bank of England, the Mansion House, the massive if funereal battlements of the Law Courts; and on the other side, Westminster Abbey and the Houses of Parliament. (*TG*: 176)

Tellingly, St Paul's Cathedral and Westminster Abbey define the boundaries of this patriarchal 'world of public life' (*TG*: 176). In her close reading of Woolf's treatment of religion in this polemic, de Gay observes that 'Woolf's analysis in *Three Guineas* focuses closely on the symbolic links between legal, political, financial and religious institutions, starting by noting the significantly close proximity of their flagship buildings' (2009: 4).

In her many and varied representations of the city, St Paul's Cathedral, Westminster Cathedral, and Westminster Abbey frequently feature as structures that define the London skyline.[9] Woolf's 1932 essay, 'Abbeys and Cathedrals', for instance, begins with the proclamation that: 'It is a commonplace, but we cannot help repeating it, that St. Paul's dominates London. It swells like a great grey bubble from a distance; it looms over us, huge and menacing, as we approach.' As the essay progresses, Woolf draws her readers' attention to 'the enormous walls of St. Paul's. Here it is again, looming over us, mountainous, immense, greyer, colder, quieter than before' (2006a: 43, 45). The repetitive description of the cathedral as a structure that 'looms' over London's inhabitants, in addition to the use of language such as 'menacing', 'mountainous', and 'immense', each combine to emphasise the inescapable propensity of such a place to overwhelm and subsume. Woolf's own view of such sites of worship might be summed up by the thoughts of Rachel Vinrace in *The Voyage Out*, as she begins to question the legitimacy of her own faith:

> One after another, vast and hard and cold, appeared to her the churches all over the world where this blundering effort and misunderstanding were perpetually going on, great buildings, filled with innumerable men and women, not seeing clearly, who finally gave up the effort to see, and relapsed tamely into praise and acquiescence, half-shutting their eyes and pursing up their lips. (*VO*: 264–5)

For Woolf, as for Rachel, the physical structure of the church comes to represent and reinforce those religious orders that oppress and dominate the individual through the command that one must unquestioningly adhere to the prescribed doctrines.

In terms of public places, it is not only the built forms of religion that concern Woolf: throughout her *oeuvre*, communal sites such as buses, libraries, parks and city streets are also understood to both represent and reinforce the societal norms and expectations of

English society in the first half of the twentieth century. Once again, it is the ways in which Woolf's characters respond to the prescriptions attached to these places – through adherence, rejection, ambiguity, apathy – that indicate and define both their relations to the Other, and their mode of Being-in-the-world. This is underscored in *The Waves*, as Bernard makes his way to work:

> Clapping my hat on my head, I strode into a world inhabited by vast numbers of men who had also clapped their hats on their head, and as we jostled and encountered in trains and tubes we exchanged the knowing wink of competitors and comrades braced with a thousand snares and dodges to achieve the same end – to earn our livings. (*TW*: 201)

In this passage, the city trains and tubes are viewed as representative arms of the work-world; as Bernard conforms to the social expectation that the role of a man is to earn a living, the trains and their stations provide the means by which such a prescription might be carried out. A lack of individuality – each of these countless and nameless men wear the same 'uniform' – demonstrates the level of conformity that is required by the social order. And while Bernard's musings reflect his self-consciousness and critical reflection, they also emphasise his awareness that resistance to such everyday expectations is ultimately futile.

That the norms and expectations of the social order come to be embedded in manifestations of place through the average everyday involvements of individuals is a notion that is also explored in *Being and Time*, where Heidegger explains that

> The 'environment' does not arrange itself in a space which has been given in advance; but its specific worldhood, in its significance, Articulates the context of involvements which belongs to some current totality of circumspectively allotted places. The world at such a time always reveals the spatiality of the space which belongs to it. To encounter the ready-to-hand in its environmental space remains ontically possible only because Dasein itself is 'spatial' with regard to its Being-in-the-world. (*BT*: 138)

Heidegger's stance reflects the understanding that 'Society is itself established and constituted through the organization of space, and so is the sociality of being-there [Dasein] expressed in spatialized form' (Malpas 2008: 88). Such societal ordering of space and place is foregrounded in Woolf's *Three Guineas*, where she uses the setting of Cambridge University as a means of exploring and critiquing the patriarchal bias and domination that provides the foundation for the British education system.

Positing the far-reaching benefits of education for all individuals, Woolf begins her essay by drawing attention to both past and present educational privations experienced by women, who have long been relegated to the home and the 'occupation' of marriage, while the education of their brothers has been encouraged and funded. Writing from the perspective of the 'educated man's daughter', Woolf draws attention to the ways in which the architecture of educational institutions provides a tangible measure of this inequality. Detailing the wealth of the men's colleges, Woolf views the dilapidated state of the women's college as representative of the ways in which social hierarchies and dichotomies come to be spacialised (*TG*: 194). Nine years earlier, in a *Room of One's Own*, Woolf had drawn attention to the representative discrepancies between the built forms of men and women's education in Britain, describing the 'raw and red and squalid' condition of the Oxbridge women's college, Fernham, which has been the site of immense struggles to raise even meagre funds, so that: 'To raise bare walls out of bare earth was the utmost they could do' (*RO*: 19, 29).

In her 1922 novel, *Jacob's Room,* Woolf's description of the British Museum again foregrounds the ways in which socially sanctioned patriarchal discourse comes to manifest itself in public space. While women are allowed access to the words and wisdom of men located in this place, they are denied a means of making their own contribution to this esteemed site of knowledge. Revealing the emphasis of the library's content, the names of 'great men' circle the Reading Room's majestic domed roof; as the gaze of 'the feminist', Julia Hedge, turns to the ceiling, she bitterly notes the absence of a woman's name, and asks, '"why didn't they leave room for an Eliot or a Brontë?"' (*JR*: 144, 145). As the day ends, and the novel's British Museum scene draws to its close, the narrative turns to a drunken woman in a nearby street who has been locked out of her home; crying in vain throughout the night, '"Let me in! Let me in!"' (*JR*: 149), this woman's plaintive callings come to represent all women who are locked out of this male-dominated place of influence and knowledge, despite superficial admittance.

Guest, stranger, outsider-within and scapegoat

While real, remembered and imagined notions of place can become means of highlighting and reinforcing our primordial state of Being-with-Others, they can also be used as a justification for divisions, demarcations and conflict between individuals. As divisions between self and Other come to be emphasised and reinforced, current systems of power and influence are not only upheld, but also strengthened. Arguably, what is most at stake as a result of a particular society's inclusionary and exclusionary expectations and practices in relation to place, is the individual's average everyday mode of Being-in-the-world.

In his study of social space in the works of both D. H. Lawrence and Woolf, Youngjoo Son asserts that these writers' representations of space raise 'issues of borders and movements, belonging and exclusion, limits and expansions, and enclosure and mobility'. Son suggests that within their writings, both 'Lawrence and Woolf simultaneously expose and disrupt the dominant social order that governs the ways in which people construct, live, and imagine space' (Son 2006: 10, 11). Such disruption is evident in *Three Guineas*, where Woolf openly questions both the relevance and validity of nationalism for the women of Britain: '"Our country" ... throughout the greater part of its history has treated me as a slave; it has denied me education or any share in its possessions'. In a powerful summation of her argument, Woolf writes: 'as a woman, I have no country. As a woman I want no country. As a woman my country is the whole world' (*TG*: 313). Woolf's proclamations make clear her belief that the women of England are more akin to guests than shareholders of this largest of places.

As discussed, for Woolf, an everyday manifestation of English society's exclusionary practices in relation to women and their education comes in the form of the physical sites of the nation's universities. As Woolf visits Fernham and is disappointed with the state of the college building and its facilities in *A Room of One's Own*, she poses the question: 'was it for a guest, a stranger (for I had no more right here in Fernham than in Trinity or Somerville or Girton or Newnham or Christchurch), to say, "The dinner was not good"' (*RO*: 22–3). Identifying herself as 'a guest, a stranger', Woolf's position in relation to Oxbridge grants her a perspective that is unlike that of either the insider or the outsider. Bauman suggests that, in terms of understandings of place, the stranger 'defies the easy expedient of spatial or temporal segregation' (1991: 59), thereby disturbing the socially sanctioned definitions that dictate who should be welcomed or expelled from particular sites. Most importantly, strangers 'do not question just one opposition here and now: they question oppositions as such, the very principle of the opposition, the plausibility of dichotomy it suggests and feasibility of separation it demands. They unmask the brittle artificiality of division' (Bauman 1991: 58–9).

In his discussion of the possibility of an individual forming a relationship or connection with the Other, including the 'stranger', Heidegger refers to the notion of 'empathy', arguing that

> 'Empathy' does not first constitute Being-with; only on the basis of Being-with does 'empathy' become possible: it gets its motivation from the unsociability of the dominant modes of Being-with . . . The special hermeneutic of empathy will have to show how Being-with-one-another and Dasein's knowing of itself are led astray and obstructed by the various possibilities of Being which Dasein possesses, so that a genuine 'understanding' gets suppressed, and Dasein takes refuge in substitutes; the possibility of understanding the stranger correctly presupposes such a hermeneutic as its positive existential condition . . . One's own Dasein, like the Dasein-with of Others, is encountered proximally and for the most part in terms of the with-world with which we are environmentally concerned. (*BT*: 162–3)

For Heidegger, empathy for the Other is not an intrinsic facet of Being-in-the-world, despite our primordial state of Being-with; rather, our ability or desire to 'understand' those around us is often thwarted by our immersion in an inauthentic theyness that prescribes a particular view of the Other. Thiele suggests that 'The stimulus for empathy may often be the desire to offset the egoistic or immoral dispositions frequently encountered in social life' (1995: 53).

Such an understanding is apparent in *Orlando*, where the protagonist becomes a stranger in her own society when he/she is unable to comply with the strict definitions of what it means to be a man 'or' a woman. Society's discomfort in the face of such ambivalence is blatantly evident upon Orlando's change from a man into a woman: 'Many people . . . holding that such change of sex is against nature, have been at great pains to prove (1) that Orlando had always been a woman, (2) that Orlando is at this moment a man' (*O*: 98). What is imperative, from the standpoint of society's need to order, categorise and demarcate, is that Orlando's sex ceases to be ambiguous; indeed, the 'female' Orlando must await the Court's ruling of her sex before she is legally considered to be a 'proper' British citizen. Ultimately, society must decide whether Orlando is a man or a woman in order to reinforce its own laws, because, as Bauman puts it: 'resistance to definition sets the limits to sovereignty, to power, to the transparency of the world, to its control, to order' (1991: 9).

Orlando's change from a man to a woman takes place while working as an ambassador in Constantinople. Upon her change of sex, Orlando flees the capital, travelling to the north-west of Turkey, where she finds sanctuary with a gypsy tribe. Within this environment, Orlando comes into contact with a culture that does not define an individual's place and role within their community according to his or her sex. Most significantly, the gypsy way of life presents Orlando with an alternative view of the individual's relationship to place: for these individuals, the land is not something that can be bought, owned or sold; rather, the land always already belongs to all people. It is from such a perspective that Orlando is not considered to be a stranger or a guest who is 'visiting' – 'the word was unknown' (O: 100) – this community, as a guest requires a host, which in turn implies some sense of ownership of place. Within such a context, notions of the insider and outsider also cease to exist: 'The gipsies followed the grass; when it was grazed down, on they moved again . . . there was not a key, let alone a golden key, in the whole camp' (O: 99–100). The gypsies view Orlando's former way of life in England, where people own property and live in houses, as 'barbarous'; Orlando proudly describes her English ancestral estate, which consists of 365 bedrooms, but the gypsies see such an accumulation of property and wealth as a source of shame.

In *Of Hospitality*, Jacques Derrida provides an in-depth discussion of the host and the foreigner/stranger/guest from the perspective of the theory of deconstruction. Derrida suggests that there is 'No hospitality, in the classic sense, without sovereignty of oneself over one's home, but since there is also no hospitality without finitude, sovereignty can only be exercised by filtering, choosing, and thus by excluding and doing violence' (2000: 55). Such an understanding has obvious implications in terms of the insider and outsider dualism, since 'any attempt to behave hospitably is also always partly betrothed to the keeping of guests under control, to the closing of boundaries, to nationalism, and even to the exclusion of particular groups or ethnicities' (Reynolds 2010: np). From such a perspective, the gypsies' refusal to extend the hand of hospitality to Orlando provides the foundation for her experience of inclusion in relation to this particular society.

Unlike her experiences among the gypsies in Turkey, when Orlando returns to London society, her change in sex comes to determine her freedom to gain access to certain places, so that Orlando finds that even her ability to walk through the Mall is compromised: 'she had forgotten that ladies are not supposed to walk in public places alone'. It is only when Orlando dons the garb of a man at night that she is free 'to walk the streets in search of adventure' (O: 134, 153). And just as the female Orlando's access to the city street is restricted due to her sex, so too are the female narrators of *A Room of One's Own* and *Three Guineas* denied free access to education and the professions. As the experience of each of these individuals attests, although an English woman is officially located within the confines of English society, she is nevertheless not granted the privileges of an insider in terms of her access to the places and opportunities that are freely accessible to her brothers.

From such a perspective, women's position within English society might be classified as that of the 'outsider-within', a term that is highlighted by Madelyn Detloff in her discussion of the ancient Greek notion of the *metic*. As Detloff explains, understood as an outsider, such an individual was 'dependent upon the goodwill of a citizen sponsor in order to remain within the *polis*'; as such, he or she could 'be dispossessed, exiled, or made a slave' (2009: 7, 17) if such patronage was withdrawn. Referring to Woolf's aforementioned assertion in *Three Guineas* that 'As I woman I want no country', Detloff observes that 'Woolf resignifies a negative condition – a gendered sense of un-belonging (because marriage trumps nationality) – into inspiration for affiliation across borders and accountability to the world beyond the provincialism of one's geographic location' (2009: 7).

Sharing affinities with the notion of the outsider-within, Jacques Derrida draws attention to the *pharmakos*, or 'scapegoat', found in ancient Greek culture. Understood as a force of evil, the scapegoat must be expelled from the city so that the purity and order of this place might be sustained (2004: 133).[10] In a footnote in *Three Guineas*, Woolf asserts that the 'ridicule, censure and contempt' (*TG*: 273) experienced by women in English society for centuries is symptomatic of their allotted role as society's scapegoat since the time of Genesis (*TG*: 396, n41). Representing an Otherness-within, the scapegoat, not unlike the English woman, must first be located within the city in order for it to be excluded, thereby disrupting the very notion of homogeneity, borders and the pure binary opposition of inside and outside that typically defines understandings of place.

In *Mrs Dalloway*, Woolf refers to Septimus Smith as 'the scapegoat, the eternal sufferer', a man who is 'a border case, neither one thing nor the other' (*MD*: 24, 84). Defined in such a way, Septimus 'must be tabooed, disarmed, suppressed, exiled physically or mentally – or the world may perish' (Bauman 1991: 59). Throughout this novel, the medical profession becomes the strong arm of societal control and policing, dictating that Septimus must be physically removed from society in order that the Other-within might be converted, suppressed or destroyed. Aware of his fate at the hands of Dr Holmes and the psychiatrist Sir William Bradshaw, Septimus must decide how he will respond:

> So he was deserted. The whole world was clamouring: Kill yourself, kill yourself, for our sakes. But why should he kill himself for their sakes? ... Besides, now that he was quite alone, condemned, deserted, as those who are about to die are alone, there was a luxury in it, an isolation full of sublimity; a freedom which the attached can never know. Holmes had won of course; the brute with the red nostrils had won. But even Holmes himself could not touch this last relic straying on the edge of the world, this outcast, who gazed back at the inhabited regions, who lay, like a drowned sailor, on the shore of the world. (*MD*: 93)

As a result of his inability to understand or adhere to the societal conventions and prescriptions that surround him, Septimus is essentially placeless and unattached. Through his belief that the world demands his sacrifice, this character is resigned to his fate as scapegoat. Just as the ancient Athenian scapegoat must be expelled from the city and sacrificed 'at critical moments (drought, plague, famine)' (Derrida 2004: 134), Septimus must be expelled from his place in society in the period of June 1923, as his shell-shocked state makes him a living symbol and reminder of the greatest calamity to befall Britain in modern times. Within such a context, Septimus must be driven out of society in the hope that such a sacrifice will bring 'a purification and a remedy to the suffering city' (Derrida 2004: 134).

As Squier recognises, albeit from an alternative perspective, 'Rather than subverting the social order' (1985: 116), Septimus's suicide ultimately reinforces it.

Conclusion – the politics of place

Throughout her writings, Woolf repeatedly emphasises the essential connection that exists between the individual and the places that he or she inhabits, remembers and imagines. A sense of this often intense and indissoluble bond is demonstrated in 'A Sketch of the Past', as Woolf describes one of her earliest formative memories:

> If life has a base that it stands upon, if it is a bowl that one fills and fills and fills – then my bowl without a doubt stands upon this memory. It is of lying half asleep, half awake, in bed in the nursery at St Ives. It is of hearing the waves breaking, one, two, one, two, and sending a splash of water over the beach; and then breaking one, two, one, two, behind a yellow blind. It is of hearing the blind draw its little acorn across the floor as the wind blew the blind out. It is of lying and hearing this splash and seeing this light, and feeling, it is almost impossible that I should be here; of feeling the purest ecstasy I can conceive. ('Sketch': 78–9)

Woolf's seemingly prosaic impressions combine to provide a powerful and poetic instance of the unification of the individual and place: light, wind, sound and objects merge in the consciousness of the child to produce a state of blissful contentment.

Whether we are excluded or welcomed, surrounded by Others, or alone and isolated, ultimately and inevitably, as individuals, we are always already situated in a place. As demonstrated throughout this chapter, for Woolf place becomes the means of navigating and experiencing our everyday lives, forming attachments and engaging with the Other. Such an approach shares affinities with Heidegger's assertion in *Being and Time* that

> it is not merely human identity that is tied to place or locality, but the very possibility of being the sort of creature that can engage *with* a world (and, more particularly, with the objects and events within it), that can think *about* that world, and that can find itself *in* the world. (Malpas 1999: 8)

For both Woolf and Heidegger, the individual's existential average everyday involvement with place, regardless of its size or configuration, is a tangible and inescapable element of Being-in-the-world and Being-with-Others.

Often drawing upon her personal experiences and translating them into her work, from her earliest writings, Woolf is preoccupied by the ways in which place can be viewed as a physical manifestation of the social order. Woolf's representations of place are largely, and fundamentally, political in nature; her writings emphasise and question the prevailing social order in terms of its relation to issues such as class, nationalism, and the insider–outsider dualism. Such an approach clearly differs from Heidegger's treatment of place in *Being and Time*, where the call for social reconfiguration that is emphasised throughout Woolf's writings is absent.

In the following chapter, the study of place will be narrowed to the notions of home and homelessness, which are representative of not only the individual's primordial condition of Being-in-the-world, but can also be viewed as emblematic of the social hierarchies and inequalities of power prevalent throughout English society in the first half of the twentieth century.

Notes

1. The philosopher Edward Casey defines place as 'an arena of action that is at once physical and historical, social and cultural' (2001: 683); Theodore R. Schatzki suggests that place can be understood by 'the ends, projects, actions, and also moods, rules, and ideas of the people living amid them' (1991: 656).
2. Such a perspective is recorded in a number of instances throughout Woolf's diaries, where she describes Monk's House as a site that is 'safe from voices & talk!' (D3: 222); 'Not a voice, not a telephone' (D5: 99). In 1932, Woolf muses that within this locale she 'can stop & wallow in coolness & downs, & let the wheels of my mind – how I beg them to do this – cool & slow & stop altogether' (D4: 132); it is this place that provides Woolf with 'a chance to brew a little quiet thought' (D3: 295).
3. While the majority of Woolf's novels are set in the city of London, such a preoccupation with the city is not unique; indeed, in *Modernism 1890–1930*, Malcolm Bradbury defines modernism as 'very much an urban phenomenon' (1976b: 183), suggesting that: 'The pull and push of the city, its attraction and repulsion, have provided themes

and attitudes that run deep in literature, where the city has become metaphor rather than place' (1976a: 97).
4. Twenty-three years later, Woolf's attachment to London is made particularly apparent in the diary entries and letters written in the midst of the devastating bombing of the city by German forces during the Blitz. In a postscript to a letter dated 12 September 1940, Woolf records her impressions after visiting the now-ravaged city:

> the passion of my life, that is the City of London – to see London all blasted, that too raked my heart. Have you that feeling for certain alleys and little courts, between Chancery Lane and the City? I walked to the Tower the other day by way of caressing my love of all that. (*Letters* 6: 431)

5. In a 1915 diary entry, Woolf remarks:

> I could wander about the dusky streets of Holborn & Bloomsbury for hours. The things one sees – & guesses at – the tumult & riot & busyness of it all – Crowded streets are the only places, too, that ever make me what-in-the-case of another-one-might-call think. (*D*1: 9)

Although a close analysis of Woolf's treatment of the female street wanderer as flâneur is outside the scope of this work, critics such as Anna Snaith and Michael H. Whitworth attest that: '*Flânerie*, as a literal and a metaphorical pursuit, was an essential fuel for her writing' (Snaith and Whitworth 2007: 1). While critics such as Victoria Rosner (2005: 148) and Janet Wolff (1985: 41) assert that the notion of the modernist flâneur best reflects male rather than female street wandering, Leslie Kathleen Hankins posits the emergence of the 'twentieth-century *flâneuse*', a street wanderer who can be found in the texts of writers such as Woolf; this individual, whom Hankins describes as 'the strid*ing* feminist', is apparent in *A Room of One's Own* in the guise of 'the intellectual, emancipated woman as trespasser and outsider' (2000: 20).

6. Such descriptions of the living conditions of the destitute are similar to those recorded in 1844 by Friedrich Engels in his polemic, *The Condition of the Working Class in England*. Like Elizabeth Barrett in Woolf's novel, Engels describes his own experience of coming across a particularly grim area of extreme poverty that was previously unknown to him:

> Everywhere heaps of debris, refuse, and offal; standing pools for gutters, and a stench which alone would make it impossible for a human being in any degree civilized to live in such a district . . . I should never have discovered it myself, without the breaks made by the railway, though I thought I knew this whole region thoroughly. (2009: 63)

7. Numerous critics have addressed Woolf's treatment of class throughout her *oeuvre*, often claiming, as Liesl M. Olson does, that 'Woolf's representation of everyday moments no doubt tends to favor the perspectives of the upper class' (2003: 59). In an attempt to account for such omissions, in her reading of 'Street Haunting', Kathryn Simpson argues that 'The limited space given to the destitute in Woolf's essay can be seen to equate to the limitations placed on the literal, economic, and political space such marginalized figures are permitted to occupy' (2010: 50).
8. Hussey briefly discusses Heidegger's understanding of 'nearness' from the perspective of Woolf's *Between the Acts* (2013: 95–6).
9. In *Jacob's Room*, 'St Paul's swells white above the fretted, pointed, or oblong buildings beside it' (*JR*: 155). In *The Waves*, St Paul's Cathedral is 'the brooding hen with spread wings from whose shelter run omnibuses and streams of men and women at the rush hour' (*TW*: 216). In *Orlando*, as the protagonist sails down the Thames upon her return to London from Constantinople, the ship's Captain points out significant architecture, including St Paul's Cathedral and Westminster Abbey (*O*: 117).
10. Arguably, the 'stranger' and the 'scapegoat' as the Other-within also share affinities with Julia Kristeva's notion of the *abject*, which represents 'above all ambiguity' (1982: 9). Not unlike the scapegoat, which is initially located within the city, the abject is located within the individual. Like the stranger, the abject is understood as the 'in-between, the ambiguous, the composite' (1982: 4).

Chapter 3

Being-at-home and Homelessness

From an existential perspective, the notion of home is arguably one of the more significant expressions of place. Not defined simply as a co-ordinate on a map, home encompasses neighbourhoods, nations, traditions, customs, narrative, myth, the tangible, the imaginable, the dream, as well as each individual's relation to Being. Home has relevance to all humans: despite its multifarious manifestations, our diverse relationships with home – whether positive, negative, or ambivalent – can be life-long and pervasive, creating and rekindling memories, inspiring desires and the imagination, shaping who we are, and how we relate to the Other. As this chapter will elucidate, each individual's involvements in, and experiences of, the various expressions of home have the potential to confirm or deny his or her fundamental sense of belonging in the world.

For the Western urban dweller, the most typical ontic manifestation of home is the built architectural form. Such physical structures can also be understood from an existential-ontological perspective, insofar as this expression of home is representative of our average everyday involvements in a world that we always already share with others, even in solitude. Characteristically, though not exclusively, such dwellings are defined by the walls that create the rooms that both enclose and divide, as well as the doors that invite or prohibit entry. Such structures are also inevitably filled with objects of various types and forms – from crockery to collectibles and furniture – each of which can be viewed as a reflection of the quotidian life of its inhabitants. It is such ordinary elements of the home that both mark, and are marked by, the daily lives of the individuals who dwell within this particular place.

Woolf's autobiographical accounts of her formative experiences of home, particularly her relationships and interactions with those with whom she shared such a space, were frequently given fictional representation. What is clear from the various forms of Woolf's writings is that, typically, the domestic spaces of the late nineteenth century and early twentieth century were sites that were entrenched in the intrusive prescriptions and expectations of the patriarchal social order. As will be discussed, this understanding is demonstrated through Woolf's frequent representations of the lived body within the context of the private sphere. Despite an intense and often desperate desire to attain a sense of Being-at-home within such spaces, for Woolf, as well as many of her female characters, the individual is repeatedly and overwhelmingly overcome by a sense of homelessness in the midst of this environment, as her agency and sense of self comes to be questioned, constrained and denied. As such, the domestic space becomes both a literal and figurative representation of not-Being-at-home. Yet, as will be emphasised in this chapter, for Woolf, the experience of homelessness is confined neither to women, nor to the geographic location of the private sphere. As Woolf's textual representations repeatedly demonstrate, for the outsider located within society, a relentless sense of homelessness is not necessarily attached to any particular space or place; rather, this mode of Being is indicative of such an individual's overarching sense of Being-in-the-world.

Throughout this chapter Heidegger's treatment in *Being and Time* of the contrasting states of 'not-being-at-home' and 'Being-at-home' (*BT*: 233) in the world will be drawn upon. As Thiele emphasises, Heidegger's understanding of Being-at-home 'has less to do with our ongoing relation to any particular plot of ground than it does with our relation to the ground of Being itself' (1995: 176). For Heidegger, the individual's average everyday mode of Being-in-the-world is typified by a sense of Being-at-home, insofar as he or she comes to be immersed in the preoccupations and prescriptions of theyness, which leads to a comfortable state of unquestioning complacency. Despite this, Heidegger asserts that each individual's primordial state of Being is in fact defined by a 'homelessness' that is the product of the radical contingency, or 'thrownness', of Being-in-the-world. As will be explored in further detail in the following two chapters, this state of thrownness refers to the fact that each of us is born into a particular world, historical context and social order that is not of our own choosing, but that nonetheless never ceases to determine and influence our present and future possibilities and potentialities. In the face of thrownness, the individual has the choice to live in authentic awareness, thereby acknowledging and appropriating the resultant possibilities and making them his or her own; or to exist in the inauthentic comfort of Being-at-home in the midst of theyness.

In *Being and Time* Heidegger explains that

> because Dasein is in each case essentially its own possibility, it *can*, in its very Being, 'choose' itself and win itself; it can also lose itself and never win itself; or only 'seem' to do so. But only in so far as it is essentially something which can be *authentic* – that is, something of its own – can it have lost itself and not yet won itself. (*BT*: 68)

As emphasised throughout this chapter, such a point of view is located throughout the various forms of Woolf's writings, where her interrogative representations of the expectations and prescriptions of the social order reflect her understanding that, although the scope of each individual's possibilities is determined by the thrown nature of Being-in-the-world, through an awareness and acceptance of our primordial state of homelessness, each of us possesses the potential to choose how we will live out and re-enact those possibilities, in order to make them our own. Apparent in both Woolf and Heidegger's treatments of homelessness is the ensuing tension experienced by the individual as he or she comes face to face with the choice between the discomfort of authentic homelessness, and the comfortable, yet tranquilised, state of Being-at-home in the world.

It is important to acknowledge that discussions of the Heideggerian notions of Being-at-home and homelessness from the perspective of Woolf's politically oriented representations of manifestations of home takes the philosopher's understanding of these terms into directions that were never intended in *Being and Time*. Nevertheless, such trajectories are arguably justifiable, as they are founded upon a question that is of fundamental concern to both Woolf and Heidegger; that is: 'How is the individual to respond to his or her primordial state of not-Being-at-home in the world?' Woolf's response to such a question will provide the principal impetus for this chapter.

From Kensington to Bloomsbury

In her 1922 memoir, 'Old Bloomsbury', Woolf describes her experience of living in 22 Hyde Park Gate, the London family home she resided in until the age of twenty-two:

> Here then seventeen or eighteen people lived in small bedrooms with one bathroom and three water-closets between them. Here the four of us were born; here my grandmother died; here my mother died; here my

father died; here Stella became engaged to Jack Hills and two doors further down the street after three months of marriage she died too. When I look back upon that house it seems to me so crowded with scenes of family life, grotesque, comic and tragic; with the violent emotions of youth, revolt, despair, intoxicating happiness, immense boredom, with parties of the famous and the dull; with rages again, George and Gerald; with love scenes with Jack Hills; with passionate affection for my father alternating with passionate hatred of him, all tingling and vibrating in an atmosphere of youthful bewilderment and curiosity – that I feel suffocated by the recollection. (2002b: 45)

As Woolf's memoir attests, home is defined by both the major and minor signposts of a lived life: it is, quite literally, the site of birth, death and everything in between. Demonstrated throughout this passage is Woolf's conviction that home is defined by the intersubjective relations that occur within its walls; indeed, after her initial brief description of small bedrooms and limited amenities, Woolf ceases to describe the physical characteristics of Hyde Park Gate, drawing attention instead to the everyday dynamics of relations between the members of this family.

Woolf's description of her family interactions at Hyde Park Gate highlights not only the topophilia – 'strong affection' – that she has for her first home, but also the topophobia, or 'aversion' (Relph 2000: 27) that can persist beyond one's physical presence in a particular place. As Relph suggests, 'The places to which we are most committed may be the very centres of our lives, but they may also be oppressive and imprisoning' (1976: 41). Such a perspective is clearly forwarded by Woolf's assertion that she could be 'suffocated by the recollection' of this site that was the stage for so much of the drama of everyday life. This view of home is granted even greater severity in a journal entry recorded by Woolf in 1903, as she cares for her father while he slowly dies of cancer:

Our modern house with its cumbersome walls & its foundations planted deep in the ground is nothing better than a prison; [ ] & more & more prison like does it become the longer we live there & wear fetters of association & sentiment, painful to wear – still more painful to break. (*PA*: 208)

Nevertheless, despite the feelings of entrapment that the environment of the family home often created for Woolf, as she and her siblings leave Hyde Park Gate for Bloomsbury upon the death of their father in 1904, Woolf's sense of loss is acute: 'For not only had the furniture been dispersed. The family which had seemed equally wedged together had broken apart too' (2002b: 46). Despite her misgivings, for Woolf, both her sense of self and connection to significant others are entwined with the physical manifestation of this place. Echoing Woolf's response to her childhood home, Relph notes that

> Our experience of place, and especially of home, is a dialectical one – balancing a need to stay with a desire to escape. When one of these needs is too readily satisfied we suffer either from nostalgia and a sense of being uprooted, or from the melancholia that accompanies a feeling of oppression and imprisonment in a place. (1976: 42)

For the rest of her life, Woolf was to experience a certain degree of discontent and discombobulation whenever she moved from one home to another. In 1923, while Woolf writes of her desperate need to relocate from Richmond to London, she also describes the 'horror' (*D2*: 249) of such a move. Such unease surfaces once more when Woolf is faced with the necessary move from Tavistock Square to Mecklenburgh Square in 1939. As Woolf remarks in 'A Sketch of the Past', 'any break – like that of house moving – causes me extreme distress; it breaks; it shallows; it turns the depth into hard thin splinters' ('Sketch': 108).[1]

When Woolf moves from Kensington to Bloomsbury, she experiences first-hand the ways in which a change of home can alter the individual's mode of Being-in-the-world; as she remarks in a diary entry fourteen years later: 'the gulf between Kensington and Bloomsbury was the gulf between respectable mum[m]ified humbug & life crude & impertinent perhaps, but living' (*D1*: 206). Woolf's more immediate impressions of the transition from the staid to 'life itself' are given fictional representation in her 1906 short story, 'Phyllis and Rosamond'. Residing in South Kensington, the sisters Phyllis and Rosamond Hibbert have been 'born of well-to-do, respectable, official parents' (1989b: 17), who expect that their daughters' greatest ambition will be to marry well. Attending a party held by the Tristram sisters in Bloomsbury, Phyllis and Rosamond engage in novel conversations about love, marriage and the professions, and in so doing are met with the uncomfortable discovery that a young woman located in English society might choose an alternative means of living her life.

Comparing South Kensington to Bloomsbury, Phyllis surmises that

> if one lived here in Bloomsbury . . . one might grow up as one liked. There was room, and freedom, and in the roar and splendour of the

Strand she read the live realities of the world from which her stucco and her pillars protected her so completely. (1989b: 24)

Reflecting Woolf's personal experience, in this short story, South Kensington epitomises the nineteenth-century Victorian social order, with its call for women's conformity, isolation and repression; in contrast, Bloomsbury represents independence, opportunities and new possibilities: it is a place where the individual can grow unfettered by the constraints of convention.[2] Woolf's representations of Kensington as a site in which its inhabitants are expected to lead 'a life trained to grow in an ugly pattern to match the staid ugliness of its fellows' (1989b: 24), shares affinities with Heidegger's notion of theyness, since both are representative of an unthinking adherence to socially prescribed expectations and modes of Being-in-the-world.

The uncanny

When Phyllis is faced with an alternative response to the control and influence of the social order that Kensington represents, she is overcome by a state of unease: 'in penetrating to her real self Phyllis had let in some chill gust of air to that closely guarded place' (1989b: 28). Such unease is akin to the Heideggerian understanding of the mood of *Angst*, or 'anxiety', described in *Being and Time*. As discussed in detail in the concluding chapter of this volume, for Heidegger, the individual always already experiences the world through the lens of moods. Heidegger notes that certain moods, including anxiety, provide the individual with the potential to experience the disclosure of that which is ordinarily concealed by average everydayness. Of particular note is the understanding that the mood of anxiety affords the individual the possibility to look beyond the societal constructs and expectations of theyness, as is the case when Phyllis begins to question her own choices, expectations and responses.

As Heidegger explains, a defining symptom of anxiety is the sense that 'one feels "*uncanny*", that is, one feels a sense of "not-being-at-home"' (*BT*: 233). In *Being and Time*, Heidegger discusses the notion of home and homelessness in some detail, suggesting that

> as Dasein falls, anxiety brings it back from its absorption in the 'world'. Everyday familiarity collapses. Dasein has been individualized, but individualized *as* Being-in-the-world. Being-in enters into the existential

'mode' of the '*not-at-home*'. Nothing else is meant by our talk about 'uncanniness' ... When in falling we flee *into* the 'at-home' of publicness, we flee *in the face of* the 'not-at-home'; that is, we flee in the face of the uncanniness which lies in Dasein – in Dasein as thrown Being-in-the-world, which has been delivered over to itself in its Being. This uncanniness pursues Dasein constantly, and is a threat to its everyday lostness in the 'they' ... *From an existential-ontological point of view, the 'not-at-home' must be conceived as the more primordial phenomenon.* (BT: 233–4)

In other words, so long as an individual adheres to the everyday constructs of the they, he or she will continue to live with a false sense of Being-at-home in the world. It is only when these socially inscribed expectations and prescriptions are recognised, questioned and abandoned that the individual's authentic self – manifested through a sense of not-Being-at-home to convention – comes to be disclosed. As the individual begins to question the social codes that once governed his or her life, a sense of homelessness ensues due to the realisation that he or she is no longer 'part of the crowd'.

Reflecting Woolf's own position within English society, a number of her characters, including Phyllis and Rosamond Hibbert, Rachel Vinrace in *The Voyage Out*, Clarissa Dalloway in *Mrs Dalloway*, and *Night and Day*'s Katharine Hilbery, are each born into an English middle- or upper-middle-class socio-economic sphere that is defined, at least in part, by an adherence to particular socially accepted norms, conventions and prescriptions. While each of these individuals experiences the constraints of the expectations, rules and limitations of their lot, each is also ultimately faced with a choice, however limited and difficult, to reject the '"at-home" of publicness' (Heidegger *BT*: 234) in the pursuit of individuality and authenticity. For Phyllis Hibbert, the recognition that she is in a position to choose how she might live her life is both uncomfortable and confronting.

As the Hibbert sisters travel home after their visit to Bloomsbury, Phyllis acknowledges that 'They were both somewhat excited; and anxious to analyse their discomfort, and find out what it meant'. Despite the beginnings of such an awakening, upon her return to her conventional home in Kensington, Phyllis finds that her resolve to understand her unease crumbles; as she goes to bed that night, Phyllis finds some comfort in the knowledge that her mother 'had arranged a full day for them tomorrow: at any rate she need not think; and river parties were amusing' (1989b: 28, 29). Reflecting Heidegger's pronouncement that one typically flees from the homelessness of individuality into the at-homeness of the they, Phyllis takes flight from unconventional Bloomsbury, back to the conformity of Kensington. Unlike Woolf, who abandons the constraints of Kensington in favour of the personal freedom of Bloomsbury, Phyllis resists change, clinging instead to the known quality of the societal conventions that have governed her life since birth.

As Heidegger emphasises in *Being and Time*, such an inauthentic mode of Being-in-the-world should be neither completely abandoned, nor denied. Thiele explains that

> Life itself, one might fairly say, depends on this habitual management and ingenious coping . . . The point is neither permanently to escape our anxious apprehension of contingency and the nothingness of Being nor self-destructively to languish in it. The problem is to live in the balance. (1995: 178)

As demonstrated in the previous chapter, such a sense of balance is acutely absent for *Mrs Dalloway*'s returned soldier, Septimus Smith, who has permanently ceased to feel the 'tranquillized self-assurance' (Heidegger *BT*: 233) that results from Being-at-home in the world. Suffering the debilitating symptoms of shell-shock upon his return to England, Septimus experiences immense unease in the face of the norms and expectations of society.

Despite the severity of his symptoms, the medical practitioner, Dr Holmes, proclaims that there is nothing wrong with Septimus: 'he brushed it all aside – headaches, sleeplessness, fears, dreams – nerve symptoms and nothing more' (*MD*: 91–2). In order to feel better, Septimus is told to immerse himself in the activities and preoccupations of everyday society: 'go to a music hall, play cricket' (*MD*: 23). Ultimately, the desired outcome of such a prescription is that this patient will once again feel at-home in society, thereby accepting, rather than questioning the prevailing social order. In his discussion of Heidegger's notion of the uncanny, Julian Young suggests that 'in anxiety one's world is experienced as a threatening, unsafe place and as such cannot constitute a "home"' (2001: 131). For Septimus, such a sense of Being-in-the-world is reinforced when Dr Holmes visits his flat; despite Septimus's refusal to see the doctor, this man of medicine will not be deterred, giving Septimus's wife,

Lucrezia Smith, 'a friendly push before he could get past her into her husband's bedroom' (*MD*: 92). Holmes's violation of the inherent sanctity and security of the Smiths' home reinforces and represents this young man's inescapable condition of hopelessness and homelessness. In her discussion of Dr Holmes, Elizabeth Clea Lamont suggests that this medical practitioner has

> geopolitical significance, symbolizing the fact that 'home' is not always necessarily a place of understanding and safety. Septimus himself recognizes the irony of his doctor's name when Bradshaw tries to commit him to an institution: 'One of Holmes [*sic*] homes?' he puns. (Lamont 2001: 172–3)

As discussed in Chapter 1, throughout *The Waves*, the characters Louis and Rhoda are also depicted as social outsiders who ultimately come to be defined by their inherent sense of homelessness. Born in Australia, and migrating to England as a child, Louis spends all his life vacillating between a desperate desire to achieve a sense of Being-at-home within English middle-class society, and disgust at the ways in which the social order constricts the individuality and agency of the self. As he sits alone in a London cafe as a young adult, Louis's internal struggle between inauthenticity and authenticity is palpable. Watching the crowds passing the shop's window, and observing his fellow customers, Louis's musings reflect his inherent sense of unease:

> 'I am an average Englishman; I am an average clerk', yet I look at the little men at the next table to be sure that I do what they do . . . Here is the central rhythm; here the common mainspring. I watch it expand, contract; and then expand again. Yet I am not included. If I speak, imitating their accent, they prick their ears, waiting for me to speak again, in order that they may place me – if I come from Canada or Australia, I, who desire above all things to be taken to the arms with love, am alien, external. I, who would wish to feel close over me the protective waves of the ordinary, catch with the tail of my eye some far horizon. (*TW*: 69, 70)

At the novel's end, Louis's life is summed up by his long-time friend, Bernard, who describes him as 'Unhappy, unfriended, in exile . . . He was without those simple attachments by which one is connected with another' (*TW*: 187, 188). Ultimately, Louis's life is defined by a perpetual state of detachment and not-Being-at-home. Reflecting

Heidegger's pronouncements regarding the importance of each individual attaining a balance between his or her sense of homelessness and Being-at-home in the world, while Louis's almost ceaseless mode of not-Being-at-home provides him with a perspective that allows for insightful observations of society and its members, ultimately such a sustained approach to Being-in-the-world does not grant the individual a happy or fulfilled life.

Not unlike Louis, who lives with an almost unrelenting sense of disconnection and unease, during her lifetime, Rhoda will 'flutter unattached, without anchorage anywhere, unconsolidated' (*TW*: 91). Just as Louis watches other men in the restaurant in order to pick up cues that will direct his own behaviour, Rhoda responds to her state of homelessness and her overwhelming desire for belonging, by emulating her friends Jinny and Susan:

> 'But since I wish above all things to have lodgment, I pretend, as I go upstairs lagging behind Jinny and Susan, to have an end in view. I pull on my stockings as I see them pull on theirs. I wait for you to speak and then speak like you.' (*TW*: 98)

Rhoda's longing for 'lodgment' reflects Heidegger's suggestion that when the individual '"understands" uncanniness in the everyday manner, it does so by turning away from it in falling; in this turning-away, the "not-at-home" gets "dimmed down"' (*BT*: 234). For Rhoda, such a sense of 'falling' is represented by her ultimately unsuccessful desire to mask her homelessness through a conscious and desperate attempt to conform to socially accepted norms and expectations.

The insider and outsider dichotomy

Just as Louis is aware of his sense of homelessness at an early age, so too does a young Rhoda realise that she inhabits the world in a manner that differs from that of her friends. This is demonstrated as Rhoda sits in a classroom, struggling to endure her mathematics lesson: what is perfectly clear to Bernard, Jinny, Neville, Susan, and even Louis, is unfathomable to this child. Rhoda becomes increasingly frustrated and overwhelmed by the figures on the blackboard that 'have no meaning for her' (*TW*: 15). As her friends hand in their answers and leave the room one by one, this child is left alone to continue her struggle. Rhoda's awareness that she occupies the place of an outsider who is condemned to be an onlooker rather than an active participant in society, is reflected in her observations as she sits in the classroom:

> I begin to draw a figure and the world is looped in it, and I myself am outside the loop; which I now join – so – and seal up, and make entire. The world is entire, and I am outside of it, crying, 'Oh save me, from being blown for ever outside the loop of time!' (*TW*: 14–15)

Such a figure represents a world of conventions and expectations that Rhoda will neither join nor understand; for this young girl, such an experience of being 'outside' is definitive of her inherent homelessness in the world.

In *Place and Placelessness,* Relph refers to 'existential outsideness' (1976: 51), a term that aptly describes Rhoda's mode of Being-in-the-world: conflating 'outsideness' with not-Being-at-home, Relph explains that such a state 'involves a selfconscious and reflective uninvolvement, an alienation from people and places, homelessness, a sense of the unreality of the world, and of not belonging' (1976: 51). Such a figure, who observes, but nevertheless remains largely detached from the world, can also be applied to the character Louis. As the novel begins, while each of the young characters – aside from Rhoda – repeatedly call Louis's name as they play together in the garden, this boy deliberately positions himself so that: 'they cannot see me. I am on the other side of the hedge. There are only little eye-holes among the leaves. Oh Lord, let them pass . . . let me be unseen' (*TW*: 7, 8). Such a propensity to remain an unseen observer continues when Louis attends boarding school: 'Peeping from behind a curtain', Louis observes the 'insider' schoolboys, and imagines 'How majestic is their order, how beautiful is their obedience!' (*TW*: 34). For Louis, both the hedge and curtain are representative of a self-imposed barrier that creates and reinforces his distance and disconnection from those whom he considers to be at-home in each situation and setting.

Gaston Bachelard suggests that 'Outside and inside are both intimate – they are always ready to be reversed, to exchange their hostility' (1994: 217–18). The notion that the inside and outside dualism is an unstable opposition has obvious implications for understandings of Being-at-home and homelessness. Throughout Woolf's various representations of individuals who return home after long absences, the fluidity of such divisions comes to be particularly marked. In *Mrs Dalloway*, for instance, upon Peter Walsh's return to London after years spent in India, he finds himself wandering the once-familiar streets, and 'the strangeness of standing alone, alive, unknown, at half-past eleven in Trafalgar Square overcame him. What is it? Where am I?' (*MD*: 51). As Relph explains, when the individual returns to a significant place that has since changed, this can have a profound effect upon his or her sense of Being-at-home: 'Whereas before we were involved in the scene, now we are an outsider, an observer' (1976: 31). Peter's lodgement in a hotel is representative of his liminal position: the hotel 'serves as Peter's domestic space but one from which he feels thoroughly alienated' (Lamont 2001: 176). Lamont suggests that Peter's sense that 'These hotels are not consoling places. Far from it' (*MD*: 157), 'expresses a traveler's sense of loneliness and displacement' (Lamont 2001: 177).

In *The Years*, North Pargiter has also recently returned to London after spending an extended time living abroad. On his way to visit his cousin Sara, North's sense of not-Being-at-home is clearly evident: 'He was always finding himself now outside the doors of strange houses. He had a feeling that he was no one and nowhere in particular'. Rather than feel that he has returned home, North perceives London as 'an unknown land' (*TY*: 228, 232). Attending his Aunt Delia's party, North feels 'an outsider . . . All these people knew each other. They called each other – he stood on the outskirts'. As he listens to a conversation dominated by the topics of 'money and politics', North distances himself from this society and its values: 'Nothing would be easier than to join a society, to sign what Patrick called "a manifesto." But he did not believe in joining societies, in signing manifestoes' (*TY*: 295, 296).

Home and the lived body

Woolf's personal circumstances also represent the malleability of the demarcation between insider and outsider: Woolf's class defines her as an insider within particular spheres of society; while, as a woman, she is deemed to be an outsider in many social arenas.

Discussing Woolf's series of *Good Housekeeping* essays, which were later republished as *The London Scene*, Squier argues that such writing reveals 'identity-in-contestation as Woolf struggles between identification with insiders (men, the upper class) and outsiders (women, the working classes)' (1991: 109). As Susan Stanford Friedman suggests, such a 'kaleidoscope of contradictions emphasizes the interplay of power and powerlessness along different axes of alterity' (1998: 22). Throughout her writings, Woolf's exploration of the social positioning of women as outsiders can be equated with the notion of not-Being-at-home in the world. This is particularly apparent in Woolf's textual representations of the 'lived body', a term that Iris Marion Young defines as

> a unified idea of a physical body acting and experiencing in a specific socio-cultural context; it is body-in-situation. For existentialist theory, *situation* denotes the produce of *facticity* and *freedom*. The person always faces the material facts of her body and its relation to a given environment . . . Her specific body lives in a specific context . . . All these concrete material relations of a person's bodily existence and her physical and social environment constitute her *facticity* . . . Like the category of sex, that of the lived body can refer to the specific physical facts of bodies, including sexual and reproductive differentiation. (2002: 415, 416)

The understanding that the lived body is a product of each individual's factical circumstance is also reflected in Heidegger's philosophy, where factors such as the body, sex and gender reflect the 'thrown' nature of the individual; that is, the radical contingency of his or her existence, insofar as each of us is born with a particular type of body, of a certain sex, but it could have easily been otherwise. Such characteristics are considered to be contingent factical elements of existence, just as birthplace and societal-historical circumstances also combine to define the factical nature of each individual's mode of Being-in-the-world. Despite the contingent nature of the lived body, both Heidegger and Iris Marion Young emphasise that from an existential-phenomenological perspective, the individual

> is an actor; she has an ontological freedom to construct herself in relation to this facticity. The human actor has specific projects, things she aims to accomplish, ways she aims to express herself, make her mark on the world, transform her surroundings and relationships. Often these are projects she engages in jointly with others. (Young 2002: 415)

As discussed, for Heidegger, the underlying condition of not-Being-at-home is disclosed to the individual through the mood of anxiety; as each of us is faced with the inextricable thrownness of our condition, we are faced with the realisation that 'The worldly stage is neither of our making nor of our choosing, and we find ourselves cast in roles beyond our power fully to direct or control' (Thiele 1995: 177). Throughout our daily lives, our conduct and actions are always measured from the perspective of a blueprint that is not entirely of our own making: the conventions, norms, transgressions, roles and possibilities that exist within a particular social context are always predetermined despite their potential future fluidity. As Heidegger emphasises in *Being and Time,* 'Dasein's facticity is such that *as long as* it is what it is, Dasein remains in the throw, and is sucked into the turbulence of the "they's" inauthenticity' (*BT*: 223). As a result, both thrownness and theyness continue to impact upon each individual's mode of Being-in-the-world for as long as he or she lives. Along similar lines, in her reference to Woolf's representations of the social order of England throughout her writings, Zwerdling remarks that

> Woolf was writing about a society in which ... seemingly absurd distinctions dictated one's fate. The individual's freedom was strictly circumscribed by the accident of birth, so that the range of his opportunities could be imagined if one had a realistic sense of his starting point. (1986: 90)

Arguably, for Woolf, one of the more significant manifestations of thrownness is the facticity of the lived body, due to its impact upon, and determination of, the average everyday lived experience of the individual.

In a section of *Being and Time* entitled 'The Spatiality of Being-in-the-world', Heidegger concedes, in parentheses, that the individual's '"bodily nature" hides a whole problematic of its own, though we shall not treat it here' (*BT*: 143). As Heidegger's concern is an existential-phenomenological analysis of Dasein's mode of Being-in-the-world, it is unsurprising that such factical elements are afforded scant attention; as Derrida remarks:

> If the neutrality of the title '*Dasein*' is essential, it is precisely because the interpretation of that being – which *we* are – is to be engaged *before* and *outside* of a concretion of that type. The first example of 'concretion' would then be belonging to one or another of the two sexes. (2001: 58)[3]

Despite this, it has been emphasised by critics that the issues of embodiment and gender are neglected areas of Heidegger's analysis in *Being and Time*.⁴ As Kevin A. Aho remarks, while Heidegger's focus is directed upon the individual's average everyday involvement in the world, he nevertheless fails 'to discuss the role of the lived-body in our everyday acts and practices' (2005: 7). In Heidegger's 1959 *Zollikon Seminars,* the philosopher is asked by Medard Boss to respond to the statement that critics 'took up the reproach of Jean-Paul Sartre, who wondered why you only wrote six lines about the body in the whole of *Being and Time*'; Heidegger's reply is in keeping with his 1927 pronouncements regarding this issue: 'I can only counter Sartre's reproach by stating that the bodily [*das Leibliche*] is the most difficult [to understand] and that I was unable to say more at that time' (Heidegger 2001: 231). In contrast to his earlier stance, within these later seminars, Heidegger does elaborate upon his understanding of the body through his emphasis that

> the *bodily limit* is extended beyond the *corporeal limit* . . . The *bodying forth [Leiben] of the body* is determined by the way of my being. The bodying forth of the body, therefore, is a way of Da-sein's being. (2001: 86–7)

Referring to the *Zollikon Seminars*, Aho explains that

> Heidegger wants to make it clear that the body, understood phenomenologically, is not a bounded corporeal thing that is 'present-at-hand', rather it is already stretching beyond its own skin, actively directed towards and interwoven with the world . . . And it is here that Heidegger makes contact with Merleau-Ponty. (2005: 10)⁵

The French philosopher, Maurice Merleau-Ponty (1908–61), is generally regarded as having subsequently provided the phenomenology of embodied experience that was lacking in Heidegger's analysis. While acknowledging the differences in the two philosophers' approaches to the body, Aho draws attention to the affinities between Heidegger and Merleau-Ponty, particularly their shared understanding that 'the body is *not* a material thing that occupies a current position in space, rather it indicates a "range" or horizon within which a nexus of things is encountered' (2005: 11). In other words, the body's relationship with the world comes to be defined by average everyday existential involvement rather than self-containment.

Of particular significance in terms of Woolf's approach to the lived body is Aho's assertion that both Heidegger and Merleau-Ponty offer 'a phenomenological description of embodied spatiality and orientation that applies to human acts and practices *generally*, as we live them "*proximally and for the most part* – in average everydayness"' (2005: 13–14). Such a perspective is reflected in Holland's discussion of 'Heidegger and the Feminine They-Self':

> If we see Dasein ... as necessarily always already immersed in a they-self, a social world of meanings, roles, games, and scripts into which it has been thrown and from which it must draw its projects insofar as they are to be recognized and valued by those around it, then the fact that the scripts and roles of any possible social context will be heavily gender differentiated will mean that gender (and in certain circumstances, race or class) cannot be phenomenologically 'secondary' ... Even if Heidegger insists that Dasein is 'a-sexual', human existentiality dictates that gender is one of the most important facts about any possible life that any Dasein might in fact live. (2001: 141–2)

Arguably, Heidegger's approach to embodiment represents a starting point that is developed further through Woolf's textual representations of the lived body. Indeed, the remainder of this section will focus upon the ways in which, in contrast to Heidegger, Woolf's treatment of the lived body always takes place within the context of '*particular* social practices' (Aho 2005: 14). The intention is not only to illuminate Woolf's understanding of the lived body within the context of Being-in-the-world; it is also hoped that 'Introducing variations of social difference to the discussion of spatiality can deepen the original insights of Heidegger' (Aho 2005: 15). Nevertheless, it must be reiterated that 'such investigations have nothing to do with Heidegger's core concern, which is fundamental ontology' (Aho 2005: 15).

Throughout Woolf's fictional and non-fictional writings, it is the domestic space that is repeatedly marked as a site that is particularly representative of the influence that the social and historical context has upon the lived bodies of women. Victoria Rosner observes that 'No social institution is more closely tied to the construction and reproduction of gender and sexual identity than the home' (2005: 14); while Emily Blair suggests that the domestic space represented in nineteenth- and twentieth-century literature 'serves as an analog for the mind and the body' (2007: 11). Detailing the daily life that she and her sister Vanessa experienced as young women located within an upper-middle-class household at the turn of the twentieth century, Woolf remarks in 'A Sketch of the Past' that: 'Every day we did battle for that which was always being snatched from us, or distorted. The most imminent obstacle, the most oppressive stone laid upon our vitality and its struggle to live was of course father' ('Sketch': 146). Woolf's struggle to attain autonomy and agency within this domestic sphere produces a sense of unease that is akin to Biddy Martin and Chandra Talpade Mohanty's discussion of 'not being home', which is defined by the realisation 'that home was an illusion of coherence and safety based on the exclusion of specific histories of oppression and resistance' (Martin and Mohanty 1986: 196).

Such a perspective is evident in Woolf's 1931 essay 'Professions for Women', where she both highlights and calls into question the notion of the 'Angel in the House' (1942d: 150), a figure that has its origins in Coventry Patmore's 1854 poem (see Patmore 2006), which glorifies 'those women still performing the unpaid work and enforced domestic servitude of wife and mother' (Goldman 2006: 116). In her essay, Woolf discusses the beginnings of her own writing career, asserting that in order to express her thoughts and opinions through her craft, she had to struggle with, and ultimately kill, this domestic Angel. In Woolf's novel, *The Years*, the eldest Pargiter daughter, Eleanor, is representative of such a figure; automatically assuming the role of housekeeper at the age of twenty-two upon the death of her mother, Eleanor willingly maintains this position for the thirty-one years that she continues to live with her father in the family home.

Reflecting the attributes of the 'Angel in the House' that are emphasised by Woolf in her essay, Eleanor is 'intensely sympathetic', 'utterly unselfish', someone who 'excelled in the difficult arts of family life', 'sacrificed herself daily', and ultimately, 'never had a mind or a wish of her own' (1942d: 150). Eleanor's liberation is only attained upon her father's death, whereupon 'her house was shut up; she had no attachment at the moment anywhere' (*TY*: 143). 'Glad to be quit of it all', Eleanor contemplates her future, musing: 'Should she take another house? Should she travel? Should she go to India, at last?' Upon consideration of each of these options, Eleanor concludes: 'No, I don't mean to take another house, not another house', whereupon 'the sense came to her of a ship padding softly through the waves; of a train swinging from side to side down a railway-line' (*TY*: 158, 156). As such imagery reflects, Eleanor's life-journey is finally to begin; freed from the constraints and expectations that maintaining a home and adhering to the expectations of the social order imposes upon the lived body of women, Eleanor finds herself free to choose how she will lead the remainder of her life.[6]

Hussey discusses Woolf's treatment of the lived body from the perspective of the notions of 'embodiment and unembodiment', insofar as such states are representative of the degree to which each individual is 'at home' (1986: 5) in his or her body. In keeping with the philosophy of Merleau-Ponty, Hussey asserts that 'The question of the way the body is lived must precede any account of self precisely because human beings *live* their bodies as their foundation in the world' (1986: 19). Hussey's study of Woolf's representation of 'the variety of ways characters are more or less "at home" in their bodies' provides a useful insight into each character's sense of Being at-home or homeless in the world, where embodiment is understood as 'a flux, conditioning the way an individual experiences the world' (1986: 5, 10). In his study of *The Waves*, Hussey explains that 'Jinny stands as the most fully embodied of all Woolf's characters, while Rhoda lies at the extreme of unembodiment' (1986: 5). Arguably, as Jinny 'is most "at home" in her body' (Hussey 1986: 5), this character is also most at-home in terms of her mode of Being-in-the-world.

In her discussion of the 'modalities of feminine bodily existence', Iris Marion Young writes that

> woman lives her body as *object* as well as subject. The source of this is that patriarchal society defines woman as object, as a mere body . . . The source of this objectified bodily existence is in the attitude of others regarding her, but the woman herself often actively takes up her body as a mere thing. She gazes at it in the mirror, worries about how it looks to others, prunes it, shapes it, molds and decorates it. (1980: 153–4)

Young's description of those women who come to view their own bodies as objects, typifies Jinny's approach to Being-in-the-world. This character lives for the admiring gaze of the Other, consciously adhering to the socially-defined prescriptions of what it means to be a 'woman'. Jinny's typical mode of Being-in-the-world is exemplified as she painstakingly prepares for her entrance at a social gathering:

> This is the prelude, this is the beginning. I glance, I peep, I powder. All is exact, prepared. My hair is swept in one curve. My lips are precisely red. I am ready now to join men and women on the stairs, my peers. I pass them, exposed to their gaze, as they are to mine . . . Our bodies communicate. This is my calling. This is my world. (*TW*: 75)

From a Heideggerian perspective, Jinny is most likely to feel at-home in the world, as she is the least likely of the characters in *The Waves* to feel the unease that results from the questioning or rejection of the prescriptions and expectations of the social order. As Hussey observes, for those characters 'whose way of living the body tends very much to complete embodiment, the world is not usually a threatening place. They are marked by a sense of security, of "belonging"' (1986: 12).

Such a sense of Being-in-the-world lies in sharp contrast to that experienced by those who do not feel at-home in their bodies, due to the understanding that 'Those who tend to unembodiment are outcasts, outsiders, and visionaries' (Hussey 1986: 8). Hussey suggests that 'at the furthest extreme of unembodiment of all Woolf's characters is Rhoda, in *The Waves*':

> Rhoda is thrown into the world by a body she hates and tries to avoid . . . She longs for 'lodgement' . . . that is, for a *home* in the world that her body does not provide . . . Her feeling of being 'committed' to life, in the sense of being committed to prison, springs from the tension inherent in the way she lives her body. (1986: 16, 17)

Although Hussey does not refer to Heidegger's philosophy in his discussion of Rhoda's relationship to her body or the world, his description of this young woman as 'thrown', and in search of a 'home', is in keeping with Heidegger's notion of Dasein's state of thrownness: through no choice of her own, Rhoda is a female born into a society with specific socially-constructed expectations concerning the lived body. It is as a result of such expectations that Rhoda feels that she must assume roles that she finds to be unnatural, uncomfortable and ultimately unsustainable.

The built form of home

The lived body can be understood not only as a site of socially inscribed norms that govern our sense of Being-at-home-in-the-world; the body can also become marked by those places that we call home. In *The Poetics of Space,* Bachelard posits the notion of bodily inscription as he explores the ways that the body retains a particular connection to the first home that it inhabited:

> [O]ver and beyond our memories, the house we were born in is physically inscribed in us. It is a group of organic habits. After twenty years, in spite of all the other anonymous stairways; we would recapture the reflexes of the 'first stairway,' we would not stumble on that rather high step. The house's entire being would open up, faithful to our own being. We would push the door that creaks with the same gesture, we would find our way in the dark to the distant attic. The feel of the tiniest latch has remained in our hands. (1994: 14–15)

Such a sense of the physical connection between the individual and built manifestations of home is evident when one considers Woolf's life-long ties to her childhood summer residence, Talland House. In a 1905 diary entry, Woolf records the first visit that she and her Stephen siblings make to Cornwall after a ten-year absence:

> We could fancy that we were but coming home along the high road after some long day's outing, & that when we reached the gate at Talland House, we should thrust it open, & find ourselves among the familiar sights again. In the dark, indeed, we made bold to humour this fancy of ours further than we had a right to; we passed through the gate, groped steadily but with sure feet up the carriage drive, mounted the little flight of rough steps, & peered through a chink in the escalonia hedge ... But yet as we knew well, we could go no further. (*PA*: 282)

The bodies of Woolf and her siblings remember this place of significance, so that they do not stumble as they make their way in the dark. Such a perspective is in keeping with that of Merleau-Ponty, who asserts that in the individual's average everyday dealings, 'the body already has a "tacit knowledge" of its place in the world because it has been habitually interwoven to a familiar concrete situation' (Aho 2005: 8–9). In contrast, Heidegger's analysis in *Being and Time* does not concern itself with 'the body's role in this spatial orientation' (Aho 2005: 8).

The sense that place inscribes the lived body is evident in Woolf's 1932 essay, 'Great Men's Houses', where she describes the hardships that Thomas Carlyle's long-suffering wife, Jane, endures as a result of living in a home 'without water, without electric light, without gas fires' (2006b: 32). The everyday involvement that is required in order to live in such a dwelling comes to mark Jane's body, so that 'Her cheeks are hollow; bitterness and suffering mingle in the half-tender, half-tortured expression of the eyes. Such is the effect of a pump in the basement and a yellow tin bath up three pairs of stairs' (2006b: 35). Emphasised in this essay is Woolf's understanding that the lived body also leaves its mark upon the domestic space through its average everyday activities and involvement:

> The stairs, carved as they are and wide and dignified, seem worn by the feet of harassed women carrying tin cans. The high panelled rooms seem to echo with the sound of pumping and the swish of scrubbing. The voice of the house – and all houses have voices – is the voice of pumping and scrubbing, of coughing and groaning. (2006b: 33)

This place becomes a tangible expression of everyday Being-in-the-world for Thomas and Jane Carlyle, and their maid, as home can be understood as 'an extension of and mirror for the living body in its everyday activity' (Young 1997: 150).

In 'Great Men's Houses', Woolf emphasises the close association between the women of different classes who live within the Carlyle household, where both 'mistress and maid fought against dirt and cold for cleanliness and warmth' (2006b: 33), each experiencing degrees of confinement and privation within the context of the domestic space. Nevertheless, it should be noted that such a conflation of different social classes is not a typical feature of Woolf's writings; although women of all classes in the first half of the twentieth century are often relegated to the domestic space in one form or another, throughout Woolf's writings, the architecture of the home frequently reflects not only gender prescriptions, but also class divides. In her discussion of Woolf's personal and textual approach to the issue of domestic servants, Light draws attention to the notion that

> For Woolf, as for many others growing up in nineteenth-century urban culture, the topography of the house lent itself as an inevitable metaphor

for bourgeois identity, with the lower orders curtained off, relegated to the bottom of the house or to its extremities, like a symbolic ordering of the body. (2007: 75)

Such an ordering is evident in 'A Sketch of the Past', as Woolf describes the living arrangements provided for the domestic staff in her childhood home at Hyde Park Gate. Describing 'the servants' sitting room', which is located in the basement, Woolf writes:

It was at the back; very low and very dark . . . The basement was a dark insanitary place for seven maids to live in. 'It's like hell,' one of them burst out to my mother as we sat at lessons in the dining room. My mother at once assumed the frozen dignity of the Victorian matron; and said (perhaps): 'Leave the room'; and she (unfortunate girl) vanished behind the red plush curtain which, hooped round a semi-circular wire, and anchored by a great gold knob, hid the door that led from the dining room to the pantry. ('Sketch': 123–4)

Such a sense that the living conditions of the servant are beneath the notice of her masters and mistresses is granted fictional form in Woolf's *The Years*. As Eleanor Pargiter prepares to vacate her family home after it has been sold, she visits the dismal quarters where their maid, Crosby, has spent the last forty years of her life: 'She had never realized how dark, how low it was, until, looking at it with "our Mr Grice," she had felt ashamed' (*TY*: 158). That Eleanor could spend so many years living in the same home as another woman, and not be aware of her living conditions, is a stark reflection of the treatment of the domestic servant during the late nineteenth and early twentieth centuries.

As noted in the opening chapter, in her essay 'Mr. Bennett and Mrs. Brown', Woolf draws attention to a perceived change in 'human character' (1966a: 320) that occurred in 1910. Reflecting upon this change, Woolf describes the association between the built form of the home and the situation of the domestic servant:

In life one can see the change, if I may use a homely illustration, in the character of one's cook. The Victorian cook lived like a leviathan in the lower depths, formidable, silent, obscure, inscrutable; the Georgian cook is a creature of sunshine and fresh air; in and out of the drawing-room, now to borrow the *Daily Herald*, now to ask advice about a hat. Do you ask for more solemn instances of the power of the human race to change? (1966a: 320)

Woolf's observations, though far from nondiscriminatory, emphasise that the politics of the home can be viewed as a significant gauge for the prevailing expectations and prescriptions of the social order. As Michael Tratner claims in his reading of this essay: 'Woolf connects her own life with the lives of working women: the same change in human relations releases the cook into the drawing room and allows a woman of genius to write books instead of scouring saucepans' (1995: 54).

In his 1951 essay, 'Building Dwelling Thinking', Heidegger discusses the inextricable connection between building and dwelling, where dwelling is representative of our primordial state of Being-in-the-world.[7] Heidegger asserts that dwelling 'is *the basic character* of Being in keeping with which mortals exist'; further to this, 'building belongs to dwelling and . . . receives its nature from dwelling' (2001: 158). In other words, buildings are both a response and manifestation of our mode of Being-in, where self and world are indivisibly connected. Nuala Hancock suggests that

> If we are to follow through this Heideggerian synchronicity, we open ourselves to the suggestion that an immersion in the inner spaces of another's dwelling might reveal unspoken and elemental aspects of their intimate ways of being in the world. (2012: 15)

Indeed, the architectural features of the built spaces that each of us inhabits and encounters in the course of our daily lives, have the potential to significantly affect our sense of Being-at-home-in-the-world. Throughout Woolf's writings, the 'door' is a recurring motif that represents and signals each individual's sense of being at-home or not-at-home within a particular situation or context. Bachelard describes the significance of the door in terms of its potential to encourage or deny entry: 'The door schematizes two strong possibilities, which sharply classify two types of daydream. At times, it is closed, bolted, padlocked. At others, it is open, that is to say, wide open' (1994: 222). In *A Room of One's Own*, such a point of view is reflected as Woolf takes her leave from Oxbridge after dining at one of the men's colleges: 'Gate after gate seemed to close with gentle finality behind me. Innumerable beadles were fitting innumerable keys into well-oiled locks: the treasure-house was being made secure for another night' (*RO*: 16–17). These gates reveal and reinforce the temporary nature of Woolf's inclusion in the male-dominated world of university education, where she is ultimately considered to be an outsider.

For Woolf, the image of the door also marks the stark divide between the private domestic space and public life in English society. In her polemic, Woolf describes the scenario of a husband returning home to his wife and children after spending his day at work:

> He would open the door of drawing-room or nursery, I thought, and find her among her children perhaps, or with a piece of embroidery on her knee – at any rate, the centre of some different order and system of life, and the contrast between this world and his own, which might be the law courts or the House of Commons, would at once refresh and invigorate. (*RO*: 112–13)

As this passage reflects, the husband, unlike his wife, is free to cross the threshold that separates the public and private domains. Indeed, Mircea Eliade suggests that 'The *threshold* concentrates not only the boundary between outside and inside but also the possibility of passage from one zone to the other' (1987: 181); while Rosner observes that 'Thresholds can threaten domestic order because they are sites of intersection and difference' (2005: 65).

The understanding that the door is representative of the degree of free passage and agency that an individual has within a particular place or sphere of society is emphasised in *Three Guineas*, as Woolf describes

> the force which in the nineteenth century opposed itself to the force of the fathers. All we can safely say about that force was that it was a force of tremendous power. It forced open the doors of the private house. (*TG*: 358)

– even as the doors to the public sphere remained firmly shut. Throughout her polemic, Woolf draws attention to the doors of patriarchal society that have long been closed; lamenting women's restricted agency as a result of their segregation from public life, Woolf writes:

> our bird's-eye view of the outside of things is not altogether encouraging ... it serves to remind us that there are many inner and secret chambers that we cannot enter. What real influence can we bring to bear upon law or business, religion or politics – we to whom many doors are still locked, or at best ajar, we who have neither capital nor force behind us? (*TG*: 181)

From such a perspective it is of note that Woolf had in mind a number of titles for the essay that eventually became *Three Guineas*; as Anne Oliver Bell notes, the alternative titles, '*The Open Door; Opening the Door; A Tap at the Door*' (D4: 6, n8) were each considered.

While the image of the locked door clearly represents the individual's exclusion from particular social spheres, Woolf also emphasises that there are certain times when the individual feels the need to close or lock his or her door as a means of keeping the prescriptions of society at bay. In *Night and Day*, for instance, Katharine only works on her hidden passion, mathematics, when she is alone in her bedroom with the door closed. Katharine is acutely aware that, 'living people were at work on the other side of the door, and the door, which could be thrown open in a second, was her only protection against the world' (*ND*: 461). This door represents and emphasises the fragility of Katharine's private space, agency and sovereignty. From a similar perspective, in *A Room of One's Own,* Woolf asserts that 'it is necessary to have five hundred [pounds] a year and a room with a lock on the door if you are to write fiction or poetry', as 'a lock on the door means the power to think for oneself' (*RO*: 137, 139). For both Katharine and Woolf, the door provides women with much-needed privacy and autonomy, as well as the means to attain and regain a sense of the unfettered self.

Bachelard emphasises the ways that the door can be viewed as a measure of the individual's lived life:

> How concrete everything becomes in the world of the spirit when an object, a mere door, can give images of hesitation, temptation, desire, security, welcome and respect. If one were to give an account of all the doors one has closed and opened, of all the doors one would like to reopen, one would have to tell the story of one's entire life.
> But is he who opens a door and he who closes it the same being? (1994: 224)

An inventory of the doors we have passed through, as well as those that have remained closed to us, becomes a blueprint of our life's journey. As the final sentence of this passage reflects, each door leaves its imprint upon the subjectivity of the individual. This is particularly apparent in terms of one's identification as an insider who feels at-home in the world, or as an outsider who is overcome by a sense of homelessness. In *The Waves,* for instance, Louis, as an Australian-born boy living in British society, describes his sense of being located 'outside' the closed doors of social acceptance and opportunity. As Louis explains, his greatest aspiration is to pass through these closed doors:

> 'I am now a boy only with a colonial accent holding my knuckles against Mr. Wickham's grained oak door . . . But I am also one who will force himself to desert these windy and moonlit territories, these midnight wanderings, and confront grained oak doors. I will achieve in my life – Heaven grant that it be not long – some gigantic amalgamation between the two discrepancies so hideously apparent to me. Out of my suffering I will do it. I will knock. I will enter.' (*TW*: 38)

As a character who defines himself as an outsider, Louis will spend his life seeking to cross those thresholds that he believes exist between himself and the social order of English society.

A room of one's own

In *Three Guineas*, Woolf uses the motif of the door to describe the impact that the 1919 Sex Disqualification (Removal) Act has upon the lives of women as they gain greater access to the public sphere of employment. As Woolf writes: 'The door of the private house was thrown open. In every purse there was, or might be, one bright new sixpence in whose light every thought, every sight, every action looked different' (*TG*: 172). Within such a context, the door signals women's escape from the confines of the private home, and the rooms that they have long been expected to inhabit. In *A Room of One's Own*, Woolf discusses women's confinement to the domestic space, suggesting that

> one has only to go into any room in any street for the whole of that extremely complex force of femininity to fly in one's face. How should it be otherwise? For women have sat indoors all these millions of years. (*RO*: 114)

The rooms that women have long been relegated to within the domestic sphere, such as 'drawing-rooms, nurseries, kitchens', have ultimately been 'rooms with no privacy' (Lee 1996: 47), and as such, no autonomy. As Rosner explains, 'Though women occasionally had a study or its equivalent, for the most part such spaces of solitary retreat and labor were seen as incompatible with women's role at the center of family life' (2005: 95). It is from such a perspective that Woolf represents the rooms within the private home as an architectural motif for women's place in society. Through her famous proclamation that 'a woman must have money and a room of her own if she is to write fiction' (*RO*: 4), Woolf asserts each woman's need for a private space in which she can determine for herself how she will spend her time. The significance of a private room within the home as a place of retreat and privacy is reflected in Woolf's first novel, *The Voyage Out*, where Helen Ambrose convinces her niece to accompany her to South America with the promise that this young woman will be supplied with

> a room cut off from the rest of the house, large, private – a room in which she could play, read, think, defy the world, a fortress as well as a sanctuary. Rooms, she knew, became more like worlds than rooms at the age of twenty-four. (*VO*: 136)

As mentioned, in *Being and Time,* Heidegger discusses the significance of the 'work-world' (*BT*: 101) as a representative site of average everyday concern and involvement. Referring to Heidegger's assertion that 'Our concernful absorption in whatever work-world lies closest to us, has a function of discovering' (*BT*: 101), Paul C. Adams explains that such 'absorption helps us to become aware of our own being-in-the-world' (2001: 407). For Woolf, 'a room of one's own' represents a revised understanding and manifestation of the work-world as it relates to women. Arguably, Woolf's emphasis upon the importance of such a private space in which to think, work and write, is in keeping with Heidegger's personal desire for a place of his own in which to carry out his philosophical work. While Heidegger's official workplace was located in the German universities where he lectured and researched throughout his academic career, the philosopher 'found the university milieu unconducive to his work' (Sharr 2006: 50). In contrast, Heidegger's preferred work-world, from 1922 until the final years of his life, was a modest and secluded hut located in the Black Forest of southern Germany.[8] It was within this isolated rural environment that Heidegger found the inspiration for his work and carried out much of his writings. As Heidegger attests in his 1934 essay, 'Why Do I Stay in the Provinces?': 'On a deep winter's night when a wild, pounding snowstorm rages around the cabin and veils and covers everything, that is the perfect time for philosophy. Then its questions must become simple and essential' (2010: 27–8). For Heidegger, within the context of this hut, self, environment and philosophy became intertwined: each informing and forming the other.

For Woolf, Monk's House in Rodmell was the site of her rural retreat and work-world. From 1919, Woolf and her husband, Leonard, 'were seasonal visitors', until the couple were forced to abandon London and permanently relocate to the countryside during the Second World War. Woolf's countryside workplace consisted of what she termed a 'lodge': a simple timber outhouse located in the garden of Monk's House. From 1921 until her death in 1941, during her stays at Rodmell, Woolf worked in this dwelling during the warmer months of the year. It was within this place that Woolf 'wrote parts of all her major novels from *Mrs Dalloway* to *Between the Acts*, many essays and reviews, and many letters' (Lee 2008).[9] Louise DeSalvo states that it was within this environment that 'Woolf found the solitude necessary to unravel the conundrums in her work' (2009: 18). Just as Heidegger valued the privacy that his retreat offered, so that 'Generally, visitors were permitted only alone or in small numbers, when work allowed' (Sharr 2006: 57), Woolf frequently viewed visitors as an intrusive interruption to her work. Much to Woolf's dismay, her lodge did not offer the same level of peace and seclusion that Heidegger enjoyed in his hut. On a daily basis, Woolf had to contend with the sounds of village life that invaded her work-world, including 'little cottage boys with the cursed shrill voices, playing cricket . . . & interrupting me . . . & I detest more & more interruption' (D3: 189).

Nevertheless, like Heidegger's hut, Woolf's lodge provided the writer with the physical, emotional and intellectual room to ruminate and create. Woolf's lodge and Heidegger's hut provide tangible expressions of the approaches that these two individuals took towards their work, insofar as home and the work-world are combined, rather than juxtaposed or segregated.

The understanding that 'a room of one's own' facilitates not only a work-world, but also a sense of freedom and autonomy for the individual, is given fictional representation by Woolf in *Night and Day*, when Katharine Hilbery visits Mary Datchet, a young woman who lives alone in a London flat. From Katharine's perspective, 'The whole aspect of the place . . . struck her as enviably free; in such a room one could work – one could have a life of one's own' (ND: 259). In *Orlando*, Woolf demonstrates that a private room is also a necessary space for men: from the perspective of the young male protagonist,

> when the feasting was at its height and his guests were at their revels, he was apt to take himself off to his private room alone. There when the door was shut, and he was certain of privacy, he would have out an old writing book... In this he would write till midnight chimed and long after. (O: 77)

Not unlike Katharine Hilbery's interest in mathematics, Orlando must partake of his poetic passion within the privacy of his own room. As a result of both characters' need to conceal and repress their true interests, desires and selves, each experiences a sense of not-Being-at-home in the face of the societal expectations and constraints that dictate the interests and vocations that young men and women are called upon to pursue.

Throughout Woolf's writings, rooms within the home also frequently represent the temporal dimensions and characteristics of place that were discussed in the previous chapter. In 'A Sketch of the Past', for instance, Woolf describes the rich history of her parents' bedroom:

> the double bedded bedroom on the first floor was the sexual centre; the birth centre, the death centre of the house. It was not a large room; but its walls must be soaked, if walls take pictures and board up what is done and said with all that was most intense, of all that makes the most private being, of family life. In that bed four children were begotten; there they were born; there first mother died; then father died, with a picture of mother hanging in front of him. ('Sketch': 125)

Woolf reflects upon her belief that this room of significance retains the memory of all that has passed within the confines of its walls. Such an understanding is in keeping with Bachelard's assertion that 'The old house, for those who know how to listen, is a sort of geometry of echoes' (1994: 60). In *Charleston and Monk's House: The Intimate House Museums of Virginia Woolf and Vanessa Bell*, Hancock discusses the significance of the 'commemorative house' (2012: 16) as a means of understanding its former inhabitants; referring to Heidegger's essay, 'Building Dwelling Thinking', Hancock draws attention to

> The mutualism inherent in both Heidegger and Bachelard between interiors and interiority... If, as Heidegger proposes, building is a 'letting dwell', then the spaces of the commemorative building have the potential to divulge something of their inhabitants' essential ways of 'being-in-the-world'. (2012: 16)

Throughout *Between the Acts,* the history of the rooms of Pointz Hall is continually emphasised. For the elderly Lucy Swithin and her brother Bartholomew Oliver, their family home provides a tangible connection to their deceased mother. In the opening pages of the novel, for instance, as Bartholomew entertains guests, he recalls that 'over sixty years ago . . . his mother had given him the works of Byron in that very room'; as Lucy sits in her bedroom one morning, she recalls 'her mother in that very room rebuking her'; and when Lucy gives William Dodge a tour of her home, she describes the morning room as the space '"Where my mother received her guests"' (*BA*: 6, 8, 43). While memories of the past provide both Lucy and Bartholomew with a greater sense of connection to this place, such recollections also provide evidence of women's confinement and connection to the domestic space, where home is represented by the maternal figure.

Home and its objects

While maternal images provide a sense of comfort and belonging to Lucy and Bartholomew, the paternal figure of 'the great poet, Richard Alardyce' (*ND*: 7) threatens to overcome Katharine Hilbery in *Night and Day*. As she and her mother sit in the study and work on her grandfather's biography, Katharine muses that

> Quiet as the room was, and undisturbed by the sounds of the present moment, Katharine could fancy that here was a deep pool of past time, and that she and her mother were bathed in the light of sixty years ago. (*ND*: 103)

Finding herself in such an environment, Katharine 'very nearly lost consciousness that she was a separate being, with a future of her own' (*ND*: 104). Describing this room, Katharine notes that it is filled with her grandfather's belongings: 'All the books and pictures, even the chairs and tables, had belonged to him, or had reference to him' (*ND*: 103). The organisation of the Hilbery residence is akin to a shrine to Katharine's grandfather, where visitors are encouraged to view the famous English poet's works and belongings. Lee suggests that the various objects in the Hilbery home, inherited from earlier generations, 'lovingly and stiflingly enclose' Katharine, so that 'In her struggle with the past Katharine Hilbery wants to go outside, find bare rooms, escape from these "dear things"' (1996: 44).

Surrounded by the objects that are representative of both the current and future expectations that have been thrust upon her, that is, her continued work upon her grandfather's biography, Katharine is overcome by a sense of not-Being-at-home within this space.

In her discussion of *The Years,* Lee suggests that 'the whole story of the middle-class daughter's servitude to her father and her brothers is embodied in the objects on the writing-table which she has inherited from her mother' (1996: 45).[10] When Eleanor Pargiter assumes possession of these objects, including a 'spotted Walrus with a brush in its back' (*ND*: 25), she also assumes her mother's position within the home. The connection between the walrus brush and Eleanor's servitude to a social order that dictates that a woman's principal role is that of homemaker and caretaker is made explicit years later when an elderly, but emancipated, Eleanor awakens from a nap: 'she was suffused with a feeling of happiness. Was it because this had survived – this keen sensation (she was waking up) and the other thing, the solid object – she saw an ink-corroded walrus – had vanished?' (*TY*: 312). For this woman, the relinquishment of her mother's objects equates to her freedom from the ties, expectations and limitations of the Victorian family home; Eleanor is, in a sense, awakened by such a parting, as she finally experiences her own life on her own terms.

The notion that the accumulation of objects within the home can create bonds that inhibit the freedom of the individual is made apparent in Woolf's response after viewing her badly damaged London residence in Mecklenburgh Square during the London Blitz in October 1940:

> Exhilaration at losing possessions – save at times I want my books & chairs & carpets & beds – How I worked to buy them – one by one – And the pictures . . . But its odd – the relief at losing possessions. I shd like to start life, in peace, almost bare – free to go anywhere. (*D5*: 331–2)

In both the closing scene of *Jacob's Room,* and the interlude of *To the Lighthouse,* Woolf uses objects within vacated spaces as a means of reflecting upon her sense of the connections between home, the individual and memory. As Bonamy stands in Jacob's room after his friend has died in combat, the bills on the table, the empty chair, the ram's skull collected as a child, letters, and the old shoes, each provide a record of Jacob's life (*JR*: 246–7).

Drawing parallels between Woolf's treatment of Jacob's shoes and Heidegger's discussion of Van Gogh's 1888 painting, 'The Old Pair of Shoes', in his 1936 lecture, 'The Origin of the Work of Art', Carmen Concilio remarks that in both examples, these pairs of shoes 'say something more than their mere objectivity' (1999: 291).[11] In his discussion of Van Gogh's painting, Heidegger refers to the image of the peasant shoes as a means by which an everyday object reveals the nature of its owner's mode of Being-in-the-world:

> From the dark opening of the worn insides of the shoes the toilsome tread of the worker stares forth. In the stiffly rugged heaviness of the shoes there is the accumulated tenacity of her slow trudge through the far-spreading and ever-uniform furrows of the field swept by a raw wind. On the leather lie the dampness and richness of the soil. (2002b: 159)

Kelly S. Walsh also draws attention to the parallels between Jacob's empty shoes and Heidegger's discussion, suggesting that 'Jacob's empty shoes, as with Heidegger's interpretation of Van Gogh's painting of the shoes, seem to constitute some sort of event or truth' (2009: 19, n23). Indeed, these worn and well-used shoes provide glimpses of the otherwise unknown everyday mode of Being-in-the-world that was experienced by both Jacob and Van Gogh's peasant.

In *To the Lighthouse,* the novel's omniscient narrator wanders through the empty house after Mrs Ramsay's death, noting that

> What people had shed and left . . . those alone kept the human shape and in the emptiness indicated how once they were filled and animated; how once hands were busy with hooks and buttons; how once the looking-glass had held a face. (*TL*: 123)[12]

In this novel, such discarded objects also provide a tangible representation of the passing of time: while the house stands vacant, 'The saucepan had rusted and the mat decayed' (*TL*: 131). As the housekeeper, Mrs McNab, attempts to clean the deserted home, the objects that she encounters trigger memories of the past, so that, spotting Mrs Ramsay's 'old grey cloak', she 'could see her with one of the children by her' (*TL*: 129, 130). Storl suggests that in this novel, 'Mrs. McNab's being and doing succinctly reveal key tenets of Heidegger's account of *Sorge* [care]' (2008: 312); while Henke briefly draws attention to affinities between the work of Woolf and

Heidegger in terms of Woolf's representation of Mrs Ramsay's death in the novel and her designation of Mrs McNab as 'a "care-taking woman"' (1999: 269, 271). The notion of 'care' is foregrounded in *Being and Time*, where Heidegger states: 'that very potentiality-for-Being for the sake of which Dasein is, has Being-in-the-world as its kind of Being. Thus it implies ontologically a relation to entities within-the-world. Care is always concern and solicitude, even if only privatively' (*BT*: 238–9). Through her 'care' of the neglected objects in the Ramsay home, Mrs NcNab's actions reflect her inevitable mode of Being-with-Others, even in solitude.

The notion that objects provide a connection between the individual and the Other through the interpenetration of past and present is also demonstrated in *Orlando*, where the objects in the protagonist's ancestral home reflect not only days gone by, but also a sense of continuity, so that

> the most ordinary movement in the world, such as sitting down at a table and pulling the inkstand towards one, may agitate a thousand odd, disconnected fragments, now bright, now dim, hanging and bobbing and dipping and flaunting, like the underlinen of a family of fourteen on a line in a gale of wind. (*O*: 55)

For Woolf, an object of such significance that reappears throughout both her fiction and autobiographical writings is the tea table. In 'A Sketch of the Past', Woolf provides a revealing and detailed description of this centre of meaning:

> The tea table, the very hearth and centre of family life, the tea table round which sat innumerable parties . . . The tea table rather than the dinner table was the centre of Victorian family life – in our family at least. Savages I suppose have some tree, or fire place, round which they congregate; the round table marked that focal, that sacred spot in our house. It was the centre, the heart of the family. It was the centre to which the sons returned from their work in the evening; the hearth whose fire was tended by the mother, pouring out tea. ('Sketch': 125)

What is clearly indicated throughout Woolf's representation of the tea table is the strict, but nevertheless interdependent divide that exists between the public and the private worlds, and the lives of men and women. The tea table becomes a motif for the private sphere that a woman is destined by the social order to inhabit, since women are expected to maintain their place within the home in anticipation of men's return to the hearth. As Iris Marion Young asserts: 'For millennia the image of Penelope sitting by the hearth and weaving, saving and preserving the home while her man roams the earth in daring adventures, has defined one of Western culture's basic ideas of womanhood' (1997: 134).

Such a perspective is affirmed at the end of Woolf's memoir when she describes those men who occupy the places around her family's tea table:

> There they were, on the verge of the drawing room, these great men: while, round the tea table, George and Gerald and Jack talked of the Post Office, the publishing office, and the Law Courts. And I, sitting by the table, was quite unable to make any connection. There were so many different worlds: but they were distant from me. I could not make them cohere; nor feel myself in touch with them. ('Sketch': 159–60)

As Lee explains, such a sense of servitude and disconnectedness is ultimately translated into Woolf's fiction, so that

> *Night and Day* begins with the daughter of the house, 'in common with many other young ladies of her class', pouring tea for elderly visitors at just such a tea-table. In *The Years*, the daughters of the family feel as if they have spent their whole life sitting around this table, waiting for 'the old-fashioned brass kettle, chased with a design of roses that was almost obliterated', to boil on its brass bowl. (1996: 42)

For Woolf, the tea table reflects women's state of not-Being-at-home, not only in relation to the domestic space, but also in terms of those unknown and unknowable 'worlds' of paid employment, education and pleasure that lay beyond the confines of the family home.

In his 1923 course, *Ontology: The Hermeneutics of Facticity*, Heidegger also draws attention to the significance of such an everyday object when he refers to his own table as representative of his family's average everyday experience of Being-in-the-world:

> What is there in *the* room there at home is *the* table (not 'a' table among many other tables in other rooms and other houses) at which one sits *in order to* write, have a meal, sew, play . . . Here and there it shows lines – the boys like to busy themselves at the table. Those lines are not just interruptions in the paint, but rather: it was the boys and it still is. This side is not the east side, and this narrow side so many cm. shorter than the other, but rather the one at which my wife sits in the evening

when she wants to stay up and read, there at the table we had such and such a discussion that time, there that decision was made with a *friend* that time, there that *work* written that time, there that *holiday* celebrated that time. (1999: 69)

While the underlying meaning of Woolf and Heidegger's tables differ – for Woolf, it is a symbol of repression and homelessness; for Heidegger, it is a largely positive record of family life – for both, such an everyday object is indicative of the individual's primordial state of Being-with-Others. The table is the place where hierarchies, roles and relations between individuals are created, reinforced and maintained on a daily basis; such objects within the home become markers of the lived lives of those who dwell within this particular site.

Conclusion – the search for home

In his discussion of Heidegger's philosophy, Thiele surmises that: 'The ongoing search for a home in our earthly homelessness defines human life' (1995: 178). Throughout Woolf's writings there is an obvious tension between her desire for the domestic space to be a site in which she can feel at-home-in-the-world, and her repeated emphasis upon the understanding that home is typically 'culturally defined' (Relph 1976: 15), since the dynamics of power within this place provide a clear and tangible reflection of the values and constructs inscribed by the patriarchal social order.

A similar tension is also present in Heidegger's approach to the states of Being-at-home or not-at-home in the world: while Being-at-home, as an inauthentic state, reflects the individual's unthinking immersion in average everyday theyness, homelessness, in contrast, is defined by a sense of unease as the individual comes face to face with his or her inevitable thrownness, that is, the realisation that one's present and future options and prospects are ultimately founded upon a factical context that was not of his or her making or choosing.

In his study of Heidegger's approach to homelessness, Thiele states that the philosopher 'proposes that we make our abode in the world in a way that acknowledges rather than ignores or denies our sense of existential displacement' (1995: 178); as emphasised throughout this chapter, such a response to the inherent and unavoidable tension between Being-at-home and homelessness is evident throughout Woolf's writings in terms of her treatment and representation of the individual's relationship to Being-in-the-world.

The following chapter continues the study of Woolf's approach to Being-in-the-world by shifting the focus to her treatment of time and temporality. From such a perspective, the discussion of the notion of thrownness is furthered through an emphasis upon the ways in which the past comes to be projected into the present and future so that it provides, for good and for bad, the possibilities that are open to both the individual and the collective. It will be demonstrated that 'we may learn to dwell in the ontological homelessness that anxiety brings to light' (Thiele 1995: 178) through the authentic appropriation of such thrown possibilities that are not simply duplicated, but are instead transformed and re-enacted anew.

Notes

1. Despite this, Woolf often initiated real-estate purchases, leases and relocations; in 1919, when faced with the forced prospect of vacating her Ouse Valley home, Asheham, Woolf records her feeling that 'the need of looking for another house is a source of great pleasure' (*D1*: 248).
2. Woolf was not the only writer to reflect upon Bloomsbury as a site of emancipation for women; as Anna Snaith observes, there are a number of literary examples during the early part of the twentieth century – including writers such as Olive Birrell, Radclyffe Hall, Violet Hunt and C. F. Keary – that deal with 'the symbolic power which a flat in Bloomsbury held for a single working woman' (2000: 29).
3. The understanding that there are only two sexes is a contested issue; as Claire Ainsworth remarks: 'The idea of two sexes is simplistic. Biologists now think there is a wider spectrum than that' (2015).
4. David R. Cerbone argues that:

> Given the prominence, and indeed the priority, of practical engagement with the world within Heidegger's conception of what it is to be human, an understanding of ourselves as *embodied* agents would seem to be a central concern, and not something whose treatment could be casually deferred. (2000: 210)

Søren Overgaard echoes this concern when he states that:

> Here we have a thinker who sets out to underscore precisely that human beings are in-the-world, and that their way of dealing with their surroundings is mainly practical, rather than contemplative – and then he refuses to discuss the phenomenon of human corporeality. (2004: 116)

Tina Chanter argues that 'in *Being and Time*, there is a progressive move away from the concrete starting point of Dasein's world and toward a disembodied understanding of Dasein' (2001: 81). Lisa L. Coleman's discussion of Heidegger's 1951 essay 'Building Dwelling Thinking' includes the observation that 'Heidegger's enquiry into being never speaks of women at all' (2012: 86); Coleman juxtaposes Heidegger's representation with that of Woolf in *A Room of One's Own*, where the author 'performs an inquiry into being, but the being it inquires into is the being of women' (2012: 86).

5. In her essay entitled 'The Body Unbound: A Phenomenological Reading of the Political in *A Room of One's Own*', Laura Doyle provides an insightful analysis of Woolf's 1929 polemic from the perspective of Merleau-Ponty's phenomenological notion of the 'chiasm'. Doyle suggests that 'Woolf reveals how the pivot or hinge inherent to this chiasmatic embodiment both opens the self to the world and allows for the world's interpellation or invasive calling-out of the self' (2001: 129).

6. Youngjoo Son draws attention to the fact that

    'one of the working titles of the novel was 'Other People's Houses' . . . This title is telling, for it reveals that Woolf was concerned with space as much as with time, and it invites us to look at the novel's concern with other people's (not merely women's) lives and houses. (2006: 128)

7. Hussey discusses the affinities between Heidegger's 'Building Dwelling Thinking' and Woolf's *Between the Acts*, where, during the pageant

    'the only thing to continue the emotion was the song' but it has become inaudible. The song is specifically connected by Woolf to building, to shelter. Heidegger describes dwelling as '*the basic character of* Being': 'we do not dwell because we have built, but we build and have built because we dwell.' (2013: 94)

    Further to this, Hussey also draws attention to the significance of the ending of Woolf's novel: '"The house had lost its shelter" and two figures find themselves without surrounds in a "night before roads were made, or houses"' (2013: 95).

8. Like Woolf, who maintained homes in both the city and countryside, Heidegger shared his time between a residence in the city – this was Freiburg from 1928 until his death in 1976 – and his much preferred abode, 'die Hütte' (Sharr 2006: 87, 3).

9. Reflecting Woolf's everyday involvement with her lodge, after his wife's suicide, Leonard Woolf remarks: 'I know that V. will not come across the garden from the lodge, and yet I look in that direction for her' (1989: 165).

10. The autobiographical nature and significance of these particular objects is reflected in Woolf's 'A Sketch of the Past', where she recalls her own mother 'writing at her table in London and the silver candlesticks, and the high carved chair with the claws and the pink seat; and the three-cornered brass ink pot' ('Sketch': 95).

11. Claudia Olk also refers briefly to Woolf's literary representation of Jacob's shoes – which 'capture Jacob's life-journey in a poetic image' – in relation to Heidegger's discussion of Van Gogh's painting (2014: 133–4). In *Recasting Social Values in the Work of Virginia Woolf*, Judy S. Reese makes reference to Heidegger's discussion of 'truth' and 'unconcealment' in 'The Origin of the Work of Art' (1996: 118–19).
12. In her reading of *To the Lighthouse*, Liesl Olson observes that in the novel's interlude: 'Domestic objects become more powerful than they once were; they seem to endure longer than humans do . . . [T]he objects in "Time Passes" represent firm elements of habitual, ordinary life, which a world war cannot stamp out' (2009: 81).

Chapter 4

Historical Dasein

> But none speaks with a single voice. None with a voice free from the old vibrations. (*BA*: 94)

The previous two chapters have considered Woolf's sense of Being-in-the-world principally from the perspective of her treatment of place. In this chapter, the focus shifts to the notion of temporality, an area of study that is granted particular emphasis in Heidegger's *Being and Time*. Specifically, Woolf's approach to history and historical discourse from the perspective of Being-in-the-world is investigated.[1] Woolf's interest in the subject of history began at an early age under the instruction of her father, the historian, biographer and man of letters, Sir Leslie Stephen.[2] A willing student in terms of her adolescent submission to her father's direction, Woolf's appreciation of the far-reaching significance of history and its representation was to continue during her lifetime, where both the subject and critique of history became recurrent themes throughout the various forms of her writings. As late as six months before her death, Woolf records in her diary 'an idea for a Common History book' (*D5*: 318); this idea was to culminate in her unfinished final essays, 'Anon' and 'The Reader'. As this chapter demonstrates, while to some extent, Woolf possessed a desire to emulate her father's approach to his work, 'she was shaped too by wanting to do *nothing* that father did. Much of how she lived and wrote was formulated in reaction against him' (Lee 1996: 72).[3]

In this chapter, Woolf's representations of history are viewed from a variety of perspectives, beginning with a discussion of her approach to the notion of 'time', which both she and Heidegger understand as the essential connectedness and interpenetration of the past, present and future.[4] Such a perspective is in marked contrast to the traditional discourse of historicism, which is founded upon an understanding of time as a series of homogeneous and successive 'nows', as reflected in 'clock-time'. For both Woolf and Heidegger, the individual is viewed as an inherently temporal, and therefore historical being, as demonstrated by Heidegger's notion of 'thrownness', which refers to the inextricable connection between the past and the projected possibilities of the present and future, for both the individual and the collective. As further evidence of Woolf and Heidegger's understanding of the temporal nature of the individual's primordial state of Being-in-the-world, the relationship between the past and the present, and the individual's most inevitable and final future possibility, death, will also be discussed.

The Heideggerian notion of authentic 'repetition', understood as the retrieval of those possibilities that are grounded in the past and re-enacted anew in the present and future, will be discussed from the perspective of Woolf's writings. Included in this discussion will be the notion of inauthentic repetition, which can be understood as the unthinking pure replication of that which has been. It is proposed that throughout her writings, Woolf draws attention to the ways in which such an inauthentic appropriation of the past comes to be reflected in those social 'traditions' that individuals are expected to maintain in the present, and preserve for the future.

This chapter also explores Woolf's responses to traditional historical discourse; in particular, her understanding that such accounts have been used not only to reinforce the exclusion and marginalisation of certain social groups, particularly women, but also as a means of strengthening the constructs and ideologies that define and empower the prevailing social order. Also discussed is Woolf's understanding that personal biographical writings – as opposed to official biographical accounts – become a means of disrupting the typical focus of historical discourse upon the deeds of 'great men' and events such as war. Through an emphasis upon the everyday dealings of those individuals who have been typically marginalised by society, such accounts become a powerful means of disclosing those historical relationships between self and world that have gone largely unseen and unacknowledged.

The individual 'as time' and 'in time'

Ricardo Quinones suggests that 'the first (but not final) task of modernism was to disrupt the temporal linearity that formed the basis of many nineteenth-century preoccupations' (1985: 88).[5] Such an understanding of time as succession has its origin in Aristotle's notion of the present, or 'now', as an impenetrable division between the past and future. For Heidegger, the discourse of historicism is viewed as representative of the metaphysical adherence to temporal linearity, since this traditional mode of historical discourse 'represents a privileging of metaphysical concepts of time, narrative, order, succession, continuity, and totality' (Bambach 1995: 11). Spiropoulou explains that 'Traditional historicism dominated historical scholarship and professional historiography in the West from the nineteenth century'; nevertheless, historicism 'was by no means a uniform trend. It encompassed the work of different and even contradictory thinkers across time and it accommodated idealist as well as objectivist epistemological principles' (Spiropoulou 2010: 39).

Critics suggest that Heidegger's dismissal of historicism was influenced by Germany's post-First World War milieu; as Bambach explains, within such a context, 'The violent destruction of political and social life left little promise for the reinstatement of civic order and historical continuity', thereby shattering the 'historicist faith in the meaning and coherence of human history' (Bambach 1995: 188).[6] Along similar lines, Julia Briggs discusses Woolf's conflation of war and 'rupture' (2001: 13) in her successive post-First World War novels, *Jacob's Room* (1922), *Mrs Dalloway* (1925), and *To the Lighthouse* (1927). In each of these texts, war results in the disruption of the historicist understanding of progress, meaning and order (Bambach 1995: 7), leaving in its stead a sense of discontinuity, as well as the disavowal of those assumptions posited upon a belief in society's inevitable progression and advancement.

In *Being and Time*, Heidegger defines time as the constant and essential co-existence of the past, present and future – understood respectively as the temporal 'ecstases' of 'thrownness', 'fallenness', and 'projection'. Bambach explains that historicism's reliance upon narrative – or 'developmental time' – conceals this temporal unity (1995: 220). Rejecting metaphysical notions of linearity, Heidegger emphasises that authentic temporality 'does not signify that ecstases come in a "succession". The future is *not later* than having been, and having been is *not earlier* than the Present' (*BT*: 401). The etymological origin of the term 'ecstasy' can be found in the Greek word 'ekstasis', which is defined as 'standing out' (Macann 1993: 141). So far as Heidegger's notion of the temporal ecstases is concerned, such a definition is representative of a position located outside the privileged metaphysical 'present'. Without making any reference to

Heidegger's philosophy, Banfield observes that in Woolf's writing, 'the impressions that make up the moment and the random configuration they assume can only be seized with the clarity required from a position outside experienced time. It requires what Woolf calls "dissociating herself from the moment"' (2003: 491). Arguably, the notion of such a 'position outside experienced time' is not unlike Heidegger's disruption of the hegemony of the homogeneous present, through his understanding that *'Temporality is the primordial "outside-of-itself" in and for itself'* (BT: 377).

Woolf's disruption of linear understandings of time can be read in an oft-quoted passage from her 1925 essay, 'Modern Fiction', in which she asserts that: 'Life is not a series of gig lamps symmetrically arranged; life is a luminous halo, a semi-transparent envelope surrounding us from the beginning of consciousness to the end' (1962b: 189). Whereas metaphysical representations of time and history posit the notion of linear progression in the form of a uni-directional series of autonomous 'nows', in her essay, Woolf uses the image of a surrounding halo in order to demonstrate that the relationship between the individual and time is defined by the ceaseless interpenetration, without hierarchy, of the past, present and future.

In her 1929 essay, 'The Moment: Summer's Night', Woolf challenges the notion of the homogeneous 'now' as she poses the question:

> Yet what composed the present moment? If you are young, the future lies upon the present, like a piece of glass, making it tremble and quiver. If you are old, the past lies upon the present, like a thick glass, making it waver, distorting it. All the same, everybody believes that the present is something, seeks out the different elements in this situation in order to compose the truth of it, the whole of it. (1981c: 9)

Woolf begins this essay by underscoring her intention to subvert the typical understanding of the present as separate and autonomous. In contrast to metaphysical notions of time that attribute a fixed definition to the present, for Woolf the 'truth' of the 'now' is that it is ever-changing, insofar as it is an essential aspect of the temporal individual's lived experience of Being-in-the-world. As such an approach emphasises, through an openness to and awareness of his or her inherent temporality, the authentic individual comes to realise that each moment includes not only the here and now, but also that which has been, as well as what is yet to come.

While Heidegger understands temporality to be the very foundation of one's Being, so that Dasein 'is' temporal, he nevertheless acknowledges that in its average everyday mode of Being-in-the-world, Dasein finds itself 'in' time rather than 'as' time, insofar as each of us ordinarily orders life according to the measurements of linear time, such as those provided by 'a calendar and a clock' (*BT*: 429). As Heidegger observes, from the perspective of metaphysical approaches to time, 'The historical is ordinarily characterized with the help of the time of within-time-ness' (*BT*: 429); that is, linear time. While Heidegger readily acknowledges that such a standpoint is not in itself unjustified – 'factual Dasein needs and uses a calendar and a clock' – his intention is to disrupt the 'exclusiveness' (*BT*: 429) of such a perspective. It should be noted that Heidegger's treatment of temporality is not to be understood as simply a critique or deconstruction of the ordinary understanding of time; rather, his approach must be considered from a phenomenological perspective: it is grounded in the description and analysis of lived experience.

Heidegger emphasises the inauthentic nature of the typical mode of Being, where such a privileging of the present means that 'the ecstatical character of primordial temporality has been levelled off' (*BT*: 377). Ricoeur labels such an ordinary sense of time as 'monumental', and explains that this term does not simply refer to clock time, but to 'all that is in complicity with it' (1986: 106). In his discussion of Woolf's *Mrs Dalloway*, Ricoeur suggests that to such 'monumental time belong the figures of authority and power' (1986: 106), and cites the medical profession as a particularly onerous example. Throughout this novel, such a view is expressed through the explicit parallels that Woolf draws between the overbearing, patriarchal medical profession and linear clock time: 'Shredding and slicing, dividing and subdividing, the clocks of Harley Street nibbled at the June day, counselled submission, upheld authority, and pointed out in chorus the supreme advantages of a sense of proportion' (*MD*: 103).

In *Mrs Dalloway*, Woolf draws particular attention to metaphysical manifestations of time, in order to both reveal and call into question the implications of such approaches for the individual located in society.[7] As Hana Wirth-Nesher notes, 'The manuscript's working title, "The Hours," indicates Woolf's focus on social time as an organizing principle' (1996: 184). The omniscient nature of monumental time is repeatedly emphasised in the narrative by the sounds of striking clocks that are heard both within and outside the private space. Such representations reflect Woolf's understanding that although monumental time is a 'public' time – that is, a prescription of time that all individuals within society are expected to accept and conform to – it also invades and inculcates the personal life and space of the individual. This is demonstrated in the novel as Clarissa Dalloway observes the movements of her elderly neighbour through her window:

> Big Ben struck the half-hour.
> How extraordinary it was, strange, yes, touching to see the old lady (they had been neighbours ever so many years) move away from the window, as if she were attached to that sound, that string. Gigantic as it was, it had something to do with her. Down, down, into the midst of ordinary things the finger fell, making the moment solemn. She was forced, so Clarissa imagined, by that sound, to move, to go – but where? (*MD*: 128–9)

The response of this woman to the sound of Big Ben striking is clearly reminiscent of a marionette whose strings are attached to the hands of a puppeteer. Asserting the authoritative nature of Big Ben, 'with his majesty laying down the law' (*MD*: 129), Woolf's language choices, which include words such as 'gigantic', 'fell', and 'forced', reinforce the invasive character of monumental time, and its insidious influence over the individual's 'ordinary' everyday mode of Being-in-the-world.

In *The Waves*, the pragmatic demands of everyday life that depend upon such monumental time are explicitly contrasted with Heideggerian ecstatic temporality as Bernard describes his visit to Neville's home, where the two friends become engrossed in a discussion of literature:

> 'Yes, but suddenly one hears a clock tick. We who had been immersed in this world became aware of another. It is painful. It was Neville who changed our time. He, who had been thinking with the unlimited time of the mind, which stretches in a flash from Shakespeare to ourselves, poked the fire and began to live by that other clock which marks the approach of a particular person. The wide and dignified sweep of his mind contracted. He became on the alert. I could feel him listening to sounds in the street. I noted how he touched a cushion.' (*TW*: 210)

In this passage, Woolf's portrayal of Bernard and Neville's interactions highlights the role of literature as a facilitator that grants the individual an opportunity to exist, albeit temporarily, outside the prescriptions and expectations of average everydayness, and the dominating forces of linear time. Woolf emphasises the transition from heterogeneous and multi-directional personal time, to an intense immersion in the present and the concerns of the everyday, as evidenced through Bernard's acute awareness as Neville 'touched a cushion'. As a result of this change in Bernard and Neville's relationship to time, the connection with the Other – both in the form of figures from the past, such as Shakespeare, and their rapport with one another – is fractured. Bernard and Neville's sense of openness to authentic Being-in-the-world suffers a contraction as these individuals' temporal mode of Being is concealed by clock time.

In *Orlando*, Woolf engages in a prolonged discussion of time through a juxtaposition of everyday approaches and understandings, and the authentic temporality of the individual:

> Time, unfortunately, though it makes animals and vegetables bloom and fade with amazing punctuality, has no such simple effect upon the mind of man. The mind of man, moreover, works with equal strangeness upon the body of time. An hour, once it lodges in the queer element of the human spirit, may be stretched to fifty or a hundred times its clock length; on the other hand, an hour may be accurately represented on the time-piece of the mind by one second. This extraordinary discrepancy between time on the clock and time in the mind is less known than it should be and deserves fuller investigation. (O: 68)

Woolf draws attention to 'the two forces which alternately, and what is more confusing still, at the same moment, dominate our unfortunate numbskulls – brevity and diuturnity' (O: 69). Teresa Prudente proposes that 'the co-presence of temporal linearity and a-linearity' is a dominant preoccupation in Woolf's writings, observing that 'the existence of two different processes of knowledge, one linear and progressive, and the other a-linear, intuitive and instantaneous, proves to be a central topic, which mirrors and integrates reflection on the experience of time' (2009: xii, 5). Subverting the metaphysical emphasis upon clock time as the sole measure of the course of an individual's life, Woolf contrasts the passive and automatic response of nature and animals to the linear passage of time with that of the conscious and inherently temporal human being.

Now a man of thirty, Orlando divides his time between fulfilling his everyday duties, and removing himself from such preoccupations in order to consider his life. It is in this latter mode of Being-in-the-world that Orlando finds that the 'the seconds began to round and fill until it seemed as if they would never fall', so that

> his whole past, which seemed to him of extreme length and variety, rushed into the falling second, swelled it a dozen times its natural size, coloured it a thousand tints, and filled it with all the odds and ends in the universe . . . Every single thing, once he tried to dislodge it from its place in his mind, he found thus cumbered with other matter like the lump of glass which, after a year at the bottom of the sea, is grown about with bones and dragon-flies, and coins and the tresses of drowned women. (*O*: 68, 69)

Connected to the world as a historical being, Orlando ceases to experience the present as autonomous and fleeting; rather it is heterogeneous and diuturnal. All that Orlando experiences in the present possesses infinite connections with that which has been. Such a representation of the relationship between time and the individual in this novel might be contrasted with Leslie Stephen's approach to historical and biographical discourse, which is highlighted as the novel draws to its close; as Woolf observes: 'The true length of a person's life, whatever the *Dictionary of National Biography* may say, is always a matter of dispute. For it is a difficult business – this time-keeping' (*O*: 211).[8] As Cuddy-Keane remarks, what Woolf 'argued *against* was the linear narrative – whether it is in fiction or whether it's in history, or whether it's in biography – that reduces all life to one single line, one single meaning' (2010a).

Just over a decade later, in 'A Sketch of the Past', Woolf reflects once again upon the varied and fluctuating ways in which individuals experience time. Demonstrating her understanding that the state of Being 'in' time, rather than 'as' time, influences the individual's awareness of his or her inherent historicity, Woolf writes:

> The past only comes back when the present runs so smoothly that it is like the sliding surface of a deep river. Then one sees through the surface to the depths. In those moments I find one of my greatest satisfactions, not that I am thinking of the past; but that it is then that I am living most fully in the present. For the present when backed by the past is a thousand times deeper than the present when it presses so close that you can feel nothing else . . . I write this partly in order to recover my sense of the present by getting the past to shadow this broken surface. Let me then,

like a child advancing with bare feet into a cold river, descend again into that stream. ('Sketch': 108)

Woolf's notion of a present that 'presses so close that you can feel nothing else', can be read as representative of the individual's absorption in the preoccupations of the everyday, which come to conceal the inherent ties that bind the present to the past and future. Woolf's musings demonstrate her understanding that the present comes to its fullest realisation when such connections are acknowledged. Here, and throughout Woolf's memoir, the metaphysical notion of the present as a homogeneous and autonomous site is called into question as it is weighed against an understanding of time as heterogeneous and fluid.

Within this memoir, one of the more overt and significant expressions of Woolf's interest in the notion of time is to be found in her descriptions of 'being' and 'non-being'; as Woolf explains:

> Every day includes much more non-being than being . . . This is always so. A great part of every day is not lived consciously. One walks, eats, sees things, deals with what has to be done; the broken vacuum cleaner; ordering dinner; writing orders to Mabel; washing; cooking dinner; bookbinding. ('Sketch': 83–4)

For Woolf, the state of non-being, which is likened to 'a kind of nondescript cotton wool' ('Sketch': 84), is representative of the individual's immersion in the present. In contrast, Woolf's sense of 'being' is concerned with the disruption of the status quo, through an uncovering of that which lies concealed by the preoccupations, expectations and prescriptions of the here-and-now.

Woolf's notions of 'being' and 'non-being' exhibit certain marked affinities with Heidegger's understanding of authentic and inauthentic modes of Being-in-the-world: each is premised upon the individual's relationship to and with time, most particularly, the present. In his discussion of the 'everyday', Michael Sheringham briefly draws parallels between the works of Woolf and Heidegger, suggesting that 'In the guise of Heidegger's *Alltäglichkeit* [average everydayness], or of what Virginia Woolf would call the '"cotton-wool" of "non-being", the everyday is, at best, a catalyst for what must transcend it' (Sheringham 2009: 27). Just as Woolf states that 'being' is defined in contrast to 'non-being' by the individual's ability to surmount his or her absorption in the concerns of the present, for Heidegger, the authentic individual acknowledges his or her condition as a temporal being through an openness to the appropriation of the past, present and future. This might be contrasted with an inauthentic mode of Being, where Dasein's involvement with the world is focused upon the concerns of the present, so that its inherent interconnectedness to the past or future comes to be concealed.

Through her representation of Eleanor Pargiter at the close of *The Years,* Woolf reflects upon the difficulty experienced by the individual who seeks to attain and maintain a grasp and awareness of his or her authentic temporality. Now an elderly woman, Eleanor is overcome by a desire to gain possession of what she terms 'life':

> She felt as if she were standing on the edge of a precipice with her hair blown back; she was about to grasp something that just evaded her . . . She held her hands hollowed; she felt that she wanted to enclose the present moment; to make it stay; to fill it fuller and fuller, with the past, the present and the future, until it shone, whole, bright, deep with understanding. (*TY*: 313)

This character's moment of 'understanding' consists of the uncovering of the temporal dimension of Being that has previously been concealed. Such 'understanding' shares certain parallels with Heidegger's perspective in *Being and Time,* where he asserts that

> whenever Dasein tacitly understands and interprets something like Being, it does so with *time* as its standpoint. Time must be brought to light – and genuinely conceived – as the horizon for all understanding of Being and for any way of interpreting it . . . This task as a whole requires that the conception of time thus obtained shall be distinguished from the way in which it is ordinarily understood. (*BT*: 39)

Despite Eleanor's recognition of her own temporal mode of Being-in-the-world, emerging from her reverie, Eleanor finds that maintaining such an authentic position is ultimately beyond her power to sustain: 'It's useless, she thought, opening her hands. It must drop. It must fall' (*TY*: 313). Just as Woolf asserts that 'a great part of every day is not lived consciously', and Heidegger suggests that Dasein's everyday mode of Being tends towards inauthenticity as the individual becomes immersed in the concerns and preoccupations of the present, so too does Eleanor inevitably revert to an inauthentic average everyday mode of Being-in-the-world.

The radical contingency of Being-in-the-world

In contrast to the everyday propensity of the individual to immerse him- or herself in the concerns of the present at the expense of a conscious awareness of his or her inherently temporal state of Being-in-the-world, Rachel Bowlby states that throughout Woolf's work, this writer 'tends to see the understanding of a person's identity in the present, both as an individual and as part of a group, as tied to their sense of a relation (or lack of relation) to the past' (1997: 162). Such a suggestion is demonstrated in *Between the Acts* as Isa Oliver enters the family stable yard during a pageant intermission. Surveying her surroundings, Isa makes explicit her historical mode of Being-in-the-world through her musings:

> The tree, whose roots went beneath the flags, was weighed with hard green pears. Fingering one of them she murmured: 'How am I burdened with what they drew from the earth; memories; possessions. This is the burden that the past laid on me, last little donkey in the long caravanserai crossing the desert. "Kneel down,", said the past. "Fill your pannier from our tree. Rise up, donkey. Go your way till your heels blister and your hoofs crack."'
> The pear was hard as stone. She looked down at the cracked flags beneath which the roots spread. 'That was the burden,' she mused, 'laid on me in the cradle; murmured by waves; breathed by restless elm trees; crooned by singing women; what we must remember; what we would forget.'
> She looked up. The gilt hands of the stable clock pointed inflexibly at two minutes to the hour. The clock was about to strike.
> 'Now comes the lightning,' she muttered, 'from the stone blue sky. The thongs are burst that the dead tied. Loosed are our possessions.'
> (*BA*: 93)

Isa's reference to the roots of the pear tree clearly represents not only the past, but also the far-reaching effects of both her personal and the collective history upon present and future circumstances. Foregrounding this character's primordial historicity, Isa's use of the term 'burden' conveys a notion of one's past and its thrown possibilities as that which the individual must unceasingly carry forth. The cracked flagstones are not only representative of the effect of the past upon the possibilities of the present; they also act as a trope for the propensity of the individual and society at large to attempt to conceal such historical connections, which nevertheless, unexpectedly surface and show forth at particular moments. Woolf's depiction of the pear as hard and inedible is symbolic of the nature of the fruits of the past that have been inherited in June 1939, as Britain stands poised for war. Highlighting the everyday propensity of the individual to deny or forget the connections between the past and present, Isa laments that although the world 'must remember' the lessons of history, particularly as war looms ever closer, inevitably it 'would forget'. Such a stance is reinforced as Isa is jolted out of her reverie and authentic mode of understanding, and back into the present, by the antithesis of authentic temporality, clock time.

In keeping with Woolf's representation of Isa's connection to the past, inherent in Heidegger's assertion that temporality underpins the very foundation of Dasein's state of Being-in-the-world is the understanding that temporality defines each individual's particular 'historicity'.[9] As Heidegger remarks in *Being and Time*:

> In analysing the historicality [historicity] of Dasein we shall try to show that this entity is not 'temporal' because it 'stands in history', but that, on the contrary, it exists historically and can so exist only because it is temporal in the very basis of its Being. (*BT*: 428)

Further to this, Heidegger explains that 'the proposition, "Dasein is historical", is confirmed as a fundamental existential-ontological assertion. This assertion is far removed from the mere ontical establishment of the fact that Dasein occurs in a "world-history"' (*BT*: 381). Heidegger states that the 'existential-ontological constitution of historicality [historicity] has been covered up by the way Dasein's history is ordinarily interpreted; we must get hold of it *in spite of* all this' (*BT*: 428).

As a means of elucidating Dasein's historicity, Heidegger draws upon the notion of 'thrownness'; as explained in Chapter 3 of this volume, the term denotes the radical contingency of each individual's existence; through no choice of our own, each of us is born into a world that will continue to determine and impact upon our present and future possibilities. In her 1917 short story, 'The Mark on the Wall', Woolf's emphasis upon the contingent nature of existence shares clear affinities with Heidegger's notion of thrownness:

> Why, if one wants to compare life to anything, one must liken it to being blown through the Tube at fifty miles an hour – landing at the other end without a single hairpin in one's hair! Shot out at the feet of God entirely naked! Tumbling head over heels in the asphodel meadows like

brown paper parcels pitched down a shoot in the post office! With one's hair flying back like the tail of a racehorse. Yes, that seems to express the rapidity of life, the perpetual waste and repair; all so casual, all so haphazard. (2003a: 60–1)

Heidegger explains that Dasein 'projects itself upon possibilities into which it has been thrown' (*BT*: 330), where being 'thrown' is representative of the individual '"going back" to the possibilities that have been' (Korab-Karpowicz 2011). The notion of 'projection' refers to the essential connection between the individual's past, present and future, since the basis of one's present and future possibilities are understood to be founded upon one's personal and collective past. From such a perspective, the individual's past can never be disengaged or denied: it is an integral element of one's state of Being-in-the-world that must be borne from conception to death; as Heidegger remarks: 'Its own past – and this always means the past of its "generation" – is not something which *follows along after* Dasein, but something which already goes ahead of it' (*BT*: 41).

Heidegger suggests that it is only through the individual's recognition of his or her temporal mode of Being-in-the-world that he or she can 'be historical in the very depths of its existence' (*BT*: 437). As such, authenticity is achieved through the individual's acceptance of his or her thrownness, and the 'inevitable' character of much of what is inherited – both 'the "fortunate" circumstances' and 'the cruelty of accidents' (*BT*: 436) – even as he or she attempts to transform these inherited contingent circumstances, characteristics and possibilities. Such an authentic mode of Being might be juxtaposed with Bernard's recollection of his response to Percival's death years earlier in *The Waves*. Having sought the company of Jinny in order to share his acute sense of loss, Bernard recalls that upon taking leave of his friend, he surveyed the surrounding streetscape and observed

> with disillusioned clarity the despicable non-entity of the street; its porches; its window curtains; the drab clothes, the cupidity and complacency of shopping women; and old men taking the air in comforters; the caution of people crossing; the universal determination to go on living, when really, fools and gulls that you are, I said, any slate may fly from a roof, any car may swerve, for there is neither rhyme nor reason when a drunk man staggers about with a club in his hand – that is all. (*TW*: 204)

As this passage reflects, Bernard is overwhelmed by an oppressive and hopeless sense that there is no organising or guiding principle in terms of how one's life might unfold. Although Percival's death has granted Bernard a greater awareness of the finite nature of his own existence, he nevertheless fails to acknowledge or comprehend the fateful connection between Britain's collective imperial history – which created the possibility that was chosen by Percival when he sought his commission in India – and his friend's death in India as a result of a fall from a horse. Any hope of attaining such awareness is dashed as Bernard, like Isa, is drawn back into the concerns of the present:

> I was like one admitted behind the scenes: like one shown how the effects are produced. I returned, however, to my own snug home and was warned by the parlourmaid to creep upstairs in my stockings. The child was asleep. (*TW*: 204)

Being-towards-death

Through Woolf's descriptions of the early deaths of her mother, half-sister Stella, and brother Thoby in 'A Sketch of the Past', the notions of thrownness and fate are clearly foregrounded from a deeply personal perspective. Woolf's memoir can be understood as an attempt to make sense of each of these losses, over which she had neither control nor warning. As Woolf writes decades after the occurrence of these deaths:

> Did those deaths give us an experience that even if it was numbing, mutilating, yet meant that the Gods (as I used to phrase it) were taking us seriously, and giving us a job which they would not have thought it worthwhile to give – say, the Booths or the Milmans? I had my usual visual way of putting it. I would see (after Thoby's death) two great grindstones . . . and myself between them. I would stage a conflict between myself and 'them'. I would reason that if life were thus made to rear and kick, it was a thing to be ridden; nobody could say 'they' had fobbed me off with a weak little feeble slip of the precious matter. ('Sketch': 141)

Woolf's guarded acceptance of the 'two great grindstones', which, from the perspective of Heideggerian philosophy, might be understood as thrownness and death, represents her understanding that while the individual possesses a freedom in terms of how he or she chooses to live his or her life, it is nevertheless a constrained freedom, insofar as those choices must be made in light of the conditions and possibilities that have been determined for each of us.

Woolf depicts the loss of both her mother and Stella as 'those two great unnecessary blunders; those two lashes of the random unheeding, unthinking flail that brutally and pointlessly killed the two people who should have made those years normal and natural, if not "happy"' ('Sketch': 140).[10] Referring to her brother's passing, Woolf laments the fact that she and her family

> had no kind of foreboding that he was to die when he was twenty-six and I was twenty-four. That is one of the falsifications – that knell I always find myself hearing and transmitting – that one cannot guard against, save by noting it. ('Sketch': 143)

For Heidegger, an authentic approach to Being-in-the-world requires that the individual accepts and anticipates its final and most inevitable possibility:

> The more authentically Dasein resolves – and this means that in anticipating death it understands itself unambiguously in terms of its ownmost distinctive possibility – the more unequivocally does it choose and find the possibility of its existence, and the less does it do so by accident. Only by the anticipation of death is every accidental and 'provisional' possibility driven out. Only Being-free *for* death, gives Dasein its goal outright and pushes existence into its finitude. Once one has grasped the finitude of one's existence, it snatches one back from the endless multiplicity of possibilities which offer themselves as closest to one – those of comfortableness, shirking, and taking things lightly – and brings Dasein into the simplicity of its *fate* [*Schicksals*]. This is how we designate Dasein's primordial historizing, which lies in authentic resoluteness and in which Dasein *hands* itself *down* to itself, free for death, in a possibility which it has inherited and yet has chosen. (*BT*: 435)

Ultimately, the individual's acknowledgement and acceptance of his or her unavoidable fate means that the decisions and choices that are made are considered with greater care and awareness. As the individual ceases to unthinkingly turn to those possibilities that are most convenient, or most in keeping with societal expectations or trends, he or she is more likely to consider and retrieve those possibilities that have been authentically handed down through his or her heritage as a temporal being.

Such an understanding of the connection between the acknowledgement of one's finitude, and one's ability to authentically grasp and realise his or her inherited possibilities, is reflected in *Night and Day*. As Katharine Hilbery and her mother continue their work upon the biography of Katharine's grandfather, Mrs Hilbery contemplates her own death, 'The depression communicated itself to Katharine. How impotent they were, fiddling about all day long with papers! And the clock was striking eleven and nothing done!' The intrusive quality of the clock clearly emphasises the passing of time and those moments that cannot be reclaimed. As Katharine becomes increasingly aware of her own finitude, 'She felt all the unfairness of the claim which her mother tacitly made to her time and sympathy, and what Mrs. Hilbery took, Katharine thought bitterly, she wasted' (*ND*: 105). As discussed, Katharine's involvement with her grandfather's biography is founded upon her mother's desires and expectations, rather than any great aptitude or interest on Katharine's part; through such an involvement in that which is simply 'closest' (*BT*: 435), Katharine covers over and relinquishes those inherited possibilities and potentialities that have yet to be authentically 'chosen' (*BT*: 435). From Heidegger's perspective, to enact an authentic future, the individual must be receptive rather than passive in terms of appropriating the past; without such authentic appropriation, certain possibilities come to be closed off.

The sense that the individual's understanding and acceptance of his or her inevitable fate as Being-towards-death significantly impacts upon the decisions and choices that he or she makes, is expressed from a personal perspective in Woolf's 1907–8 memoir, 'Reminiscences'. Reflecting upon the characteristics of her deceased mother, Julia Stephen, Woolf observes that

> she seemed to watch, like some wise Fate, the birth, growth, flower and death of innumerable lives all round her, with a constant sense of the mystery that encircled them . . . She kept herself marvellously alive to all the changes that went on around her, as though she heard perpetually the ticking of a vast clock and could never forget that some day it would cease for all of us . . . 'Let us make the most of what we have, since we know nothing of the future' was the motive that urged her to toil so incessantly on behalf of happiness, right doing, love. (2002c: 7–8)

Julia Stephen's decision not to live a life of 'comfortableness, shirking, and taking things lightly' (*BT*: 435), reflects Heidegger's description of an authentic appropriation of one's fate, where the individual lives with the knowledge and acceptance that each day may be his or her last, and that the choices that each of us makes deserves thoughtful contemplation, rather than blind adherence to the status quo.

The notion of one's finitude – 'the possible impossibility of its existence' (*BT*: 310) – is a reality that individuals typically flee from, choosing instead to divert and conceal such an inevitability through an immersion in the concerns of the present. Such a propensity is made evident in *Mrs Dalloway*, as an ageing Peter Walsh refuses to acknowledge the unavoidable nature of his own demise. As Peter makes his way through the streets of London, the striking of St Margaret's clock signals the unrelenting passage of time, prompting Peter to imagine Clarissa's death, as he recalls her weakened state of health following a bout of influenza:

> It was her heart, he remembered; and the sudden loudness of the final stroke tolled for death that surprised in the midst of life, Clarissa falling where she stood, in her drawing-room. No! No! he cried. She is not dead! I am not old, he cried, and marched up Whitehall, as if there rolled down to him, vigorous, unending, his future. (*MD*: 49)

As this passage illustrates, Peter's concern is not focused solely upon Clarissa's mortality; the striking of the clock also signals his own fate; one that he brushes aside, choosing instead to believe that his prospects are 'unending'.

Former possibilities re-enacted anew

As Peter continues his march up Whitehall, he is overcome by a sense of 'escaping (only of course for an hour or so) from being precisely what he was'. In such a state, Peter experiences an

> irrepressible, exquisite delight; as if inside his brain, by another hand, strings were pulled, shutters moved, and he, having nothing to do with it, yet stood at the opening of endless avenues down which if he chose he might wander. (*MD*: 51)

As Peter renounces his personal identity, he also relinquishes any responsibility for his future possibilities, so that the 'endless avenues' of choice bear no relation to Peter's personal past and inherited present and future prospects. Not unlike his disavowal of his own mortality,

Peter's sense that he 'was utterly free' (*MD*: 51) of his former ties and responsibilities reflects a misguided and ultimately inauthentic mode of Being-in-the-world.

In his discussion of the authentic appropriation of one's state of thrownness, Heidegger suggests that 'If *Being*-as-having-been is authentic, we call it *"repetition"*' (*BT*: 388). Heidegger's understanding of repetition refers to a retrieval of elements of the past that are then projected as a repository of meaning to be re-enacted anew. As Macquarrie and Robinson explain in their translation of *Being and Time*, such repetition 'does not mean either a mere mechanical repetition or an attempt to reconstitute the physical past; it means rather an attempt to go back to the past and retrieve former *possibilities*, which are thus "explicitly handed down" or "transmitted"' (*BT*: 437, n1). In Woolf's *The Waves*, the motif of the 'wave' shares similarities with Heidegger's notion of repetition: each wave represents an eternal recurrence that embraces individual variation, giving fresh life to that which has been. Focalised from the perspective of an elderly Bernard, such an understanding is underscored on the final page of the novel:

> 'Dawn is some sort of whitening of the sky; some sort of renewal. Another day; another Friday; another twentieth of March, January, or September. Another general awakening. The stars draw back and are extinguished. The bars deepen themselves between the waves. The film of mist thickens on the fields. A redness gathers on the roses, even on the pale rose that hangs by the bedroom window. A bird chirps. Cottagers light their early candles. Yes, this is the eternal renewal, the incessant rise and fall and fall and rise again.
>
> 'And in me too the wave rises. It swells; it arches its back. I am aware once more of a new desire, something rising beneath me like the proud horse whose rider first spurs and then pulls him back.' (*TW*: 228)

Through his emphasis upon the individual as the site of repetition, Bernard's ruminations demonstrate the temporal character of Being-in-the-world. Also highlighted throughout Bernard's musings is the sense that repetition does not necessarily result in the pure duplication of that which has been; rather, it provides the impetus for the appropriation of 'new desires' that are founded upon projected possibilities from the past.

The inherent connection between repetition and future possibilities is also stressed in Woolf's final novel, *Between the Acts*. As Detloff suggests, set on the cusp of the Second World War, when England's involvement is still to be finally and officially determined, this novel invests 'the historical moment of June 1939 with many possibilities' (2009: 35). Drawing upon Michael André Bernstein's notion of 'sideshadowing' – which might be understood as '"a gesturing to the side, to a present dense with multiple, and mutually exclusive, possibilities for what is to come"' (Detloff 2009: 35) – Detloff explains that Woolf's choice of temporal setting reinforces the sense that the individual and the collective must take responsibility for the choices that are made in the present (2009: 35). Describing what can be understood as an inauthentic approach to the past and its projected possibilities within the context of June 1939, Detloff asserts that 'When we foreclose attempts to imagine different alternatives to war . . . we foreclose our ability to "think peace into existence"' (2009: 40).

Such a perspective possesses particular significance for the generation living in England during the period between the two World Wars. In her discussion of *Between the Acts,* Gillian Beer describes the character Giles Oliver as 'outraged by his knowledge that war approaches and that he is powerless to prevent it, refusing to understand his own historical complicity in aggression' (2000: xxvi). Not unlike Bernard's inability to perceive the connection between Percival's death in India and Britain's imperial history, Giles fails to acknowledge the role that his own nation's history has had upon the present-day political climate. The novel prompts such a reading through the inclusion of the historical pageant, which 'encourages its dual audiences (the 1939 audience of the novel's historical pageant and the present-day audience of the novel) to react to national history in ways that promote political accountability rather than patriotic identification' (Detloff 2009: 34).

In contrast to the individual's personal relationship to the past, understood as 'fate', Heidegger uses the term 'destiny' to refer to the ties that connect the collective to the past, asserting that 'if fateful Dasein, as Being-in-the-world, exists essentially in Being-with Others, its historizing is a co-historizing and is determinative for it as *destiny* [*Geschick*]. This is how we designate the historizing of the community, of a people' (*BT*: 436). At this point it is important to emphasise a significant dissimilarity between the approaches of Woolf and Heidegger: as highlighted in the second chapter, Woolf's stance throughout her writings clearly reflects an anti-imperialist, pacifist stance, whereas Heidegger's approach to historical repetition can be read from an imperialist perspective, particularly when one considers his future support for the Nazi revolution of the Third Reich as a means of realising Germany's 'destiny'.

As thrown, the individual encounters war as a manifestation of a collective past that determines present and future possibilities. Such an understanding of the inevitable and inextricable connection that exists between different individuals within a given societal and historical context as a result of collective destiny is clearly evident in Woolf's final novel, where war provides a tangible expression of the sense that the possibilities and agency of the individual are always tethered to some degree to the 'social, cultural and personal history that make up an individual's present situation' (Mulhall 2003: 169–70). As the character William Dodge laments, with '"The doom of sudden death hanging over us," . . . "There's no retreating and advancing" . . . "for us as for them"' (*BA*: 70): friends and enemies alike are united by this common destiny.

In this novel, Woolf uses rain as an analogy for the ubiquity of collective destiny within a pre-wartime setting:

> No one had seen the cloud coming. There it was, black, swollen, on top of them. Down it poured like all the people in the world weeping. Tears, Tears. Tears.
> 'O that our human pain could here have ending!' Isa murmured. Looking up she received two great blots of rain full in her face. They trickled down her cheeks as if they were her own tears. But they were all people's tears, weeping for all people. Hands were raised . . . The rain was sudden and universal. (*BA*: 107)

As this passage emphasises, war is indeed 'universal' in terms of its impact upon all individuals. Just as Miss La Trobe and Lucy Swithin are unable to forecast with any certainty whether it will or will not rain on the day of the pageant, so too must the world await the outcome of its shared destiny.

The inherent connection between war and collective destiny is highlighted by Woolf in *Mrs Dalloway*; set five years after the end of the First World War, tears again provide a symbol for the ties between members of English society and their projected possibilities. As the novel opens, Clarissa walks through the streets of London, aware that 'This late age of world's experience had bred in them all, all men and women, a well of tears. Tears and sorrows; courage and endurance; a perfectly upright and stoical bearing' (*MD*: 7). Reflecting the preoccupations of its 1923 setting, Woolf alludes not only to the devastating effects of the First World War, but also to the ensuing sense of uncertainty for the future that is experienced by the individual and the collective alike, 'as if some august fate, known to them, awaited without fear, were about to sweep them into complete annihilation' (*MD*: 57). Such a sense of Being-in-the-world indicates the temporal unity of past, present, and future, where thrown possibilities are projected into the future.

The understanding that the individual's possibilities are bound to his or her historical and societal context is also demonstrated in Woolf's *Orlando*. While the protagonist's sense of self remains 'fundamentally the same' (*O*: 163) throughout her lifetime, this character's possibilities are very much governed by the different historical periods in which she lives. As the mock-biographer describes Orlando after she changes from a man into a woman, she asserts that 'The change of sex, though it altered their future, did nothing whatever to alter their identity' (*O*: 98). Woolf makes explicit the understanding that while Orlando's change from a man into a woman does not alter her core identity, it is society's perceptions and treatments of gender within the context of different historical epochs that impacts upon the possibilities and potentialities available to each individual. As Elizabeth Grosz asserts, any attempt to define women in isolation from their historical situation risks essentialism, where such a term 'refers to the existence of fixed characteristics, given attributes, and ahistorical functions that limit the possibilities of change and thus of social reorganization' (1995: 48).

Inauthentic repetition as pure duplication

Throughout her *oeuvre*, Woolf calls into question the propensity of the social order to encourage the repetition of that which has gone before as a means of maintaining and strengthening certain political and ideological perspectives, including the discourse of patriarchy. In *Three Guineas*, for instance, Woolf discusses women's ongoing battles as they pursue access into male-dominated professions and education. Drawing parallels between the present-day 1938 impasse, and women's earlier struggles to gain admittance to the Royal College of Surgeons, Woolf writes:

> The whole proceeding is so familiar that the battle of Harley Street in the year 1869 might well be the battle of Cambridge University at the present moment. On both occasions there is the same waste of strength,

waste of temper, waste of time, and waste of money. Almost the same daughters ask almost the same brothers for almost the same privileges. Almost the same gentlemen intone the same refusals for almost the same reasons. It seems as if there were no progress in the human race, but only repetition. We can almost hear them if we listen singing the same old song, 'Here we go round the mulberry tree, the mulberry tree, the mulberry tree'. (*TG*: 248–9)

Such a sense of replication without variation might be contrasted with Heidegger's understanding of authentic repetition:

The simple reduplication which reproduces something already actualized is precisely a movement away from the origin, precisely the *de-generation* which is the source of the inauthentic, the second-hand, the fallen. Repetition is always an originary operation by means of which Dasein opens up possibilities latent in the tradition, bringing forth something new. (Caputo 1987: 90)

In Woolf's passage, her critique of the propensity of the patriarchal social order to rely upon pure repetition as means of control and exclusion is performatively emphasised through her own repetition of the word 'same' seven times. In contrast to authentic repetition, which involves 'bringing forth something new', such 'de-generation' becomes a means of negating those new possibilities and outcomes that would call into question the status quo, such as the inclusion of women in the male-dominated areas of education and the professions.

The critique of such inauthentic de-generation is foregrounded in Woolf's polemic as she draws attention to the notion of repetition in her discussion of the connections between war and patriarchal ideology. Referring to calls on the wireless by the daily press for women to return to their traditional place in the home, so that the public world of employment might become once more the exclusive dominion of men, Woolf suggests that

As we listen to the voices we seem to hear an infant crying in the night, the black night that now covers Europe . . . But it is not a new cry, it is a very old cry. Let us shut off the wireless and listen to the past. We are in Greece now; Christ has not been born yet, nor St Paul either. But listen. (*TG*: 362)

Woolf asks her readers to be attentive to the parallels between the views broadcast on the wireless in the present time, and the voice of history in the form of 'Creon, the dictator' in Sophocles's *Antigone*. Describing Creon's dictate that 'We must support the cause of order, and in no wise suffer a woman to worst us', Woolf likens the leader's treatment of Antigone – who is shut in a tomb, not 'a concentration camp, but in a tomb' – to society's current demand that women remain within the confines of the domestic space. Emphasising the connection between patriarchal discourse and war, Woolf explains that, not unlike the leaders of her present-day world, Creon's actions 'scattered the land with the bodies of the dead' (*TG*: 363). Woolf finishes her reference to this classic play with the ironic and sobering proclamation:

> It seems, Sir, as we listen to the voices of the past, as if we were looking at the photographs again, at the picture of dead bodies and ruined houses that the Spanish Government sends us almost weekly. Things repeat themselves it seems. Pictures and voices are the same today as they were 2,000 years ago. (*TG*: 363)[11]

As Woolf draws her polemic to a close, she concludes by responding to the educated man who initially sought her opinion regarding how women might participate in the prevention of war:

> since we are different, our help must be different ... as a result the answer to your question must be that we can best help you to prevent war not by repeating your words and following your methods but by finding new words and creating new methods. (*TG*: 366)

Woolf warns that the individual and the collective must listen to the voice of the past, and in so doing, choose wisely from the possibilities that history provides for the present and future: the alternative is to face the devastating consequences that can ensue when society unthinkingly repeats, without variation, the acts of history.

Detloff observes that Woolf's interrogation of nationalism and war throughout her *oeuvre* can be viewed as a means of advocating 'a wholesale change in the way we think about ingrained traditions, beliefs, and norms' (2009: 32). Woolf's textual approach to the far-reaching effects of patriarchal discourse upon women in society is also founded upon the questioning and dismissal of the notion of tradition. This is particularly evident in *Three Guineas*, where Woolf describes the widely divergent experiences of men and women located within English society, arguing that such differences are based upon their vastly different educational opportunities, access to the paid workforce, and rights in terms of property ownership. Woolf asserts that such a polarity of experience comes to be 'influenced by memory and tradition' to such a degree that, 'Though we see the same world, we see it through different eyes' (*TG*: 175).

In much the same way that repetition in the form of pure duplication is considered by Heidegger to be inauthentic, throughout her writings, Woolf repeatedly calls into question the propensity of tradition to construct a rigid and prescriptive framework that constrains both the individual and the collective in terms of their ability to appropriate as their own, those thrown possibilities that each inherits.[12] As demonstrated in both *Three Guineas* and *A Room of One's Own*, for Woolf, it is tradition that provides the social order with an excuse to exclude women from various social spheres and roles; and it is tradition that relegates women – who are deemed to be neither Fellows nor Scholars – to walk on the gravel path rather than the grass, 'which has been rolled for 300 years in succession' (*RO*: 7) at Oxbridge.

From Woolf's perspective, the defining characteristic of tradition as unchanging and unyielding means that individuality comes to be inhibited and repressed, while societal conformity and obedience are strengthened. This is in contrast to an individual's authentic appropriation of his or her heritage, where the past – which includes former meanings and cultural possibilities – is projected forward in order to be transformed and re-enacted anew. Such a perspective is reflected in a *Room of One's Own*, as Woolf discusses the difficulties faced by those aspiring early nineteenth-century female novelists who 'had no tradition behind them, or one so short and partial that it was of little help. For we think back through our mothers if we are women'. Through her assertion that 'such a lack of tradition, such a scarcity and inadequacy of tools, must have told enormously upon the writing of women' (*RO*: 99, 100), Woolf emphasises the understanding that, in contrast to their male counterparts, the authentic possibilities and opportunities open to these female novelists were both restricted and compromised.

As politically conservative, Heidegger emphasises the importance of tradition; nevertheless, he, like Woolf, also warns of the danger for Dasein when

> tradition keeps it from providing its own guidance, whether in inquiring or in choosing ... When tradition thus becomes master, it does so in such a way that what it 'transmits' is made so inaccessible, proximally and for the most part, that it rather becomes concealed. Tradition takes

what has come down to us and delivers it over to self-evidence; it blocks our access to those primordial 'sources' from which the categories and concepts handed down to us have been in part quite genuinely drawn. Indeed it makes us forget that they have had such an origin, and makes us suppose that the necessity of going back to these sources is something which we need not even understand. (*BT*: 42–3)

For both Heidegger and Woolf, it is crucial that tradition does not become a means of covering over the individual's authentic thrown possibilities. In *Night and Day*, Woolf's representation of her protagonist, Katharine Hilbery, provides an example of the ways that tradition can conceal, limit and inhibit the thrown possibilities available to the individual. As the novel begins, it is clear that Katharine believes that her life holds few future possibilities beyond working on her grandfather's biography, or marrying William Rodney – a man whom she does not love. Involving herself in her grandfather's biography, despite the fact that she has admittedly 'no aptitude for literature', Katharine dismisses the possibility of pursuing a career in her chosen field of study, mathematics: 'Perhaps the unwomanly nature of the science made her instinctively wish to conceal her love of it. But the more profound reason was that in her mind mathematics were directly opposed to literature'. Coming as she does from a literary family, Katharine feels that 'There was something a little unseemly in thus opposing the tradition of her family; something that made her feel wrong-headed, and thus more than ever disposed to shut her desires away from view and cherish them with extraordinary fondness' (*ND*: 35, 37–8).

Woolf's critique of the propensity of tradition to restrict the individual's access to authentic projected possibilities is evident in *The Waves*, through her representation of Australian-born Louis. Having graduated from school, Louis is possessed by the certainty that he and his fellow classmates

have forged certain links. Above all, we have inherited traditions. These stone flags have been worn for six hundred years. On these walls are inscribed the names of men of war, of statesmen . . . Blessings be on all traditions, on all safeguards and circumscriptions! (*TW*: 42)

As noted, due to his colonial background, Louis constantly struggles with the sense of being an outsider within English society. As a schoolboy, he is conscious of those students who appear to possess a sense of ease and belonging; describing these classmates as the 'boasting boys',

Louis asserts: 'I shall envy them their continuance down the safe traditional ways under the shade of old yew trees while I consort with cockneys and clerks, and tap the pavements of the city' (*TW*: 49). Desperate to attain a sense of belonging, Louis clings unquestioningly and pathetically to those traditions that he believes will validate his place in the social order.

In terms of her own childhood and adolescence, in 'A Sketch of the Past' Woolf describes her sense that she and her sister Vanessa were 'trapped' within the confines of Victorian tradition. Describing their relationship to a dominating father who ran his household based on nineteenth-century prescriptions and expectations, Woolf writes:

> We looked at him with eyes that were looking into the future ... But while we looked into the future, we were completely under the power of the past. Explorers and revolutionists, as we both were by nature, we lived under the sway of a society that was about fifty years too old for us ... If I had the power to lift out of the past a single day as we lived it about 1900, it would give a section of upper middle class Victorian life, like one of those sections with glass covers in which ants and bees are shown going about their tasks. ('Sketch': 149–50)

Given Woolf's personal experiences, it is unsurprising that she possessed a lifelong abhorrence of the propensity of tradition to restrict and define the possibilities open to individuals within English society.

Historical discourse and exclusion

Just as Woolf highlights the ways in which tradition can be used as an excuse for the confinement and exclusion of women in terms of their place and role within particular social spheres and contexts, throughout her writings, Woolf emphasises her belief that traditional historical discourse becomes a means of justifying and reinforcing those dualisms that marginalise certain groups within society, particularly women. This is evinced in her first novel, *The Voyage Out*, through Woolf's repeated references to the work of the renowned eighteenth-century historian, Edward Gibbon (1737–94).[13] As Woolf introduces the young Cambridge man, St John Hirst, in her novel, he is described as 'reading the third volume of Gibbon's *History of the Decline and Fall of Rome* ... while a whole procession of splendid sentences entered his capacious brow and went marching through his brain in order' *(VO: 116)*. Such a description of chronological 'order' can be viewed as representative of the inherent connection between such traditional historical discourse and the metaphysical notions of linearity and causality. As the novel progresses, this arrogant and insecure individual attempts to make conversation with the unworldly Rachel Vinrace; upon learning that Rachel has never read Gibbon's work, Hirst openly refers to the historian's writings as a means of measuring this young woman's mental aptitude: '"D'you think you'll be able to appreciate him? He's the test, of course. It's awfully difficult to tell about women," he continued, "how much, I mean, is due to lack of training, and how much is native incapacity"' (*VO*: 172).

As de Gay observes, in Woolf's earliest novel, Gibbon's work not only 'becomes a form of currency in the cultural economy of Rachel's circle'; such writings become 'a means of dividing male and female experience, and asserting male dominance' (2007b: 21). Such a perspective is reflected in Woolf's subsequent novel, *Night and Day*, as she describes the experience of Cassandra Otway, a young woman who feels compelled to read Lord Macaulay's *The History of England* upon the advice of her future husband, William Rodney. While Rodney feels a compulsion to 'educate' (*ND*: 414) Cassandra, it is of note that Macaulay's works were similarly recommended to the fifteen-year-old Woolf by her father as a means of educating his daughter (*PA*: 69). Unlike Cassandra, who fails to read any of Macaulay's history, in her 1897 diary, Woolf proudly records her experience of reading the five volumes of the historian's work within the space of a month, using attributes such as 'cherished' and 'beloved' (*PA*: 79, 80) to describe the writer who was personally acquainted with her father. From the perspective of the fictional representations of Rachel Vinrace and Cassandra Otway, and the lived experience of young Virginia Stephen, traditional historiography becomes not simply a means of instigating societal inculcation; such discourse is also utilised as an exclusionary tool of the patriarchal social order.

Yet, as Woolf attests in *Three Guineas*, it is not only women's access to historical writings that both demonstrate and reinforce their position of social exclusion; perhaps even more telling is the absence of women and other marginalised members of society from historical discourse itself. In marked contrast to such omissions, in her 1925 diary Woolf records her intention to 'read voraciously & gather material for the Lives of the Obscure – which is to tell the whole history of England in one obscure life after another' (*D3*: 37), an ambition that ultimately results in a series of essays. As Anne Olivier Bell remarks, by 1927 Woolf 'had already published two such "Lives" (reprinted in *The Common Reader*)' (*D3*: 129, n7). At that time Woolf's interest and intention to write such a history still remained: 'I shall write memoirs; have a plan already to get historical manuscripts & write Lives of the Obscure' (*D3*: 129). Comparing Woolf's approach to history with that of her father, Sabine Hotho-Jackson suggests that: 'If for Stephen, the obscure were the rank and file of history, without which the great men could not have achieved their historical impact, for Woolf they were history itself' (1991: 310).

Throughout Woolf's fiction and non-fictional writings, her interest in marginalised lives was to remain a preoccupation. This is demonstrated in *A Room of One's Own*, where the issue of the obscurity and marginalisation of women's lives within historical discourse is a dominant concern. As Woolf satirically observes, the lives of women are 'all but absent from history'. Woolf draws attention to the stark contrast between the copious representations of women in fiction, and their lack of a presence in history: 'Imaginatively she is of the highest importance; practically she is completely insignificant' (*RO*: 56). As Woolf surveys the chapter headings in G. M. Trevelyan's 1926 *History of England*, she is met with the usual signposts of history such as war, education, politics and religion; areas in which women have been traditionally excluded. As Woolf ironically observes, 'by no possible means could middle-class women with nothing but brains and character at their command have taken part in any one of the great movements which, brought together, constitute the historian's view of the past' (*RO*: 57–8).

Turning to the study of the Elizabethan woman, Woolf considers the difficulty of catching a glimpse of this figure's everyday life, as, unlike some of her male counterparts, she leaves behind neither plays nor poems, and 'never writes her own life and scarcely keeps a diary'. Calling for the rewriting of history, Woolf facetiously asks whether a record of the obscure lives of such women could be added as

> a supplement to history? calling it, of course, by some inconspicuous name so that women might figure there without impropriety? For one often catches a glimpse of them in the lives of the great, whisking away into the background, concealing, I sometimes think, a wink, a laugh, perhaps a tear. (*RO*: 58)

Lamenting the unrecorded state of women's everyday lives, Woolf notes that 'Nothing remains of it all. All has vanished. No biography or history has a word to say about it.' Emphasising her desire to gain an understanding of such lives, Woolf turns her thoughts to the image of a girl serving behind a shop counter and proclaims, 'I would as soon have her true history as the hundred and fiftieth life of Napoleon or seventieth study of Keats and his use of Miltonic inversion which old Professor Z and his like are now inditing' (*RO*: 116, 117–18).

The lack of attention devoted to the lives of women in traditional historical discourse is foregrounded in *The Voyage Out*, as Terence Hewet discusses the absence of the voice of women within representations of history with his young fiancée, Rachel Vinrace:

> 'Just consider: it's the beginning of the twentieth century, and until a few years ago no woman had ever come out by herself and said things at all. There it was going on in the background, for all those thousands of years, this curious silent unrepresented life. Of course we're always writing about women – abusing them, or jeering at them, or worshipping them; but it's never come from women themselves. I believe we still don't know in the least how they live, or what they feel, or what they do precisely . . . the lives of women of forty, of unmarried women, of working women, of women who keep shops and bring up children, of women like your aunts or Mrs Thornbury or Miss Allan – one knows nothing whatever about them . . . It's the man's view that's represented, you see.' (*VO*: 245)

Hewet's assertion that history is viewed, interpreted and represented purely through the male gaze finds expression five years earlier in Woolf's 1910 essay, 'Modes and Manners of the Nineteenth Century', where she describes men as the authors of history, noting that, 'At any rate, we are left out, and history, in our opinion, lacks an eye' (1986b: 331).

Hélène Cixous suggests not only that 'Woman must write her self', but that by seizing 'the occasion to *speak*', she will achieve 'her shattering entry into history, which has always been based *on her suppression*' (1980: 245, 250). In the late 1930s, Woolf seizes such an occasion as she presents her memoir, 'Am I a Snob?', to the Memoir Club – a group that consisted of 'thirteen "old Bloomsbury" friends' who 'met at intervals' in order to 'read out amusing, carefully polished narratives of their lives' (Briggs 2005: 350). Foregrounding history's typical response to the voice of women, Woolf states:

> I am not the most widely lived or the most richly memoried. Maynard, Desmond, Clive and Leonard all live stirring and active lives; all constantly brush up against the great; all constantly affect the course of history one way or another. It is for them to unlock the doors of their treasure-houses and to set before us those gilt and gleaming objects which repose within. Who am I that I should be asked to read a memoir? (2002a: 62)

As an established writer at the time of her presentation, Woolf's assertions appear deliberately ironic and self-effacing. Although Woolf is not an official participant in those areas of society that traditionally 'affect the course of history', such as war, politics and religion, as a woman, it is only by asserting and reasserting her own voice alongside all who have been marginalised and excluded from historical discourse, that a rethinking of the definition of history might begin. As Cixous proclaims: 'It is time for women to start scoring their feats in written and oral language' (1980: 251).

In her essay, 'The Art of Biography', Woolf draws attention to history's traditional preoccupation with the lives and deeds of 'great men'. Posing the question of how one comes to define and determine whose lives are deemed worthy of record, Woolf writes:

> since so much is known that used to be unknown, the question now inevitably asks itself, whether the lives of great men only should be recorded. Is not anyone who has lived a life, and left a record of that life, worthy of biography – the failures as well as the successes, the humble as well as the illustrious? And what is greatness? And what smallness? He must revise our standards of merit and set up new heroes for our admiration. (1942a: 125)

In *Flush*, such an absence of the obscure in records of history is performatively addressed and redressed by Woolf as the life of Elizabeth Barrett Browning's dog becomes the focus of biographical concern. Along similar lines, through her inclusion of references to Miss Barrett's maid, Lily Wilson, in the novel's endnotes, Woolf draws attention to the marginalised position of the working classes in historical accounts. Discussing Wilson's future had she decided not to accompany her mistress to Italy, Woolf explains that this domestic worker would certainly have been dismissed from her position: 'And what then would have been her fate? Since English fiction in the 'forties scarcely deals with the lives of ladies' maids, and biography had not then cast its searchlight so low, the question must remain a question' (*Flush*: 111, n6). Noting that 'The life of Lily Wilson is extremely obscure and thus cries aloud for the services of a biographer' (*Flush*: 109, n6), Woolf refers to the difficulty involved in creating a thorough sketch of such an individual:

> there can have been no lack of thoughts in Wilson's old head as she sat at the window of the Palazzo Rezzonico in the evening. But nothing can be more vain than to pretend that we can guess what they were, for she was typical of the great army of her kind – the inscrutable, the all-but-silent, the all-but-invisible servant maids of history. (*Flush*: 113, n6)

In a similarly performative style, in *Three Guineas,* Woolf again refers to the unrecorded life of the domestic servant in the form of an endnote: 'It is much to be regretted that no lives of maids, from which a more fully documented account could be constructed, are to be found in the *Dictionary of National Biography*' (*TG*: 390–1, n36). Such a reference to Leslie Stephen's edited publication becomes a scarcely veiled criticism of her father's decision-making process in terms of who is deemed worthy of inclusion in the biographical pages of history.

The marginalisation of the everyday

Throughout her *oeuvre*, Woolf frequently presents biography as a form of historiography, a perspective that may well have been influenced by her father's early and extensive instruction regarding 'the interrelations of biography, history, and literature' (Hill 1981: 353). As Robert I. Rotberg suggests, accounts of the lives of individuals provide the foundation for history:

> Biography is history, depends on history, and strengthens and enriches history. In turn, all history is biography. History could hardly exist without biographical insights – without the texture of human endeavor that emanates from a full appreciation of human motivation, the real or perceived constraints on human action, and exogenous influences on human behavior. (2010: 305)

Despite her agreement with such a perspective, Woolf observes that official biographical accounts often fail to provide an authentic representation of the individual's lived experience of Being-in-the-world. In her 1927 essay, 'The New Biography', for instance, Woolf reflects upon the propensity of Victorian biographies to focus upon subject matter that has little relevance to the individual's average everyday mode of Being. As a means of illustrating her point, Woolf calls upon her readers to

> Consider one's own life; pass under review a few years that one has actually lived. Conceive how Lord Morley would have expounded them; how Sir Sidney Lee would have documented them; how strangely all that has been most real in them would have slipped through their fingers. (1994: 478)

Five years later, in her essay, 'Great Men's Houses', Woolf again highlights the propensity of Victorian biography to fail to document 'all that has been most real' in the life of its subjects, as she calls into question the biographical representation of the nineteenth-century writer, historian and biographer, Thomas Carlyle:

> Take the Carlyles, for instance. One hour spent in 5 Cheyne Row will tell us more about them and their lives than we can learn from all the biographies. Go down into the kitchen. There, in two seconds, one is made acquainted with a fact that escaped the attention of Froude, and yet was of incalculable importance – they had no water laid on. Every drop that the Carlyles used . . . had to be pumped by hand from a well in the kitchen. (2006b: 32)

Unlike representations of the Carlyles provided by James Anthony Froude, Woolf's essay uncovers the everyday mode of Being-in-the-world that was experienced by the Carlyle couple, one that was founded upon – to at least some degree – the gender and class prescriptions of the social order.

In *The Waves*, Woolf emphasises the propensity of traditional biographical discourse to focus its attention upon the so-called signposts of life, which ultimately fail to provide a true account of the individual's average everyday experiences. Focalised from the perspective of an elderly Bernard, as he imagines the way that a biographer would record his life, Woolf writes:

> 'About this time Bernard married and bought a house [. . .] His friends observed in him a growing tendency to domesticity [. . .] The birth of children made it highly desirable that he should augment his income.' That is the biographic style, and it does to tack together torn bits of stuff, stuff with raw edges . . . one cannot despise these phrases laid like Roman roads across the tumult of our lives, since they compel us to walk in step like civilised people with the slow and measured tread of policemen though one may be humming any nonsense under one's breath at the same time . . . 'He attained some success in his profession [. . .] He inherited a small sum of money from an uncle' – that is how the biographer continues, and if one wears trousers and hitches them up with braces, one has to say that, though it is tempting now and then to go blackberrying; tempting to play ducks and drakes with all these phrases. But one has to say that. (*TW*: 199–200)

Bernard's musings demonstrate Woolf's view of the incomplete and superficial style of traditional biography. As indicated by the inclusion of multiple ellipses, as well as Bernard's notion of 'raw edges', it is the unrecorded spaces that exist in between the usual signposts of life, such as marriage and the birth of children, which reflect what it means to Be-in-the-world. The sense that the societal expectations and prescriptions of theyness dictate how the life of the individual should be recorded is strongly indicated through Bernard's allusions to walking 'in step', while inwardly wishing to forgo the well-worn path, and silently humming a tune that runs counter to the march.

For Woolf, the propensity of official biographical and historical discourse to marginalise the everyday life of the individual, conceals rather than reveals the relationship between self and world. In response, throughout the various forms of her writings, Woolf's textual representations of the past privilege the ordinary, or everyday, as the principal focus of concern. As Lyndall Gordon writes, for Woolf, 'At the centre of history . . . are the acts of the obscure between the acts of kings and warriors' (2001: 163). Referring to Woolf's *oeuvre*, Gillian Beer states that 'history in her writing is a matter of textures (horse-hair or velvet), changing light (flambeaux or gas-light), not of events or "dominant figures of the age"' (1996: 8).

Despite the validity of such observations, as highlighted, Woolf, like Heidegger, openly calls into question the everyday mode of Being-in-the-world, equating it to 'non-being', due to the individual's propensity to become immersed in the concerns of the present and the constructs of theyness. From such a perspective, it would seem reasonable to question why Woolf would place an emphasis upon average everydayness as the most significant source of historical enquiry. In his discussion of Heidegger's treatment of the everyday, Thiele makes a number of significant observations that can also be applied directly to Woolf's work:

> Heidegger defines the everyday as the realm of the inauthentic. But that is not to say that he remains blind or deaf to the greatness and mystery of that which is unadorned with ceremony or fame. Quite the opposite is true. He maintains that Being may shine forth most clearly when attention is not diverted by the grandiosity of events and things . . . What lies hidden in the everyday solicits ontological rediscovery. (1995: 237, 238)[14]

In keeping with his existential analysis of Dasein, Heidegger explains that in order to best understand the life of the individual, one must reflect upon his or her most typical mode of Being-in-the-world, that is, average everydayness. Although Heidegger is not referring to biography or history in such a pronouncement, arguably such an understanding can be applied to both of these forms of discourse. From Woolf's perspective, it is the individual's everyday mode of Being that represents the political and ideological sway of the social order upon all facets of life. As average everydayness represents the individual's typical mode of Being-in-the-world, in order to gain a thorough understanding and representation of both personal and collective history, the ordinary everyday aspects of life must be revealed and considered.

Reflecting upon the importance of the everyday in terms of understandings of the past, in her 1935 article, 'The Captain's Death Bed', Woolf suggests that

> no living writer, try though he may, can bring the past back again, because no living writer can bring back the ordinary day. He sees it through a glass, sentimentally, romantically; it is either too pretty or too brutal; it lacks ordinariness. (1978: 41)

For Woolf, in order to comprehensively understand and connect with that which has been, one must understand the somewhat elusive manifestations of the everyday. Such a perspective is also stressed in 'The Art of Biography', where Woolf asserts the importance of everyday '"authentic information"', such as

> When and where did the real man live; how did he look; did he wear laced boots or elastic-sided; who were his aunts, and his friends; how did he blow his nose; whom did he love, and how; and when he came to die did he die in his bed like a Christian, or [. . .] (1942a: 125, 126)

As Woolf states, the capacity of the biographer to impart such everyday details provides a reality that 'does more to stimulate the imagination than any poet or novelist save the very greatest' (1942a: 126).

The significance of such ordinary details as a means of understanding the past is given fictional representation early in Woolf's career in her short story, 'Phyllis and Rosamond'. Arguing that it is time to look behind and beyond the traditionally dominant figures of history, Woolf proposes that the true sources of influence throughout society may in fact be those 'obscure figures' who 'occupy a place not unlike that of the showman's hand in the dance of the marionettes' (1989b: 17). Woolf suggests that in order to understand the grand events and great men of history, one must understand the everyday lives of those who exist in their orbit and in their shadow.

Written during the same year as 'Phyllis and Rosamond', Woolf's short story 'The Journal of Mistress Joan Martyn' highlights and subverts the marginalisation of the everyday within the official pages of history. Divided into two sections, the first part of this story is focalised from the perspective of the female historian, Miss Rosamond Merridew, and describes the circumstances that have provided this woman with the opportunity to gain access to a sixteenth-century journal written by a young woman named Joan Martyn. In contrast with the typical focus that traditional male historians place upon great men and grand events, the reader is introduced to Miss Merridew's keen interest in the everyday as a means of accessing and understanding both the life of the individual and the events of history. Demonstrating the significance of the everyday as a means of providing a broader understanding of the past, Woolf writes of Miss Merridew's view that

> A sudden light upon the legs of Dame Elizabeth Partridge sends its beams over the whole state of England, to the King upon his throne; she wanted stockings! and no other need impresses you in quite the same way with the reality of mediaeval legs; and therefore with the reality of mediaeval bodies, and so, proceeding upward step by step, with the reality of mediaeval brains; and there you stand at the centre of all ages: middle beginning or end. (1989a: 34)

As Cuddy-Keane observes, the first section of Woolf's short story defies conventional representations of history through 'a conversation – in fact, a debate – between two different definitions of history: the one privileging objective facts and focused on issues of genealogy, property and ownership, the other giving equal weight to personal, subjective recordings of daily life' (1997: 66).

In the second part of Woolf's short story, the reader is introduced to the contents of Joan's journal, which provide a picture of the young woman's everyday experiences and observations during a period of political unrest. Acknowledging and lamenting her own emphasis upon seemingly mundane matters throughout her journal, Joan ironically confesses that 'truly, there is nothing in the pale of my days that needs telling'. While this young woman is aware of 'the state of the country . . . dreadful stories of the plots and the battles and the bloody deeds that are going on all round us' (1989a: 61, 47), in contrast with traditional representations of history, throughout this journal war and politics form a backdrop as opposed to the central focus of recorded concern.

In *Three Guineas*, Woolf reflects upon the potential of personal, rather than official, biographical accounts to unveil the truth of the lived life that is so often concealed throughout traditional historical discourse.[15] As Morag Shiach explains in her capacity as editor of the combined volume of *A Room of One's Own* and *Three Guineas,* Woolf 'develops her argument in *Three Guineas* through readings of a very wide range of biographies, memoirs, and literary texts' (*TG*: 422). In her attempt to understand what it means to be a member of the paid workforce, Woolf turns to the biographical accounts of a number of professional men, including a barrister, politician, bishop, doctor and journalist.

Throughout these personal records of working life, Woolf finds a recurrent sense of weariness and despondency that is indicative of the heavy sacrifices and deprivations that are demanded by society, and endured by the individual. Woolf compares such personal biographical accounts with the records of history contained in an official volume such as *Whitaker's Almanack*:

> What then do these quotations from the lives of successful professional men prove, you ask? They prove, as Whitaker proves things, nothing whatever. If Whitaker, that is, says that a bishop is paid five thousand a year, that is a fact; it can be checked and verified. But if Bishop Gore says that the life of a bishop is 'an awful mind-and-soul-destroying life' he is merely giving us his opinion . . . These quotations then prove nothing that can be checked and verified; they merely cause us to hold opinions. And those opinions cause us to doubt and criticize and question the value of professional life – not its cash value; that is great; but its spiritual, its moral, its intellectual value. (*TG*: 257–8)[16]

Initially appearing to disparage the subjective nature of the biographical form, Woolf in fact provides an ironic testament to the value of such personal expressions as a powerful means of revealing elements of both the status quo and the average everyday life of the individual, which usually remain unquestioned and concealed throughout traditional historical records.

Spiropoulou states that such a privileging of the personal and non-official as a worthy record of the past is contrary to 'the historiographical practice of traditional historicism', which is 'based on formal documents which as a rule express the official point of view, excluding much personal, visual or oral evidence as well as marginal presences and ideas' (2010: 40).[17] Like Woolf's representation of Joan Martyn's journal as a means of calling into question the typical focus of traditional historical discourse, Gordon observes that Woolf's own diary was in fact 'her most sustained counter to history: a private document of her times' (2001: 171). The significance of the diary as a historical artifact that uniquely reveals the average everyday life of the individual is made evident in Woolf's two-part 1932 essay, 'Two Parsons', where she notes that the 'question of diary-keeping' is often 'the one mysterious fact in a life otherwise as clear as the sky and as candid as the dawn' (1986d: 93). In keeping with Joan Martyn's emphasis upon the everyday, in his diary, Parson James Woodforde (1740–1803) records his observation that: 'Far away guns roar; a King falls; but the sound is not loud enough to scare the rooks here in Norfolk' (1986d: 98).

Woolf's desire to subvert the emphasis of traditional historical discourse upon grand events in favour of the everyday is also evident in *The Years,* where she explicitly uses dates as chapter headings as a means of signposting the narrative's particular location in history, even as she 'marginalises and/or approaches obliquely' (Peach 1999: 192) those major historical events, such as war, that form the foundations of traditional representations of history.[18] Such a disruption of war as a traditional subject of history is particularly marked in *To the Lighthouse* through the novel's interlude, 'Time Passes'. As Gordon suggests, within this section, the omission of 'battles, gore, and political justification', acts as a 'critique of what histories and newspapers accustom us to define as memorable' (2001: 161). When war is directly referred to, it is encased in parentheses: '[A shell exploded. Twenty or thirty young men were blown up in France, among them Andrew Ramsay, whose death, mercifully, was instantaneous.]' (*TL*: 127). The use of such punctuation provides a performative representation of Woolf's attitude to war as a focus of history: as Lynn Truss explains, brackets have a number of functions, one of which is to 'half-remove the intruding aside, half-suppress it' (2005: 160).[19] Woolf's sustained critique of war as a principal focus of concern throughout official recorded history reflects her broader desire to redefine what actually constitutes 'history', in order that those individuals, movements and events that have long been overlooked and excluded from traditional historical discourse might take their rightful place within the collective memory, rather than be forgotten.

Conclusion – there is no such thing as an ordinary day

Throughout her writings, Woolf consistently draws attention to the propensity of the social order to turn to the past as a means of justifying and maintaining the prevailing status quo, particularly through traditions that are often heavily imbued with a patriarchal bias. Along similar lines, Woolf views traditional historical discourse as representative of both the past and present marginalisation of particular members of society, such as women and those belonging to the working class. The absence of the marginalised in the official pages of history means that the voices of such individuals are effectively silenced and erased. Woolf draws attention to the understanding that official biographical and historical accounts fail to demonstrate an authentic view of past worlds, as their emphasis upon grand men and grand events comes at the expense of the individual's everyday dealings, which, for both Woolf and Heidegger, is a defining and inextricable characteristic of Being-in-the-world.

Based upon their shared view of the individual as a temporal being, both Woolf and Heidegger proffer a rethinking of the relationship between the individual and history. Through their sustained emphasis upon the past as determinative of the present and future possibilities and potentialities of both the individual and the collective, Woolf and Heidegger reject the metaphysical understanding of time that privileges the present as autonomous and homogeneous. For both writer and philosopher, the individual's authentic connection to the world is neither limited to, nor defined by, an autonomous present and its particular preoccupations and concerns.

In his discussion of the individual's authentic appropriation of the past, Heidegger states that 'when historicality [historicity] is authentic, it understands history as the "recurrence" of the possible, and knows that a possibility will recur only if existence is open for it fatefully, in a moment of vision, in resolute repetition' (*BT*: 444). Significantly, Heidegger's understanding of the essential connection between the individual's authentic mode of Being-in-the-world and the 'moment of vision' shares marked affinities with Woolf's notion of the 'exceptional moment' that is introduced in her memoir, 'A Sketch of the Past'. The textual approaches of both Woolf and Heidegger to such 'moments' will provide the foundation for discussions in the following chapter. Such authentic moments are defined by a disruption of the individual's everyday immersion in the present, which is replaced by an awareness and acceptance of his or her temporal mode of Being-in-the-world. In terms of the relationship between past, present and future, for both Woolf and Heidegger, 'The moment, *Augenblick* . . . is the place, the gateway, *where* these three dimensions come together' (Elden 2001: 45): the individual, as a temporal being, comes to be the site of this collision.

In *Being and Time,* Heidegger suggests that 'the temporality of authentic historicality [historicity], as the moment of vision of anticipatory repetition, *deprives* the "today" of its character *as present*' (*BT*: 443–4). Along similar lines, James Hafley states that

> If Joyce used the single day as a unity, Virginia Woolf used it as a diversity. Joyce attempted to show all that a single day can hold; Virginia Woolf, to show that there is no such thing as a single day. (1963: 73)

Hafley's proclamation eloquently conveys Woolf's preoccupation with the temporal nature of Being-in-the-world that has been emphasised throughout this chapter, where each moment in time is representative of that which is, that which-has-been, and that which-is-yet-to-come.

Notes

1. In her 2010 monograph, *Virginia Woolf, Modernity and History: Constellations with Walter Benjamin*, Angeliki Spiropoulou asserts that 'Woolf's "philosophy of history" and historiographical practices have not been systematically examined to date' (2010: 5); from such a perspective, Spiropoulou provides a brief outline of what she considers to be relevant Woolfian criticism dating from 1988 (2010: 179, n15).
2. Katherine C. Hill discusses Woolf's early apprenticeship in history that arose as a result of her father's insistence that 'a solid background in history and biography is necessary to the appreciation of literature' (1981: 353). In their 'Forum' letters published under the heading, 'Virginia Woolf and Leslie Stephen', Louise A. DeSalvo and Alice Fox question Hill's claim that Leslie Stephen was influential in shaping Woolf's writing career (DeSalvo *et al.* 1982). Despite such concerns, I am largely in agreement with Hill's statements regarding Stephen's influence. It must be emphasised, however, that this influence did not result in imitation; rather, as will be discussed throughout this chapter, Stephen's approach inspired Woolf's critique of traditional historical discourse.

3. Along similar lines, Jane de Gay (2007a) provides a convincing argument that Woolf's representation of history in *Orlando* can be read as a reaction against Stephen's treatment of literary history.
4. Referring to Woolf's writings, Julia Briggs observes that:

   > As a novelist centrally concerned with how to represent consciousness and subjectivity, she was intensely aware of time, both as an impersonal force and as a personal experience, as shared time and individual time, as the regulated and measurable time of clocks, public and private, and of seasons and stars . . . Even the titles of her books suggest her sense of its passage – *Night and Day* (1919), *Monday or Tuesday* (1921), 'The Hours' (published as *Mrs Dalloway*, 1925), *The Waves* (1931), *The Years* (1937), *Between the Acts* (1941). (2001: 3)

5. At this point it is important to keep in mind Melba Cuddy-Keane's warning that the 'Modernist period . . . was itself heterogeneous'; from such a perspective, Woolf's writing 'must be located diversely as "like" some Modernist strands and "unlike" others' (1997: 64).
6. Further to this, Bambach suggests that during this period, 'German culture was experiencing a "crisis" concerning its own fundamental history and identity, a crisis that threatened the meaning and continuity of the historicist tradition' (1995: 189). Such a view is affirmed by Jeffrey Andrew Barash, who explains that 'The period following World War I, above all, constituted a watershed in German thought, when historical methods of understanding were subjected to searching interrogation in the German universities' (1988: 2).
7. In 'Mrs. Dalloway's Existential Temporality', Jason Wakefield provides a lengthy, and at times contentious, discussion of Woolf's novel from the perspective of Heidegger's understanding of Dasein as a temporal being; Wakefield pronounces that 'The characters in Mrs. Dalloway illustrate the difference between an authentic and an inauthentic relation to the temporality of being' (2013: 60).
8. The *Dictionary of National Biography* was Leslie Stephen's 'major life's work' (Lee 1997: 7).
9. Jeffrey Andrew Barash makes the point that in their translation of *Being and Time*, Macquarrie and Robinson define Heidegger's term, *Geschichtlichkeit*, as 'historicality' rather than 'historicity'. Barash argues that 'historicity' is the better translation, and cites David Farrell Krell's *Basic Writings* and David Couzens Hoy's essay 'History, Historicity and Historiography in *Being and Time*' as examples of Heideggerian scholars who have also preferred this translation (1988: 184, n22). As I am in agreement with Barash's rationale, the term 'historicity' will be included in square brackets in all quotations from Macquarrie and Robinson's edition of *Being and Time* that refer to the term 'historicality'.

10. An equally dark understanding of thrownness is imparted through the perspective of the shell-shocked soldier, Septimus Smith, in *Mrs Dalloway*; haunted by the images of death and a sense of meaninglessness as a result of his involvement in the First World War, Septimus cowers under the impression that 'The world has raised its whip; where will it descend?' (*MD*: 12).
11. It is of some significance that Heidegger also draws upon the literature of Sophocles as a means of commenting 'in tragic terms about the history of the West, finding ancient analogues to the modern situation in the plights of Oedipus and Antigone' (Bambach 1995: 262).
12. Along similar lines, Pauline Johnson argues that: 'Like the feminist, the modernist refuses to credit the merely traditional with the authority of a "second nature". In their various capacities, both offer a provocative challenge to the supposedly self-evident certainties of an unquestioned existence' (2004: 104).
13. In the leading article of the *Times Literary Supplement* dated 24 April 1937, entitled 'The Historian and "The Gibbon"', Woolf discusses her impressions of Edward Gibbon and his work.
14. As Zygmunt Adamczewski asserts:

    > historians may not accept as historical that which happens to private individuals in everyday life; Heidegger does – but he does not consider it as privately their own. It is buried deeper and rather than own, it is owing in the human being as such: owing – to being. Therefore those who think of being must search for a sense of history. (1970: 300)

15. Cuddy-Keane remarks that Woolf 'was fascinated by history and biography and in fact most of her reviews of books are of biographies, memoirs, diaries, letters. She considered those very important because, in particular, they were one way of getting to know women's lives' (2010a).
16. Woolf critiques the 'factual', patriarchal and linear nature of *Whitaker's Almanack* in her 1917 short story, 'The Mark on the Wall' (2003a: 63, 65–6, 67). Sim refers to Woolf's short story, remarking that:

    > The masculine point of view is linked to social and political hierarchies of power, symbolized by the 'philosophy of Whitaker' which informs us 'who follows whom' in that hierarchy of power . . . This encyclopaedic and linear view of society recalls the form of Mr Ramsay's mind and Leslie Stephen's *Dictionary of National Biography*. (2010: 44)

17. In her discussion of Woolf's disruption of Western historiography, Cuddy-Keane observes that it is Woolf's

    > actual historical practice that most effectively overturns the prevailing historiographical assumptions. The significance that she accords to unpublished and noncanonical works; her hybrid conflation of literary,

social, and economic history; her focus on historical questions rather than on historical patterns; and perhaps most importantly, her situating of literary judgments in terms of an historical text and an historical reader. (1997: 61)

18. Spiropoulou observes that:

    Although *The Years* covers a time span when important events, such as the Great War, and the death of Parnell and King Edward take place, these occur offstage and are only alluded to, as in *To the Lighthouse*. Rather . . . Woolf highlights 'the everyday' as the prime site of human history. (2010: 123)

19. Poole provides a sustained discussion of the use of 'brackets' in 'Time Passes' (1991: 83–7).

Chapter 5

Moments of Being and the Everyday

> Here is nothing out of the way . . . a dull young man is talking to rather a weakly young woman on the stairs as they go up to dress for dinner . . . But, from triviality, from commonplace, their words become suddenly full of meaning, and the moment for both one of the most memorable in their lives. It fills itself; it shines; it glows; it hangs before us, deep, trembling, serene for a second; next, the housemaid passes, and this drop, in which all the happiness of life has collected, gently subsides again to become part of the ebb and flow of ordinary existence. (Woolf 1962a: 178)

The preceding chapters have explored Woolf's emphasis throughout her writings on the notion that the individual's average everyday mode of Being-in-the-world comes to be defined and 'held in place' ('Sketch': 92) by the typically veiled forces, conventions and prescriptions of the social order, including the often overlapping discourses of patriarchy, religion, nationalism and history. As discussed, such an approach to the relationship between self and world may be contrasted with Heidegger's ontological emphasis in *Being and Time*. In this chapter, the focus shifts to the crucial role that moods and sensations play in Woolf's textual representations of the individual's experience of Being-in-the-world. This notion will be explored from the perspective of Heidegger's understanding that

> Dasein's openness to the world is constituted existentially by the attunement of a state-of-mind . . . Indeed *from the ontological point of view* we must as a general principle leave the primary discovery of the world to 'bare mood'. (*BT*: 176, 177)

As Heidegger's assertion reflects, moods provide the potential means by which each individual's relationship to the world comes to be disclosed. Thiele observes that, from a Heideggerian perspective, 'Far from standing between us and our world, moods are what first and foremost bring us into the world, into our "there"' (1997: 497). In *Being and Time*, Heidegger emphasises that 'we are never free of moods' (*BT*: 175); as such, the individual always already finds him or herself in one mood or another. Such an understanding of moods as the inevitable, inescapable and ever-changing conduit through which the individual's relationship to the world is situated and revealed is also reflected throughout Woolf's writings.

The sense that moods consistently colour and inform the individual's state of Being-in-the-world is demonstrated in Woolf's first novel, *The Voyage Out,* when she describes the responses of the young protagonist, Rachel Vinrace, as she falls in love for the first time; receiving a series of notes from the object of her affection, Terence Hewet, Rachel

> would read them, and spend the whole morning in a daze of happiness ... In these moods she found it impossible to read or play the piano, even to move being beyond her inclination. The time passed without her noticing it ... As unreflecting and pervasive were the moods of depression. Her mind was as the landscape outside when dark beneath clouds and straitly lashed by wind and hail. Again she would sit passive in her chair exposed to pain, and Helen's fantastical or gloomy words were like so many darts goading her to cry out against the hardness of life. Best of all were the moods when for no reason again this stress of feeling slackened, and life went on as usual, only with a joy and colour in its events that was unknown before; they had a significance like that which she had seen in the tree: the nights were black bars separating her from the days; she would have liked to run all the days into one long continuity of sensation. (*VO*: 258–9)

As this passage illustrates, in her writings Woolf does not always draw a marked and conscious distinction between moods and sensations. In contrast, Heidegger warns that to conflate mood and sensation, as though both were 'subjective' phenomena, is to miss the basic orienting role of mood as a way of disclosing aspects of the world in meaningful ways. Stanley Corngold explains that, for Heidegger, 'mood stands for a disclosive power whose reach cognitive understanding cannot attain' (1994: 210); as will be demonstrated, Woolf's rendering of the individual's moods and sensations throughout her writings also fulfils such a role. Indeed, despite differences in their respective approaches, throughout this chapter, attention will be drawn to the marked affinities between Woolf and Heidegger's textual representations of particular sensations and moods, particularly the ways in which these moods and sensations carry the potential to provide the individual with a glimpse of the typically unseen 'reality' of the extraordinary that is always already located in the ordinary.

The understanding that certain moods and sensations allow for the unconcealment of that which is ordinarily shrouded by the concerns of average everydayness is reflected in Woolf's 1926 diary, where she describes her impressions of the state of marriage:

> Arnold Bennett says that the horror of marriage lies in its 'dailiness'. All acuteness of relationship is rubbed away by this. The truth is more like this. Life – say 4 days out of 7 – becomes automatic; but on the 5th day a bead of sensation (between husband & wife) forms, wh. is all the fuller & more sensitive because of the automatic customary unconscious days on either side. That is to say the year is marked by moments of great intensity. Hardy's 'moments of vision'. How can a relationship endure for any length of time except under these conditions? (*D3*: 105)

In her sketch of this historically and culturally widespread institution, Woolf not only demonstrates her interest and awareness of the propensity of average everydayness to obscure; she also emphasises the role of sensation as a means of casting aside – albeit temporarily – those preoccupations that numb and blunt one's relationship not only with the surrounding world – both tangible and intangible – but also with the Other.

Of particular interest within the context of this chapter are the ways that certain types of moods trigger what will be termed 'epiphanal moments'; as will be explored from a variety of perspectives, such moments provide the individual with the potential to see through the 'cotton wool' of average everydayness. As discussed in the preceding chapter, Woolf uses the motif of cotton wool in 'A Sketch of the Past' ('Sketch': 84) as a means of exploring the notions of theyness and inauthenticity in relation to the individual's everyday mode of Being-in-the-world. Woolf's moments of non-Being are automatic and unquestioning, and as the image of cotton wool suggests, this mode of Being is also insulating, unvarying and, most significantly, opaque, insofar as one is unable to see that which lies beneath or beyond its surface. Notably, each of the forms of Woolf's writings, including her fiction, memoirs, diaries, letters, essays and reviews, are rich with examples of such moments.

Throughout this chapter, the focus of interest is Woolf's propensity to locate such moments of Being in the midst of the quotidian. Owing to the repeated emphasis upon the inauthentic nature of average everydayness throughout this book, such a reading might appear somewhat self-contradictory. However, as touched upon at the end of the previous chapter, for Heidegger, 'The mundane is pregnant with Being. This pregnancy, to borrow a Socratic image, calls us to midwifery' (Thiele 1995: 238). In other words, the extraordinary nature of the ordinary is always already present, it merely awaits discovery by an individual whose mode of Being-in-the-world is defined by 'resoluteness', which Heidegger describes as 'letting oneself be summoned out of one's lostness in the "they"' (*BT*: 345). As Thiele explains, such 'Resoluteness detaches one from convention and habit not to deliver one into a realm of abstract principles or future projects, but precisely to bring one authentically into the populated present' (1995: 235–6). Such a mode of Being-in-the-world is typified by an existential involvement with the quotidian that is posited upon authentic openness, receptivity and disclosure; this state lies in sharp contrast to the average everyday inauthentic mode of Being, in which the individual comes to be immersed in the distractions, diversions and concealments of theyness, rather than discovering the wonder that typically lies obscured.

As a means of examining such moments, and their relationship to Being-in-the-world, the structure of this chapter consists of what are essentially two sections, beginning with an examination of the literary epiphany and, most particularly, its relationship to Romantics such as William Wordsworth. This is followed by an exploration of Woolf's representations of 'moments of Being' from the perspectives of both childhood, and mental and physical illness. In the second section of this chapter, emphasis is placed upon Heidegger's philosophy, as his understandings of 'anxiety', 'nothingness', 'boredom', 'wonder' and the 'numinous' are examined from the perspective of the epiphanal moment, revealing parallels in terms of Woolf and Heidegger's respective desire to uncover that which is ordinarily concealed by the individual's immersion in average everydayness. Running throughout this chapter will be the recurring notion that the artist and the artwork are privileged origins and sites of epiphanal moments of Being.

The epiphany

Throughout Woolf's fiction and non-fictional writings, and within Heidegger's *Being and Time*, an emphasis is placed upon the notion of the authentic 'moment' as a means of disrupting the individual's everyday absorption in the present, and the ensuing unconscious conformity that is typified by theyness. For Woolf, such moments are termed 'moments of being' or 'exceptional moments' ('Sketch': 86, 85); while for Heidegger, these are understood as 'moment[s] of *vision*' (*BT*: 376). In her extensive discussion of 'the Woolfian moment', Sim suggests that 'Moments of being are one of the most important categories of experience in terms of both Woolf's life and her art' (2010: 137). Both Woolf and Heidegger's moments may be defined as epiphanal, since each represents 'a manifestation in and through the visible world of an invisible life' (Nichols 1987: 2); indeed, as Ashton Nichols explains, the origin of the term 'epiphany' can be found in the Greek word *phainein*, meaning '"to bring to light" or "cause to appear"' (1987: 5).

The exceptional moment as a literary device is not unique to Woolf as a modernist writer; James Joyce's 'epiphany', Thomas Hardy's 'moments of vision', and Joseph Conrad's 'moments of awakening' (Losey 1989: 48) are each examples of writings that incorporate the epiphanal moment to varying degrees.[1] Nichols observes that 'momentary manifestations of significance in ordinary experience have become a defining characteristic of twentieth-century fiction' (1987: 1). In *Epiphany in the Modern Novel,* Morris Beja states that the significance of the epiphany as a defining literary device first emerges in modern fiction; despite this, instances of the epiphanal moment can also be found in the earlier writings of authors such as Charles Dickens, George Eliot and Thomas Hardy. Beja claims that, as novelists, Joseph Conrad and Thomas Hardy were the principal influences in terms of Woolf's moments of vision (1971: 19, 117).

Such a perspective is reflected in Woolf's 1923 essay, 'Mr. Conrad: A Conversation', where she observes that this writer's 'books are full of moments of vision' (1981d: 77). A year later, in her essay, 'Joseph Conrad', Woolf discusses Conrad's writings from the perspective of his fictional alter ego, Marlow, a character who possesses a heightened propensity to experience moments of Being; as Woolf explains: 'He had a habit of opening his eyes suddenly and looking – at a rubbish heap, at a port, at a shop counter – and then complete in its burning ring of light that thing is flashed upon the mysterious background' (Woolf 1924: 493).

Citing a passage from *Lord Jim,* in which Conrad describes Marlow's response as he overhears a French officer exclaim, '"Mon

Dieu! how the time passes!"' (1924: 493), Woolf observes Conrad's approach to the epiphanal moment:

> Nothing could have been more commonplace than this remark; but its utterance coincided for me with a moment of vision. It's extraordinary how we go through life with eyes half shut, with dull ears, with dormant thoughts. Perhaps it's just as well; and it may be that it is this very dullness that makes life to the incalculable majority so supportable and so welcome. Nevertheless, there can be but few of us who had never known one of these rare moments of awakening when we see, hear, understand ever so much – everything – in a flash – before we fall back again into our agreeable somnolence. I raised my eyes when he spoke, and I saw him as though I had never seen him before. (Conrad 2008: 104)

It is of note that this quotation also appears in Woolf's 1917 review of Conrad's *Lord Jim*, where she suggests that such passages are of interest 'almost more for what they reveal of the writer than for any light they throw on the story'. Woolf states that such writing reflects Conrad's propensity to experience 'a "moment of vision" in which he sees people as if he had never seen them before; he expounds his vision, and we see it, too. These visions are the best things in his books' (1917: 355). As the passage from *Lord Jim* clearly demonstrates, triggered by the commonplace and ordinary, the moment of vision is epitomised by its capacity to awaken the individual to the typically unconscious, unthinking nature of average everyday Being-in-the-world. This defining feature of the literary epiphany is highlighted by Nichols, who explains that 'the emphasis is not on seeing a new thing but on seeing a familiar thing in a new way' (1987: 28).

Emphasised in the passage from Conrad's novel is the understanding that moments of vision are ephemeral in nature, so that the individual only ever experiences a momentary escape from his or her everyday mode of Being. This understanding is reflected in Woolf's 1928 leading article in the *Times Literary Supplement*, entitled 'Thomas Hardy's Novels'; discussing Hardy's epiphanal moments, Woolf writes:

> His own word, 'moments of vision,' exactly describes those passages of astonishing beauty and force which are to be found in every book that he wrote. With a sudden quickening of power which we cannot foretell, nor he, it seems, control, a single scene breaks off from the rest ... Vivid to the eye, but not to the eye alone, for every sense participates, such

scenes dawn upon us and their splendour remains. But the power goes as it comes. The moment of vision is succeeded by long stretches of plain daylight. (1928: 33)

Drawing attention to the parallels between Hardy's 'unconscious' manner of writing and his moments of vision, Woolf foregrounds the uncontrollable and ultimately transient nature of those exceptional moments that come to be located in the midst of average everydayness.

An understanding of the fleeting nature of the epiphanal moment is also evident in Woolf's own writings. In the final line of *To the Lighthouse*, the artist, Lily Briscoe, proclaims: 'I have had my vision' (*TL*: 198); as Hussey observes, this statement reflects the impermanent and finite nature of such a moment: 'Lily's present perfect tense shows that the vision cannot be prolonged' (2001: 45). In Woolf's final novel, *Between the Acts*, the pageant's director and creator, Miss La Trobe, also acknowledges the ephemeral quality of such moments as she contemplates the way that the play and its music have brought together those who are typically separate and detached: 'still for one moment she held them together – the dispersing company. Hadn't she, for twenty-five minutes, made them see? A vision imparted was relief from agony [. . .] or one moment [. . .] one moment' (*BA*: 60).

In her 1928 review, 'Half of Thomas Hardy', Woolf refers to Hardy's recorded memories of his early life, observing that they 'have the quality of moments of vision.' Woolf draws attention to Hardy's observation in 1887 that '"people are somnambulists – the material is not the real – only the visible, the real being invisible optically"' (1981b: 62, 65). It is of note that in her discussions of both Hardy and Conrad's literary epiphanal moments, Woolf's choices of illustrative passages refer to the state of somnolence, indicating that for both Hardy and Conrad, the individual's everyday mode of Being-in-the-world is characterised by an unconscious, dream-like state that masks the 'real' world. For Conrad and Hardy, the epiphanal moment shatters the stupor of average everydayness, replacing it with a momentary wakeful awareness of the extraordinary nature of the ordinary that is typically concealed. For both writers, such moments possess an acutely aesthetic, as well as existential quality. Such moments of awakening are also evident throughout Woolf's writings, where somnolence is viewed from a pronounced socio-political perspective that is understood as a symptom of inauthenticity, insofar as the individual lacks an awareness of the constructs and ideologies of the social order that define and determine his or her everyday mode of Being-in-the-world.

Romantic influences

While the influence of both Conrad and Hardy upon Woolf's understanding of the moment of vision is clearly reflected in Woolf's essays, the earlier works of the English Romantic poet, William Wordsworth, also shaped Woolf's conception and representation of such moments.[2] Describing the Romantic period as the age in which the secular epiphany arises, Beja proclaims Wordsworth's 'Preface' to the *Lyrical Ballads* to be 'the most influential Romantic statement on inspiration'; one that demonstrates 'an awareness of the poetic value of moments of illumination' (1971: 32).[3] Woolf's long association with Wordsworth's writings began in childhood, when her father would recite the poet's works of an evening. Suggesting that 'Woolf's engagement with Wordsworth helped her articulate her concept of "moments of being"', de Gay cites a number of critics who also draw 'close parallels between Woolf's "moments of being" and Wordsworth's "spots of time"' (de Gay 2007b: 166). Originating in his autobiographical poem, *The Prelude*, the phrase 'spots of time' denotes Wordsworth's literary use of epiphany, as demonstrated in the following passage:

> There are in our existence spots of time
> Which with distinct preeminence retain
> A fructifying virtue, whence, depressed
> By trivial occupations and the round
> Of ordinary intercourse, our minds –
> Especially the imaginative power –
> Are nourished and invisibly repaired;
> Such moments chiefly seem to have their date
> In our first childhood. (1995: 16)[4]

Reflected in this extract is Wordsworth's preoccupation with those 'spots of time' that uncover and surmount the average everydayness of non-Being. What is also explicitly emphasised is his Romantic sense that such epiphanal moments are most palpable during the years of childhood. In terms of Woolf's own writings, *The Waves* provides the clearest illustration of childhood as a period of heightened susceptibility to such moments.⁵ As Sim observes, Woolf's representation of the six characters at the beginning of the novel 'recalls Romantic representations of the child, particularly Wordsworth's and Blake's presentation of the child's superior capacity for states of awe and wonder at common objects' (2010: 143). Gordon remarks that in the novel, the children's 'imaginations sever them from lessons so that they are able to make their own worlds, in Wordsworthian terms "to be"' (2001: 207).

From the perspectives of these children, the early morning light; a spider's web; the shapes of leaves; a caterpillar and a snail; reflections on the window-pane; and stones under bare feet are just some of the ordinary everyday elements that are looked upon anew in the first pages of Woolf's novel. Later, as the group of friends, who are now in their early twenties, come together to farewell Percival as he leaves for India, Neville refers to their shared childhood as '"The furtive days of secrecy and hiding, the revelations on staircases, moments of terror and ecstasy"' (*TW*: 93). Neville's description inspires each of these friends to provide examples of such moments, which include both the uplifting and the horrifying:

> 'Old Mrs. Constable lifted her sponge and warmth poured over us,' said Bernard. 'We became clothed in this changing, this feeling garment of flesh.'
> 'The boot-boy made love to the scullery-maid in the kitchen garden,' said Susan, 'among the blown-out washing.'
> 'The breath of the wind was like a tiger panting,' said Rhoda.
> 'The man lay livid with his throat cut in the gutter,' said Neville. 'And going upstairs I could not raise my foot against the immitigable apple tree with its silver leaves held stiff.'
> 'The leaf danced in the hedge without anyone to blow it,' said Jinny.
> 'In the sun-baked corner,' said Louis, 'the petals swam on depths of green.'
> 'At Elvedon the gardeners swept and swept with their great brooms, and the woman sat at a table writing,' said Bernard.
> 'From these close-furled balls of string we draw now every filament,' said Louis, 'remembering, when we meet.' (*TW*: 93)

For these characters, the epiphanal moments of childhood are inspired by the most quotidian of events, which come to be viewed through a sudden heightened awareness and openness to the world. Reinforcing the individual's inherent temporality, such moments provide the foundations and web-like strands from which not only the self and Other come to be inherently connected, but so too the past, present and future. Indeed, as discussed in the previous chapter, such an approach to time is a defining characteristic of Woolf's writings.

As one reads Woolf's autobiographical writings, particularly her memoirs, it is clear that she views her own childhood as fertile ground for the various moments of revelation that never ceased to affect and influence her sense of Being-in-the-world. In 'A Sketch of the Past', for instance, Woolf relates her two earliest recollections of such moments, observing that 'each was very simple'. Describing her immediate impressions during these moments, Woolf writes:

> I am hardly aware of myself, but only of the sensation. I am only the container of the feeling of ecstasy, of the feeling of rapture. Perhaps this is characteristic of all childhood memories; perhaps it accounts for their strength. Later we add to feelings much that makes them more complex; and therefore less strong; or if not less strong, less isolated, less complete. ('Sketch': 81)[6]

Juxtaposing everyday non-Being with moments of Being, Woolf describes her childhood experiences during the summers she spent at the family's holiday house in St Ives, Cornwall. Drawing a distinction between the responses and receptiveness of adults and children to 'exceptional moments', Woolf writes:

> As a child then, my days, just as they do now, contained a large proportion of this cotton wool, this non-being. Week after week passed at St Ives and nothing made any dint upon me. Then, for no reason that I know about, there was a sudden violent shock; something happened so violently that I have remembered it all my life . . . I only know that many of these exceptional moments brought with them a peculiar horror and a physical collapse; they seemed dominant; myself passive. This suggests that as one gets older one has a greater power through reason to provide an explanation; and that this explanation blunts the sledgehammer force of the blow. I think this is true, because though I still have the peculiarity that I receive these sudden shocks, they are now always welcome; after the first surprise, I always feel instantly that they are particularly valuable. ('Sketch': 84, 85)

Demonstrating the varied nature of the epiphanal moment, Woolf presents three instances of such childhood experiences in 'A Sketch of the Past', only one of which is cast in a positive light, in the sense that it results in a sense of 'discovery' and 'satisfaction'. In contrast, the remaining moments that Woolf refers to are conveyed as 'violent moments of being' ('Sketch': 84, 85, 91).[7] The first of these moments occurs when Woolf comes to blows with her brother, Thoby:

> We were pommelling each other with our fists. Just as I raised my fist to hit him, I felt: why hurt another person? I remember the feeling. It was a feeling of hopeless sadness. It was as if I became aware of something terrible; and of my own powerlessness. ('Sketch': 84)

The second violent epiphanal moment is triggered when Woolf overhears the news of the suicide of a former St Ives guest, Mr Valpy; as she wanders in her garden that evening, Woolf finds herself before an apple tree: 'I could not pass it. I stood there looking at the grey-green creases of the bark ... in a trance of horror' ('Sketch': 84). As Woolf's personal accounts reflect, while the epiphanal moment is often viewed as a positive and uplifting disclosure and manifestation of that which ordinarily goes unseen, such moments can also be negative and unwelcome, consisting of what Robert Langbaum terms, 'insights into the abyss' (1983: 339).

In her detailed discussion of Woolf's moments of Being, Karen Schiff draws attention to the writer's repeated reference to the violence of her experiences. In order to account for such an emphasis, Schiff turns her attention to Woolf's essay, 'De Quincey's Autobiography'; likening Woolf's 'violent moments of being' to De Quincey's discussion of the autobiographer's capacity 'to pierce the haze which so often develops' (Woolf 1986a: 135), Schiff writes:

> The word 'piercing' indicates violation of a barrier; the haze is like a veil of protection that gets abruptly broken.
> An abrupt piercing creates a conduit between one's consciousness and the outside. It builds a perceptual bridge at the same time that it violates a protective barrier. (1997: 181)

As Woolf's memoir demonstrates, any 'piercing' of the cotton wool of the everyday, which typically covers over what is ordinarily concealed, has the potential to overwhelm the individual with a sense of shock and vulnerability that can be characterised as violent in nature.

Such a perspective is expressed by Woolf in her 1918 review entitled 'Moments of Vision', where she writes that such moments can be at times 'almost menacing with meaning' (1965: 75). Referring to Woolf's essay, Jane Goldman states that Woolf's 'phrase "menacing with meaning" has not survived into the common lexis of debate: rather, the Woolfian moment is considered a moment of pure being, a mystical experience beyond the everyday, beyond history, and beyond meaning' (1998: 1). Such widely held views of Woolf's textual approach to moments of Being are clearly at odds with that conveyed in her 1929 essay, 'The Moment: Summer's Night', where the writer describes a brutal scene of domestic violence and poverty that is firmly grounded in the everyday:

The moment runs like quicksilver on a sloping board into the cottage parlour ... Liz comes in and John catches her a blow on the side of her head as she slopes past him, dirty, with her hair loose and one hairpin sticking out about to fall. And she moans in a chronic animal way; and the children look up ... Let us do something then, something to end this horrible moment, this plausible glistening moment that reflects in its smooth sides this intolerable kitchen, this squalor; this woman moaning; and the rattle of the toy on the flags, and the man munching. Let us smash it by breaking a match. There – snap. (1981c: 12)

In her reading of this passage, Goldman asserts that 'Woolf exposes a moment of illumination as also one of oppression' (1998: 5). As Woolf emphasises in her childhood accounts of those moments of Being that result in the disclosure of the violent and the overwhelming, such experiences are of value in that they provide a view of reality that typically goes unseen, unknown and therefore unchallenged. Such an understanding is conveyed through Goldman's observations concerning Woolf's political critique in this essay, where she surmises that 'In advocating the smashing of this "horrible moment" of illumination, Woolf seems also to advocate the rupture of the oppressive social and familial relations it brings' (1998: 5).

Acknowledging those moments of Being that have been a defining feature of her life from early childhood, the 57-year-old Woolf remarks: 'I go on to suppose that the shock-receiving capacity is what makes me a writer. I hazard the explanation that a shock is at once in my case followed by the desire to explain it' ('Sketch': 85). Such a view is akin to that of Romantics such as Wordsworth, who attest that the poet is uniquely equipped to experience the epiphanal moment, since such an individual 'is somehow more attuned than the ordinary person to what he sees, that his gaze is qualitatively different, better' (Covey 1995: 143). From the perspectives of Woolf and Wordsworth, the artist becomes a site in which the authentic moment comes to be both realised and potentially expressed.

In his discussion of *To the Lighthouse,* Beja observes that it is the artist Lily Briscoe who experiences the greatest number of moments of vision, 'for as an artist she is peculiarly sensitive to sudden spiritual manifestations' (1971: 144). Describing her own writing process, Woolf reflects upon the inherent connection between art and epiphany, suggesting that

> there is a pattern hid behind the cotton wool. And this conception affects me every day. I prove this, now, by spending the morning writing, when I might be walking, running a shop, or learning to do something that will be useful if war comes. I feel that by writing I am doing what is far more necessary than anything else. ('Sketch': 85–6)

In his 1936 essay, 'The Origin of the Work of Art', Heidegger emphasises the connection between art and the epiphanal moment, asserting that 'art breaks open an open place, in whose openness everything is other than usual' (2002b: 197); that is, a site where the ordinary is defamiliarised and seen afresh. Such a perspective is highlighted nine years earlier – during the same year that *Being and Time* was published – in Heidegger's Marburg lecture course, *The Basic Problems of Phenomenology,* where he suggests that: 'Poetry, creative literature, is nothing but the elementary emergence into words, the becoming-uncovered, of existence as being-in-the-world' (1982: 171–2). In keeping with both Woolf and Wordsworth's approaches, Julian Young explains that in this lecture series, Heidegger also asserts that 'It takes the "original" eye of the artist to "thematize", to render "expressly visible", that of which we are, in our "average everydayness", unaware'. For Woolf, Wordsworth and Heidegger, art reveals and explains 'a world *which is already in existence*' (Young 2001: 33). For Heidegger, the German Romantic poet Friedrich Hölderlin (1770–1843) epitomises the ideal of the artist whose work reveals the extraordinary nature of that which lies concealed in the midst of average everydayness.[8]

The understanding of art as an impetus and trigger for moments of vision is granted fictional form by Woolf in *The Waves,* as the writer, Bernard, makes his way into an art gallery in order to feel the 'influence of minds like mine outside the sequence' (*TW*: 117). Desiring co-existence with the minds of those fellow artists who view and understand the world from a perspective that differs from the status quo, Bernard believes that art will allow him to 'find something unvisual beneath' (*TW*: 118). As he gazes at the work of Titian, Bernard becomes aware that

> 'something is added to my interpretation. Something lies deeply buried. For one moment I thought to grasp it. But bury it, bury it; let it breed, hidden in the depths of my mind some day to fructify. After a long lifetime, loosely, in a moment of revelation, I may lay hands on it, but now the idea breaks in my hand . . . I am glutted with sensations' (*TW*: 119)

Arguably, Woolf's use of the term 'fructify', which is employed in a similar context in Wordsworth's *Prelude*, signifies her desire to draw parallels between Bernard's moment of vision and Wordsworth's spots of time; for both Wordsworth and the character, Bernard, this term signifies their shared understanding that such moments of Being, while not always immediately grasped or understood, possess the potential to bear a fruit that will in time reveal that which is presently concealed from view and comprehension.

'Madness' and illness

During a self-described bout of depression in 1932, Woolf writes of the artist's need and propensity to record his or her feelings, sensations, concerns and impressions as a means of attempting to make sense of his or her relationship to and with the world:

> Lord how I suffer! What a terrific capacity I possess for feeling with intensity . . . I'm screwed up into a ball; cant get into step; cant make things dance; feel awfully detached . . . All is surface hard; myself only an organ that takes blows, one after another; the horror of the hard raddled faces in the [Chelsea] flower show yesterday; the inane pointlessness of all this existence; hatred of my own brainlessness & indecision: the old treadmill feeling, of going on & on & on; for no reason . . . the hardness & competitiveness of life; no space which one can expand in & say Time stand still here . . . worst of all is this disjected barrenness . . . Shall I make a book out of this? It would be a way of bringing order & speed again into my world. (*D4*: 102–3)

In the midst of this particularly depressive state of mind, Woolf finds herself standing outside the everyday order, and in doing so, gains an alternative perspective of Being-in-the-world – albeit painful, detached and pessimistic.

Fredrik Svenaeus refers to Heidegger's philosophy in *Being and Time* as a means of exploring the ways in which the individual's state of physical and mental health impacts upon his or her experience of Being-in-the-world. Writing from a phenomenological perspective, Svenaeus rejects 'the dualistic cleavage of mind from body', asserting that 'Illness is never entirely "mental" or entirely "somatic", illness is unhomelike being-in-the-world of *Dasein* including both aspects as inter-nested' (2011: 336). Noting that Heidegger 'in fact never wrote anything substantial about health or illness' (2000a: 127), Svenaeus nevertheless asserts the validity of applying Heidegger's philosophy to the subject of illness, arguing that Heidegger's principal aim is to provide a '*general* understanding of the pattern of being-in-the-world, and not of different *particular*, everyday ways of being-in-the-world' (2000a: 125–6). Indeed, throughout this book, the approach to Heidegger's philosophy in *Being and Time* in relation to Woolf's textual approach to Being-in-the-world is based upon a similar proposition and foundation.

Sharing marked parallels with Woolf's recorded state of estrangement from the everyday in the diary entry above, Svenaeus explains that the individual struck by poor health often experiences a sense of life 'getting "out of tune"', so that 'where there was earlier a homelike attunement, there is now the growing despair of uncanniness' (2000b: 12). As detailed in the third chapter, the individual's authentic mode of Being is defined by a sense of not-Being-at-home in the world. Woolf's recorded personal experiences of mental illness are typified by a sense of being jolted out of the comfortable, unreflective home-like state that is characteristic of periods of good health, prompting her to look at the world anew.[9] As Woolf repeatedly emphasises in her personal writings, episodes of mental illness provide a foundation and impetus for her creativity, a perspective that is typified in a diary entry that directly follows the 1932 entry above: 'And now today suddenly the weight on my head is lifted . . . Perhaps this is the beginning of another spurt' (*D4*: 103).

While not attempting to trivialise the significant emotional and physical pain that Woolf experienced during her repeated bouts of mental illness – episodes that led to incapacitation, confinement, multiple suicide attempts and, ultimately, her untimely death in 1941 – it is clear that Woolf's state of mind during these periods of illness frequently provided a positive impetus in relation to both her ensuing literary creativity, and her experiences of moments of revelation and illumination. As Woolf observes in her 1919 diary: 'I always remember the saying that at one's lowest ebb one is nearest a true vision' (*D1*: 298). In a 1930 diary entry, Woolf provides a detailed and lengthy account of the effect of her illnesses upon her writing:

> Once or twice I have felt that odd whirr of wings in the head which comes when I am ill so often – last year for example, at this time I lay in bed constructing A Room of One's Own (which sold 10,000 two days ago). If I could stay in bed another fortnight (but there is no chance of that) I believe I should see the whole of The Waves . . . I believe these illnesses are in my case – how shall I express it? – partly mystical. Something happens in my mind. It refuses to go on registering impressions. It shuts itself up. It becomes chrysalis. I lie quite torpid, often with acute physical pain – as last year; only discomfort this. Then suddenly something springs. Two nights ago, Vita was here; & when she went, I began to feel the quality of the evening – how it was spring coming: a silver light; mixing with the early lamps; the cabs all rushing through the streets; I had a tremendous sense of life beginning; mixed with that emotion, which is the essence of my feeling, but escapes description . . . Well, as I was saying, between these long pauses (for I am swimmy in the head, & write rather to stabilise myself than to make a correct statement), I felt the spring beginning, & Vita's life so full & flush; & all the doors opening; & this is I believe the moth shaking its wings in me. I then begin to make up my story whatever it is; ideas rush in me; often though this is before I can control my mind or pen. (*D3*: 286–7)

Woolf's pronouncements provide a foundation for Lee's claim that through the writing process, Woolf 'transforms illness into a language of power and inspiration' (1996: 194). Woolf's description of the torpidity that is symptomatic of such bouts of mental illness might be likened to a state of hibernation, in that Woolf finds herself distanced from average everyday involvements, concerns and preoccupations. No longer immersed in the cotton wool of daily life, Woolf finds that such states of mind are succeeded by an abundant flow of creativity, as quotidian features, such as lamp light and 'cabs rushing through streets', come to excite and inspire.

The propensity for mental illness to result in a heightened awareness that rises above and beyond the everyday mode of perception is given fictional form in *Mrs Dalloway*, through Woolf's representation of the shell-shocked character, Septimus Smith. Mirroring Woolf's personal experience, a symptom of Septimus's 'madness' is his repeated access to that which normally goes unseen. Throughout this novel, Woolf not only calls into question whether those who are diagnosed as 'mad' are categorised as such due to their defiance of societal conventions and expectations, but also whether such individuals are in fact in possession of a truer grasp of reality than supposedly 'saner' members of society. As Septimus sits in Regent's Park, he experiences a moment of vision in which everyday experiences and objects become sites of truth and beauty:

> To watch a leaf quivering in the rush of air was an exquisite joy. Up in the sky swallows swooping, swerving, flinging themselves in and out, round and round, yet always with perfect control as if elastics held them; and the flies rising and falling; and the sun spotting now this leaf, now that, in mockery, dazzling it with soft gold in pure good temper; and now and again some chime (it might be a motor horn) tinkling divinely on the grass stalks – all of this, calm and reasonable as it was, made out of ordinary things as it was, was the truth now; beauty, that was the truth now. Beauty was everywhere. (*MD*: 69)

In *Being and Time*, Heidegger explains that 'What we indicate *ontologically* by the term "state-of-mind" is *ontically* the most familiar and everyday sort of thing; our mood, our Being-attuned' (*BT*: 172). In this passage, Septimus's attunement to the world through the sound of a motor horn is manifested in visual form, so that 'it cannoned from rock to rock, divided, met in shocks of sound which rose in smooth columns (that music should be visible was a discovery)' (*MD*: 68). Such an impression is symptomatic of the state of synaesthesia, a term that has its origin in the Greek '*syn* (union) plus aisthesia (sensation)' (Harrison and Baron-Cohen 1994: 343).[10] Nichols suggests that epiphanal moments 'often employ synesthesia because they strive to go beyond the categories imposed by the five senses' (1987: 59). In this novel, Woolf's representation of the capacity of Septimus Smith – who is condemned by society as insane – to experience such acute sensitivity to the world, can be viewed as a reflection of her own attitude to mental illness and its possibilities, potentialities and socially-defined limitations.

In her 1926 essay, 'On Being Ill', Woolf provides a detailed discussion of her understanding and approach to the relationship between illness and the individual's mode of Being-in-the-world. Drawing attention to the defamiliarising and disclosive effects of illness that are largely unavailable to those in good health, Woolf writes:

> how astonishing, when the lights of health go down, the undiscovered countries that are then disclosed, what wastes and deserts of the soul a slight attack of influenza brings to view, what precipices and lawns sprinkled with bright flowers a little rise of temperature reveals, what ancient and obdurate oaks are uprooted in us by the act of sickness . . . how the world has changed its shape; the tools of business grown remote; the sounds of festival become romantic like a merry-go-round heard across far fields; and friends have changed, some putting on a strange beauty, others deformed to the squatness of toads, while the whole landscape of life lies remote and fair. (1981e: 14, 16)

Capable of initiating and foregrounding both uplifting and depressive impressions, for Woolf, the effects of illness, not unlike that of moods, have the potential to colour all aspects of the individual's experience and view of the world – including one's relationship with the past – as priorities shift and a transformed view of reality emerges.

As her essay progresses, Woolf discusses her perception that illness redefines the individual's position within society, so that he or she comes to be viewed as an outsider:

> Directly the bed is called for . . . we cease to be soldiers in the army of the upright; we become deserters. They march to battle. We float with the sticks on the stream; helter-skelter with the dead leaves on the lawn, irresponsible and disinterested and able, perhaps for the first time for years, to look round, to look up – to look, for example, at the sky . . . This then has been going on all the time without our knowing it! (1981e: 18)

Clearly aligning her own position with that of the individual experiencing ill health, Woolf emphasises the benefit, albeit painfully experienced, of stepping outside the somnolence of average everydayness, so that the extraordinary nature of the ordinary comes to be revealed. Here, as elsewhere in her writings, Woolf assigns positive attributes to the societal outsider who is privy to a perspective that is unattainable by the individual who is so immersed in the activities, expectations and preoccupations of everyday life, that he or she has neither the time nor the presence of mind to question or acknowledge his or her mode of Being-in-the-world.

In 'On Being Ill', Woolf observes that

> All day, all night the body intervenes; blunts or sharpens, colours or discolours, turns to wax in the warmth of June, hardens to tallow in the murk of February. The creature within can only gaze through the pane – smudged or rosy; it cannot separate off from the body like the sheath of a knife or the pod of a pea for a single instant. (1981e: 14–15)

Such pronouncements highlight Woolf's understanding of embodiment as a defining element of the individual's mode of Being-in-the-world. Woolf indicates that those individuals experiencing good health tend to remain largely unaware of their essential embodiment; in contrast, during bouts of illness, the body's vulnerability is inescapably foregrounded, alongside one's ultimate and inevitable state of Being-towards-death. As Woolf explains, 'It is only the recumbent who know what, after all, Nature is at no pains to conceal – that she in the end will conquer' (1981e: 19).[11] As discussed in the previous chapter, for both Woolf and Heidegger, it is only when the individual is mindful that every moment could be his or her last that a state of attentiveness is achieved, in which the decisions that he or she makes are granted particular consideration and significance.

Anxiety and nothingness

In *Being and Time,* Heidegger asserts that the individual's awareness of his or her inevitable finitude is brought to the fore through the mood of *Angst,* or 'anxiety', insofar as this state of mind 'arises out of Being-in-the-world as thrown Being-towards-death' (*BT*: 395). Through a conscious acknowledgement of one's unavoidable state of Being-towards-death, an awareness is awakened that provides the individual with the potential to see through and past his or her immersion in average everyday concerns. As Heidegger states, the mood of anxiety liberates the individual '*from* possibilities which "count for nothing" ["nichtigen"], and lets him become free *for* those which are authentic' (*BT*: 395). Hubert L. Dreyfus remarks that, from the perspective of the individual experiencing the mood of anxiety: 'Social action now appears as a game which there is no point in playing since it has no intrinsic meaning' (1991: 180).

Such a point of view is apparent in *Mrs Dalloway*, where the character Septimus Smith is overwhelmed by the perception that 'it might be possible that the world itself is without meaning' (*MD*: 88). Prior to his engagement in the First World War, Septimus strives to carry out and fulfil the expectations, actions and achievements that are most valued by English society during the first half of the twentieth century. This young man not only possesses a love of Shakespeare, and seeks career advancement; he also voluntarily enlists in the armed forces in order to defend his nation. Yet, despite the war medals that he earns, and the public fulfilment of 'duty' to his country, such achievements, when laid bare, appear without sense or meaning to an individual who has been repeatedly faced with the unavoidable reality of both his own and others' inevitable state of Being-towards-death.

Heidegger explains that only certain moods, including that of anxiety, provide the individual with the potential to question his or her everyday mode of Being-in-the-world through a moment of vision. As the philosopher emphasises, 'Anxiety merely brings one into the mood for a *possible* resolution. The Present of anxiety holds the moment of vision *at the ready*' (*BT*: 394). In his 1929 lecture, 'What is Metaphysics?', Heidegger observes that

> Original anxiety can awaken in existence at any moment. It needs no unusual event to rouse it. Its sway is as thoroughgoing as its possible occasionings are trivial. It is always ready, though it only seldom springs, and we are snatched away and left hanging. (2002d: 106)

Like the epiphanal moment, the mood of anxiety emerges unbidden, triggered suddenly and unexpectedly by ordinary and unexceptional everyday happenings and circumstances. Referring to the moments of Being contained in Woolf's 'A Sketch of the Past', Lee observes that 'the moments themselves happen "without any effort", as though an alchemical conversion were taking place of its own volition. Something solid or opaque or impenetrable is changed into something "transparent": something shadowed or dormant is "quickened" or "intensified"' (1984: 13).

Heidegger observes that 'Anxiety "does not know" what that in the face of which it is anxious is' (*BT*: 231). Such indeterminacy is reflected in *The Voyage Out* as Helen Ambrose travels on an expedition along a river in South America:

> inwardly she was a prey to an uneasy mood not readily to be ascribed to any one cause . . . She did not like to feel herself the victim of unclassified emotions, and certainly as the launch slipped on and on, in the hot morning sun, she felt herself unreasonably moved. Whether the unfamiliarity of the forest was the cause of it, or something less definite, she could not determine. (*VO*: 324)

A similar sense of inexplicable unease is imparted by Woolf from a personal perspective in a diary entry recorded in March 1937:

> I wish I could write out my sensations at this moment. They are so peculiar & so unpleasant . . . A physical feeling as if I were drumming slightly in the veins: very cold: impotent: & terrified. As if I were exposed on a high ledge in full light. Very lonely . . . Very useless. No atmosphere round me. No words. Very apprehensive . . . And I am powerless to ward it off: I have no protection. And this anxiety & nothingness surround me with a vacuum . . . And I want to burst into tears, but have nothing to cry for . . . And I know that I must go on doing this dance on hot bricks till I die. This is a little superficial I admit. For I can burrow under & look at myself displayed in this ridiculous way & feel complete submarine calm: a kind of calm moreover which is strong eno' to lift the entire load: I can get that at moments; but the exposed moments are terrifying. (*D5*: 63)

In this passage, Woolf refers twice to a sense of being 'exposed' while under the sway of what she terms a 'sensation'. In this state of mind, Woolf feels that she has been placed in the uncomfortable, and even terrifying, position of being physically, emotionally and spiritually naked, as the average everyday pretences, habits and fabrications are cast aside, leaving her vulnerable and without 'protection'. Just as Heidegger suggests that 'Anxiety robs us of speech' (2002d: 101), Woolf is robbed of words to describe an experience that language appears unable to express or explain. In keeping with Heidegger's claim that in the midst of this mood one does not know what one is anxious about, Woolf is overcome by the sense that she has 'nothing to cry for'.

The notion of 'nothing' or 'nothingness' that Woolf refers to in her diary entry can be equated with Heidegger's statement in *Being and Time* that 'The "nothing" with which anxiety brings us face to face, unveils the nullity by which Dasein, in its very *basis*, is defined; and this basis itself is as thrownness into death' (*BT*: 356). Ruotolo outlines the affinities between Woolf's literary and Heidegger's philosophical engagements with nothingness in *Six Existential Heroes: The Politics of Faith* (1973) and *The Interrupted Moment: A View of Virginia Woolf's Novels* (1986). Moore also draws brief parallels between Woolf and Heidegger's sense of nothingness (1980); while Lackey notes that: 'In the first half of the twentieth century, modernist writers and post-Husserlian phenomenologists commonly ontologized nothingness' (2000: 350).

Reflecting Heidegger's proclamation that nothingness 'unveils' the individual's Being-towards-death, in the interlude of *To the Lighthouse*, the 'nothing' that Woolf repeatedly refers to is representative of the deaths of Mrs Ramsay and her adult children, Prue and Andrew. As the surviving members of the family abandon the once-loved home, the motif of death as 'nothingness' becomes a ubiquitous presence:

> Nothing, it seemed, could survive the flood, the profusion of darkness . . . Sometimes a hand was raised as if to clutch something or ward off something, or somebody groaned, or somebody laughed aloud as if sharing a joke with nothingness.
> Nothing stirred in the drawing-room or in the dining-room or on the staircase. (*TL*: 119–20)[12]

Two years later, in a 1929 diary entry, Woolf reveals and explores the everyday propensity of the individual to cover over the 'nothing':

> And a sense of nothingness rolls about the house; what I call the sense of 'Where there is nothing.' This is due to the fact that we came back from France last night & are not going round in the mill yet. Time flaps on the mast – my own phrase I think. There are things I ought to do . . . I ought to write several dull silly letters; to gentlemen in Maidstone & Kingston who tell me facts about dahlias . . . But I cant – not for five minutes or so. Time flaps on the mast. And then I see through everything. Perhaps the image ought to have been one that gives an idea of a stream becoming thin: of seeing to the bottom. Lytton once said, – I connect it with a visit to Kew Gardens – that we can only live if we see through illusion . . . Now time must not flap on the mast any more. Now I must somehow brew another decoction of illusion . . . I must make human illusion – ask someone in tomorrow after dinner. (*D3*: 233, 234)

Hussey draws parallels between Woolf's notion of 'the nothing' in this diary entry and Heidegger's discussion of the nothing and anxiety in 'What is Metaphysics?' (1986: 162, n3); demonstrating parallels with Woolf's observations in her diary, Heidegger attests: 'That in the malaise of anxiety we often try to shatter the vacant stillness with compulsive talk only proves the presence of the nothing' (2002d: 101). As Woolf's account demonstrates, during the individual's immersion in the preoccupations of average everydayness, an awareness of the 'nothing' is typically concealed. Emphasised in this passage is the sense that the individual must distance him or herself from such concerns in order that the experience and reality of 'nothingness' might be felt and acknowledged, and with it, the moment of revelation in which one is able to 'see through everything' that was previously opaque. Woolf once again acknowledges that those moments in which one is capable of 'seeing to the bottom' possess an ephemeral quality, as the individual is inevitably beckoned back to average everydayness and the concerns and illusions that typically conceal the reality of his or her inevitable state of Being-towards-death.[13]

As noted, Woolf's depressive episodes often provided her with the potential for a heightened awareness and greater sense of clarity in terms of her view and understanding of the world. In a 1929 description of one such experience, Woolf emphasises the accompanying sense of nothingness, where all that society holds most valuable – work, family life, our 'relations with people' – is drained of meaning or purpose:

> And so I pitched into my great lake of melancholy. Lord how deep it is! What a born melancholiac I am! The only way I keep afloat is by working . . . Directly I stop working I feel that I am sinking down, down. And as usual, I feel that if I sink further I shall reach the truth. That is the only mitigation; a kind of nobility. Solemnity. I shall make myself face the fact that there is nothing – nothing for any of us. Work, reading, writing are all disguises; & relations with people. Yes, even having children would be useless. (*D3*: 235)

Apprehended through the mood of anxiety, for Woolf, the 'nothing' belongs to one and all. Nevertheless, as emphasised in the discussion of Being-towards-death in the previous chapter, such a truth is typically disguised by socially-defined priorities and values, which, ultimately, do nothing to alter the fact that the time each of us has on this earth is finite.

The sense that Woolf's state of anxiety allows her to come face to face with nothingness is reflected three years earlier in her 1926 diary, as she describes what she terms

> Intense depression: I have to confess that this has overcome me several times since September 6th (I think that, or thereabouts was the date.) It is so strange to me that I cannot get it right – the depression, I mean, which does not come from something definite, but from nothing. 'Where there is nothing' the phrase came <back> to me, as I sat at the table in the drawing room. (*D3*: 111)

As Gordon surmises, through such accounts of her experiences of depression, Woolf 'suggests that what a depressed intelligence sees may not be unrealistic, merely unendurable. In that state, we are awake, as Eliot shows in *The Waste Land*, to our customary oblivion' (2001: 55); that is, our Being-towards-death.

In contrast to those unbidden and unforeseen moments when the individual is overcome by the sense of nothingness that ensues in the mood of anxiety, throughout the various forms of her writings, Woolf also reflects upon the ways in which literal manifestations of death can result in moments of revelation. Just as the individual's acknowledgement of his or her inevitable state of Being-towards-death was described in the previous chapter as a means of authentically disclosing that individual's inherent temporality, so too does death become a means of revealing that which everydayness typically conceals. In *Mrs Dalloway*, Clarissa's immersion in theyness – epitomised by the society party that preoccupies this character throughout the novel – is severely disrupted as she hears the news of Septimus Smith's suicide:

> Oh! thought Clarissa, in the middle of my party, here's death . . . They went on living (she would have to go back; the rooms were still crowded; people kept on coming). They . . . they would grow old. A thing there was that mattered; a thing, wreathed about with chatter, defaced, obscured in her own life, let drop every day in corruption, lies, chatter. This he had preserved. Death was defiance. Death was an attempt to communicate, people feeling the impossibility of reaching the centre which, mystically, evaded them. (*MD*: 186, 187)

Foregrounded in this passage is Clarissa's sense that the significance of our inevitable finitude is something that is concealed, 'defaced' and 'obscured' in the midst of average everydayness. In her reading of Woolf's novel, Genevieve Lloyd suggests that, through Septimus's death, 'Clarissa, without herself dying, takes on . . . something of the perception of death as the background against which life becomes visible' (1993: 155). Nevertheless, as is characteristic of the fleeting nature of such moments of revelation, inevitably, Clarissa 'would have to go back' to her everyday inauthentic mode of Being-in-the-world.

Just as death triggers a moment of revelation in fictional form in *Mrs Dalloway,* in her memoir, 'A Sketch of the Past', Woolf emphasises the effect of her mother's death upon her own sense of Being-in-the-world. As Woolf writes:

> my mother's death unveiled and intensified; made me suddenly develop perceptions, as if a burning glass had been laid over what was shaded and dormant. Of course this quickening was spasmodic. But it was surprising – as if something were becoming visible without any effort. ('Sketch': 103)

In this account, Woolf draws attention to those moments of illumination that came to be embedded in a period in which 'a dark cloud settled over' ('Sketch': 104) the surviving family members. As her memoir suggests, for Woolf, the notion that death is a means of making visible that which was previously concealed, is a reality as opposed to an abstract theoretical proposition.

In terms of Woolf's fiction, the fifth section of her experimental novel, *The Waves,* provides a sustained examination of the potentially illuminating effects of death. Through the chapter's opening line: '"He is dead"' (*TW*: 114), the reader is immediately alerted to the fact that the effect of Percival's passing upon his surviving friends will be the focus of concern. Jackson draws parallels between Woolf's representation of death in the final chapter of *The Waves* and Heidegger's understanding of Being-towards-death, remarking that, 'Bernard's image of riding directly but ambivalently . . . toward the "indefinite certainty" of death brings him "*face to face* with the 'nothing' of the possible impossibility of [his] existence"' (1994: 159–60). Henke also marks the affinities between Heidegger's understanding of nothingness and Woolf's 1931 novel, in that 'Dread hangs on the edge of *The Waves,* ready to surge up and overwhelm the novel's characters' (1989: 461).

For Rhoda, the disclosive nature of death is made starkly apparent upon learning of Percival's untimely passing:

'Now I will walk down Oxford Street envisaging a world rent by lightening; I will look at oaks cracked asunder and red where the flowering branch has fallen ... Look now at what Percival has given me. Look at the street now that Percival is dead. The houses are lightly founded to be puffed over by a breath of air. Reckless and random the cars race and roar and hunt us to death like bloodhounds. I am alone in a hostile world' ... 'Percival, by his death, has made me this present, has revealed this terror.' (*TW*: 120–1)

Focalised from Rhoda's perspective, Woolf imparts an image of a world that is 'torn open' by the recognition of death; as Rhoda deliberately attempts to resume her everyday mode of Being-in-the-world through the immersion in the everydayness exemplified by the busy thoroughfare of Oxford Street, her focus is nevertheless drawn to an ensuing tear that grants a vision of a reality that ordinarily goes unseen. Rhoda's typical state of homelessness and detachment, as described in detail in the third chapter, is confirmed and reinforced. As Piotr Hoffman suggests, alongside the individual's recognition of his or her state of Being-towards-death, comes the realisation that the social world in which he or she exists can do nothing to provide protection against the inevitable future: 'this world *as a whole* proves to be unreliable. The tie between the individual and his public world is broken' (2011: 230). Signalled in Rhoda's response is her recognition of the inherent thrownness that defines Being-in-the-world – nothing is permanent, and death may have its way at any time.

Reacting to the death of his childhood friend, Bernard feels a need for 'silence, and to be alone and to go out, and to save one hour to consider what has happened to my world, what death has done to my world' (*TW*: 115). Newly awakened to the sights and experiences that Percival will never again behold, Bernard views the world afresh. Henke suggests that in the final section of *The Waves*, Bernard is faced with 'an ingenuous wonder at the ontological mystery revealed' (1989: 467), which arises as a result of his experience of Heideggerian nothingness. Yet, as discussed in the first chapter, and as indicative of the transient nature of the moment of vision, the everyday societal machine refuses to abdicate its influence for long, so that Bernard begins to yearn for the comfort of the everyday after the uncomfortable view of reality afforded by an immersion in nothingness: '"But now I want life round me, and books and little ornaments, and the usual sounds of tradesmen calling on which to pillow my head after this exhaustion, and shut my eyes after this revelation"' (*TW*: 120).

The mood of boredom

Reflecting Bernard's return to the everyday mode of Being-in-the-world, Heidegger asserts that when we choose a lifestyle in which 'we busy ourselves' in order to cover over the disclosive propensity of moods, we avoid the 'inner terror that every mystery carries with it and that gives Dasein its greatness' (*FC*: 164). In contrast to Bernard's response to the nothingness that an acknowledgement of one's Being-towards-death reveals, in her diary, Woolf discusses the value of immersing herself in those frightening moments of Being, where she is afforded a view of a reality that is unlike that experienced in everydayness. Woolf describes her tendency to find herself located in such moments during those periods when she is least preoccupied with everyday concerns and distractions, such as her writing, or the busy pace and abundant social engagements of London life. While staying at her countryside home in Rodmell during the summer of 1926, Woolf records the effect of such a suspension of her everyday involvement in the world, particularly the ensuing state of 'blankness' (*D3*: 111):

> it is always a question whether I wish to avoid these glooms. In part they are the result of getting away by oneself, & having a psychological interest which the usual state of working & enjoying lacks. These 9 weeks give one a plunge into deep waters; which is a little alarming, but full of interest. All the rest of the year one's (I daresay rightly) curbing & controlling this odd immeasurable soul. When it expands, though one is frightened & bored & gloomy, it is as I say to myself, awfully queer. There is an edge to it which I feel of great importance, once in a way. One goes down into the well & nothing protects one from the assault of truth. Down there I cant write or read; I exist however. I am. (*D3*: 112)

Further to this, two days later Woolf writes:

> I wished to add some remarks to this, on the mystical side of this solitude; how it is not oneself but something in the universe that one's left with. It is this that is frightening & exciting in the midst of my profound gloom, depression, boredom, whatever it is: One sees a fin passing far out. (*D3*: 113)

In both diary entries, Woolf refers to the notion of 'boredom', as she describes the uncomfortable sensation of descending beneath the average everyday view of the world to a truth that lies in wait to be noticed or revealed. In Woolf's second diary entry, this is clearly represented by the motif of a 'fin', which indicates the unsettling presence of the unseen. For Woolf, it is only when she is in a position to abandon the comfort of habitual life, and embrace instead the somewhat 'alarming' and 'frightening' experience of boredom, that such moments of revelation become a possibility.

Typically, boredom is accorded negative connotations; there is a common perception that boredom, or even the appearance of boredom, is a deficient mode of Being: one to be avoided at all costs. The individual's average everyday tendency to reject and evade boredom is represented in Woolf's earliest novel, *The Voyage Out*, as a party of English men and women embark upon a South American river expedition. As these individuals prepare to leave their boat, 'For protection against boredom, Helen put a book of memoirs beneath her arm, and Mrs Flushing her paint-box, and, thus equipped, they allowed themselves to be set on shore on the verge of the forest' (*VO*: 314). In *To the Lighthouse*, society's view of boredom as an undesirable mood that must be concealed is demonstrated as a number of the characters sit around the dining-room table conversing:

> Lily was listening; Mrs. Ramsay was listening; they were all listening. But already bored, Lily felt that something was lacking; Mr. Bankes felt that something was lacking. Pulling her shawl round her, Mrs. Ramsay felt that something was lacking. All of them bending themselves to listen thought, 'Pray heaven that the inside of my mind may not be exposed.' (*TL*: 87)

This socially-prescribed propensity to cover up one's experience of boredom is also made apparent in Woolf's 1922 memoir, 'Old Bloomsbury', as she recalls the numerous occasions when her eldest brother, George Duckworth, would compel his younger sisters to '"try not to look so bored"' (2002b: 52) as they accompanied him to various society gatherings.

In their introduction to the edited collection, *Essays on Boredom and Modernity*, Barbara Dalle Pezze and Carlo Salzani explain that 'the noun *boredom*' made its first appearance 'in the second half of the nineteenth century'; Pezze and Salzani suggest that the advent of this term was a result of 'A new social, economical and political reality' that 'engendered a new psychological situation which needed a new terminology and a new representation' (2009: 10). Although the experience of boredom was not new, as Thiele remarks, this particular state of mind 'achieved its notoriety only in modernity' (1997: 493). Elizabeth S. Goodstein provides a detailed account of the connections between boredom and modernity, observing that 'In the mid-nineteenth century, as industrialization and urbanization transformed the European landscape, the problem of boredom emerged as a mass phenomenon' (2005: 101).

In his 1929/30 lecture course, *The Fundamental Concepts of Metaphysics: World, Finitude, Solitude*, Heidegger (1995) provides an extensive analysis of boredom as a fundamental mood of world-disclosure. Reflecting upon the connections between Heidegger's emphasis upon the temporal nature of Dasein in *Being and Time*, and the philosopher's subsequent discussion of boredom, Matthew Boss explains that

> the metaphysical significance of boredom is that it gives us direct access of an extraordinary kind to the original phenomenon of time (temporality) rather than the more ordinary 'levelled down' sort. *Sein und Zeit*, motivated by the same metaphysical problems, contains its own investigation and conceptual clarification of temporality in which the principal phenomenon is that of death experienced in the mood of Angst . . . Of course, the analysis of boredom is not intended to be independent of this investigation or to replace it; on the contrary, if anything it presupposes the concepts that are first brought to light in *Sein und Zeit*. Rather than proceeding independently, the analysis of boredom represents *another* 'way' towards the elaboration of the question of being, just as *Sein und Zeit* itself is described as merely '*one*' way. (2009: 102)

Describing three types of boredom in his lecture series, Heidegger emphasises that only one of these might be understood as 'profound', insofar as it has the potential to initiate the individual's 'fundamental attunement' (*FC*: 132) to and with the world. Just as Woolf describes her sense that in the midst of the experience of boredom, 'There is an edge to it which I feel of great importance' (*D3*: 112), Heidegger states that profound boredom 'wishes to tell us something, and indeed not something arbitrary or contingent' and asserts that the attunement that is proffered by the mood of profound boredom is 'rooted in time – in the time that we ourselves are' (*FC*: 135, 133). In the midst of such a mood, the individual's usual attachment to the world and its concerns is disrupted so that one's immersion in the present or 'now' is replaced by the authentic temporality that consists of the co-existence of past, present and future. As Heidegger explains, profound boredom

> can take hold of us in an instant like a flash of lightning, and yet precisely in this instant the whole expanse of the entire time of Dasein is there and not at all specifically articulated or delimited according to past and future. Neither merely the present nor merely the past nor merely the future, nor indeed all these reckoned together – but rather their *unarticulated unity* in the simplicity of this unity of their horizon all at once. (*FC*: 148)

The propensity of profound boredom to disturb the individual's captivation by the present is reflected in Woolf's aforementioned 1926 diary entries detailing her experiences at Rodmell, where she is granted a glimpse of the reality that typically lies concealed by the average everyday preoccupations and prescriptions. In *Modernism, Feminism, and the Culture of Boredom*, Allison Pease devotes a chapter to a study of the 'multiple boredoms' depicted in Woolf's *The Voyage Out*. Pease suggests that 'Woolf presents boredom much in the way that Martin Heidegger described profound boredom' (2012: 101).

In contrast to profound boredom, Heidegger refers to a form of boredom that he terms 'becoming bored by something' (*FC*: 103). Unlike the effect of profound boredom, the individual who is under the sway of this type of boredom is well aware of the source of his or her state of mind: 'What bores us and is boring is quite specific, something with which we are acquainted' (*FC*: 108). Such a form of boredom is illustrated in *The Waves* as an elderly Bernard recalls his schoolboy days, where 'immense dullness would descend unbroken, monotonous. Nothing, nothing, nothing broke with its fin that leaden waste of waters. Nothing would happen to lift that weight of intolerable boredom. The terms went on' (*TW*: 189). In contrast to Woolf's reference to the motif of a fin in her 1926 diary entry, in this instance the fin represents continued concealment rather than disclosure, thereby indicating the absence of the moment of revelation, a deficiency that can be understood to define this type of boredom.[14] As Heidegger attests, such boredom fails to result in a moment of vision due to the individual's propensity to 'shout down the boredom by passing the time so that we *do not need to listen to it*' (*FC*: 136).

While profound boredom possesses the propensity to disclose to the individual his or her inherently temporal mode of Being-in-the-world, 'becoming bored by something' results in 'the sense of now-time, measurable with a clock' (Boss 2009: 98). Such a manifestation is evident in *To the Lighthouse*, as William Bankes sits at the Ramsays' dining table, musing that his time could be better spent:

> if he had been alone dinner would have been almost over now; he would have been free to work. Yes, he thought, it is a terrible waste of time . . . How trifling it all is, how boring it all is, he thought, compared with the other thing – work . . . What a waste of time it all was to be sure! (*TL*: 82)

As Heidegger suggests, in the midst of experiencing this type of boredom, the individual feels that he or she cannot escape, so that, as William Bankes's response attests, one becomes 'increasingly stuck with having to wait, which becomes less and less interesting and increasingly burdensome for us' (*FC*: 108).

Throughout her non-fictional writings, Woolf records her own propensity to become 'bored by' other individuals and particular social settings. Woolf's diaries frequently provide cutting testimonies to her personal experience and awareness of boredom at the hands of various individuals – famous and obscure – with whom she comes into contact. Such an encounter is described in a 1917 diary entry:

> I own that I sounded the very depths of boredom with Barbara. She gives out facts precisely as she received them – minute facts about governesses & houses. And no doubt of her own adequacy crosses her mind; all so nice, honest, sensible, how can there be a flaw? Indeed, one figures her nature as a flawless marble, impervious, unatmospheric. And the time passed; she missed her train; waited on for another – waited until 6.10; & we were to dine at 7 – & my evening fretted away without sensation, save of one standing under the drip of a water spout. (*D1*: 90)

In keeping with Heidegger's description of the symptoms of this type of boredom, in this passage Woolf emphasises her accumulating sense of frustration as she feels increasingly trapped in a situation where her heightened awareness of clock time results in an intense desire for time to pass more swiftly.

From a fictional perspective, in *Between the Acts*, the library of Pointz Hall becomes something of a monument to 'being bored by'; as Mrs Swithin enters this room, she muses that '"Books are the mirrors of the soul"' (*BA*: 12), to which the narrator wryly adds:

> In this case a tarnished, a spotted soul. For as the train took over three hours to reach this remote village in the very heart of England, no one ventured so long a journey, without staving off possible mind-hunger, without buying a book on a bookstall. Thus the mirror that reflected the soul sublime, reflected also the soul bored. (*BA*: 13)

As the responses of the train passengers suggest, in the midst of 'being bored by' the individual does all within his or her power to stave off this state of mind, which in this case consists of immersing him or herself in 'shilling shockers' (*BA*: 13).

In his lecture series, Heidegger describes a final type of boredom, understood as 'being bored with', which, unlike 'becoming bored by' (*FC*: 108), is not the result of a particular incident or person, but rather stems from 'a *slipping away, away from ourselves* toward whatever is happening' (*FC*: 118). As a means of illustrating this type of boredom, Heidegger describes a scenario that is reminiscent of various social scenes depicted by Woolf throughout her fiction, diaries, memoirs and letters:

> We have been invited out somewhere for the evening ... There we find the usual food and the usual table conversation, everything is not only very tasty, but tasteful as well. Afterward people sit together having a lively discussion, as they say, perhaps listening to music, having a chat, and things are witty and amusing. And already it is time to leave ... There is nothing at all to be found that might have been boring about this evening, neither the conversation, nor the people, nor the rooms. Thus we come home quite satisfied. We cast a quick glance at the work we interrupted this evening, make a rough assessment of things and look ahead to the next day – and then it comes: I was bored after all this evening. (*FC*: 109)

As this passage illustrates, this category of boredom arises as the individual becomes preoccupied by the present influences, concerns and conventions of average everydayness, so that an awareness of his or her temporal mode of Being-in-the-world comes to be concealed. As Heidegger explains: 'Entirely present for whatever is happening, we are cut off from our having-been and from our future' (*FC*: 124). As a result, unlike profound boredom, which provides the individual with the potential to become attuned to that which lies concealed by average everydayness through the moment of vision, 'being bored with' is defined by 'a *not wanting to listen*' (*FC*: 136).

The state of 'being bored with' is apparent in *Mrs Dalloway* through Woolf's representation of the marginal character, Lady Bradshaw, the wife of the Harley Street psychiatrist, Sir William Bradshaw:

> Fifteen years ago she had gone under. It was nothing you could put your finger on; there had been no scene, no snap; only the slow sinking, water-logged, of her will into his. Sweet was her smile, swift her submission; dinner in Harley Street, numbering eight or nine courses, feeding ten or fifteen guests of the professional classes, was smooth and urbane. Only as the evening wore on a very slight dullness, or uneasiness perhaps, a nervous twitch, fumble, stumble and confusion indicated, what it was really painful to believe – that the poor lady lied ... she cramped, squeezed, pared, pruned, drew back, peeped through: so that without knowing precisely what made the evening disagreeable, and caused this pressure on the top of the head ... disagreeable it was. (*MD*: 101)

As evidenced through Lady Bradshaw's mode of Being-in-the-world, this type of boredom arises as the individual's authentic sense of self becomes overshadowed and concealed through his or her preoccupation with the concerns of the present. Just as Lady Bradshaw unconsciously experiences a 'nervous twitch' while acting as hostess, so too does Heidegger describe the 'repeated, though suppressed yawning' (*FC*: 110) of the bored individual at the dinner party.[15]

Lady Bradshaw's immersion in the conventions of the everyday results in a sense of disillusionment and a mode of Being that distances this woman from her 'proper self' (*FC*: 120); as Heidegger attests, at social gatherings such as those described:

> We go along with things, we *chat* away, perhaps for some restful relaxation. Yet precisely our seeking nothing more from the evening is what is decisive about our comportment. With this 'seeking nothing more' something is *obstructed* in us. In this chatting along with whatever is happening we have, not wrongly or to our detriment, but legitimately,

left our proper self behind in a certain way. In this seeking nothing further here, which is self-evident for us, we *slip away* from ourselves in a certain manner . . . In this casualness of *leaving ourselves behind in abandoning ourselves* to whatever there is going on, *an emptiness can form.* (FC: 119)

The characteristic of 'seeking nothing more' – a phrase that is repeated three times in this passage – can clearly be understood as the antithesis of profound boredom's propensity to uncover and reveal that which is hidden from the individual's average everyday view and understanding.

The wonder of Being-in-the-world

The desire to 'seek more' in order to uncover that which has ordinarily gone unseen is given literal and figurative representation in Woolf's 'A Sketch of the Past', as she refers to a particular childhood experience that culminates in a moment of Being:

> I was looking at the flower bed by the front door; 'That is the whole', I said. I was looking at a plant with a spread of leaves; and it seemed suddenly plain that the flower itself was a part of the earth; that a ring enclosed what was the flower; and that was the real flower; part earth; part flower . . . I felt that I had made a discovery. ('Sketch': 84)

In keeping with Woolf's use of the motif of the fin, in this instance, Woolf's revelation consists of an awareness of the inherent connections that exist between the visible and the unseen, that is, the flower and the earth. This autobiographical moment is granted fictional representation in *Between the Acts*, as young George Oliver plays in the garden:

> The little boy had lagged and was grouting in the grass . . . George grubbed. The flower blazed between the angles of the roots. Membrane after membrane was torn. It blazed a soft yellow, a lambent light under a film of velvet; it filled the caverns behind the eyes with light. All that inner darkness became a hall, leaf smelling, earth smelling, of yellow light. And the tree was beyond the flower; the grass, the flower and the tree were entire. Down on his knees grubbing he held the flower complete. (*BA*: 9–10)

In a moment of Romantic childhood wonder, George's 'grubbing' reflects his desire to uncover the whole, the root, 'the flower complete.' As R. W. Hepburn suggests, such a sense of 'wonder can stimulate a person to enquiry: it may be intensified when the enquiry succeeds and the enigmatic in nature becomes intelligible' (1980: 2). While George is ultimately forced to abandon his discovery – '"Leave off grubbing"' (*BA*: 9), cries his nurse – not unlike Hepburn's observation, in her memoir, Woolf feels she has made a 'discovery' upon her comprehension of the plant as a whole. For Woolf, the pursuit of further discovery of that which is typically concealed becomes a principal motivating force throughout both her private life and her writings.

Such a sense of discovery and child-like wonder in the midst of the everyday is emphasised in Woolf's 1920 short story 'Solid Objects', which begins as two adult friends, John and Charles, sit on a beach. As they converse, John absentmindedly

> began burrowing his fingers down, down, into the sand. As his hand went further and further beyond the wrist, so that he had to hitch his sleeve a little higher, his eyes lost their intensity, or rather the background of thought and experience which gives an inscrutable depth to the eyes of grown people disappeared, leaving only the clear transparent surface, expressing nothing but wonder, which the eyes of young children display. (1989c: 102–3)

Upon his find of a 'lump of glass', John becomes increasingly intoxicated by the unknown qualities that lie hidden within the ordinary and everyday. Eventually foregoing his political career, John embarks on a full-time quest in search of the wonder of discarded objects, finding himself 'often astonished . . . by the immense variety of shapes to be found in London alone, and there was still more cause for wonder and speculation in the differences of qualities and designs' (1989c: 105).

In her examination of the etymological origins of the word 'wonder', Mary-Jane Rubenstein discovers a possible connection between its conventional meaning, and that of a '*wound*' (2011: 9). Emphasising characteristics that are in keeping with the epiphanal moment, Rubenstein posits the notion that wonder, in a sense, wounds the everyday, in that this state of mind opens up this site, revealing that which lies typically unseen. Nevertheless, also like both a wound and the epiphanal moment, wonder is transient, inevitably closing and fading (2011: 10). Such an understanding of wonder can be applied to Woolf's fictional and non-fictional representations of moments of Being, which have the potential to shatter or wound the average everyday mode of Being-in-the-world. Like the mood of anxiety, that which wonder most disrupts is our understanding of the everyday and the ordinary through its transformation of the 'wonderer's relationship to *this* unusually usual world, revealing the extraordinary *through* the ordinary, precisely by revealing the ordinary as extraordinarily strange' (Rubenstein 2006: 16).

In his 1937–8 Freiburg lectures, published as *Basic Questions of Philosophy: Selected 'Problems' of 'Logic,'* Heidegger states that, from the perspective of the early Greeks, the 'origin of philosophy' is in fact 'wonder' (1994: 135). In contrast to his suggestion that the mood of boredom is representative of the age of modernity, Heidegger asserts that the mood of wonder is lost in this age, having been replaced by curiosity (1994: 135). In *Being and Time*, Heidegger briefly refers to the mood of wonder, emphasising that it must not be conflated with curiosity, since

> Curiosity has nothing to do with observing entities and marveling at them – θαυμάζειν [wonder]. To be amazed to the point of not understanding is something in which it has no interest. Rather it concerns itself with a kind of knowing, but just in order to have known. (*BT*: 216–17)

As Brad Elliott Stone explains, the propensity of modernity to reify curiosity instead of wonder is grounded upon a privileging of present concerns and preoccupations at the expense of the individual's authentic temporality (2006: 222).

Towards the end of *The Waves*, an aged Bernard experiences and defines the mood of wonder as that which is no longer tempered by curiosity:

> When I look down from this transcendency, how beautiful are even the crumbled relics of bread! What shapely spirals the peelings of pears make – how thin, and mottled like some sea-bird's egg. Even the forks laid straight side by side appear lucid, logical, exact; and the horns of the rolls which we have left are glazed, yellow-plated, hard. I could worship my hand even, with its fan of bones laced by blue mysterious veins and its astonishing look of aptness, suppleness and ability to curl softly or suddenly crush . . .

> Immeasurably receptive, holding everything, trembling with fullness, yet clear, contained – so my being seems, now that desire urges it no more out and away; now that curiosity no longer dyes it a thousand colours. (*TW*: 223–4)

As evidenced in this passage, Bernard's musings are representative of the notion that '*Wonder opens up a space, a clearing [a* Lichtung] *in which beings reveal their be-ing*' (Stone 2006: 213). In keeping with the mood of wonder, and in contrast to curiosity, Bernard does not attempt to reach definitive understandings or conclusions regarding that which fascinates; rather, reflecting the authentic mode of Being-in-the-world that arises from this mood, Bernard possesses a pure openness to that which surrounds him.

Drawing attention to the affinities between Woolf's treatment of wonder and Heidegger's notion of '*Thaumazein*', Hussey suggests that 'Wonder at simply being at all is the starting point of Woolf's exploration of the human situation' (1986: xv, 100).[16] As a means of demonstrating such a preoccupation, Hussey refers to a passage from Woolf's first novel, *The Voyage Out,* where, having spent the morning reading, and with her mind 'contracting and expanding', the young protagonist, Rachel Vinrace

> was next overcome by the unspeakable queerness of the fact that she should be sitting in an armchair, in the morning, in the middle of the world. Who were the people moving in the house – moving things from one place to another? And life, what was that? It was only a light passing over the surface and vanishing, as in time she would vanish ... Her dissolution became so complete that she could not raise her finger any more, and sat perfectly still, listening and looking always at the same spot. It became stranger and stranger. She was overcome with awe that things should exist at all. (*VO*: 138–9)[17]

In keeping with Bernard's response to the mood of wonder, Rachel is content to pose questions without necessarily expecting answers. Notably, it is while sitting 'perfectly still' that Rachel, in a sense, absents herself from the hectic distractions of the everyday, so that the extraordinary located within the ordinary might shine forth and be revealed.

In *To the Lighthouse*, a sense of wonder at the extraordinary nature of the ordinary is evoked as Lily Briscoe attempts to finish the painting that was begun years earlier:

> Her mood was coming back to her . . . One wanted, she thought, dipping her brush deliberately, to be on a level with ordinary experience, to feel simply that's a chair, that's a table, and yet at the same time, It's a miracle, it's an ecstasy. (*TL*: 191–2)

Hussey states that in this passage, 'Lily finally reveals the ecstasy of the ordinary' (2001: 46); while Sim suggests that 'Lily's desire for a dual mode of apprehending the world, as familiar and ordinary, yet also extraordinary and ecstatic, informs much of Woolf's thought and writing' (2010: 13). For both Lily and Rachel Vinrace, art provides a trigger for the mood of wonder: literature and the visual arts each proffers a window through which the ordinary might potentially be seen anew, not only by the artist, but also by the individual who comes into contact with the work. Such an understanding is demonstrated as Rachel finishes her reading of Henrik Ibsen's work in *The Voyage Out*:

> she shut the book sharply, lay back, and drew a deep breath, expressive of the wonder which always marks the transition from the imaginary world to the real world.
> 'What I want to know,' she said aloud, 'is this: What is the truth? What's the truth of it all?' (*VO*: 136)

Reflecting Heidegger's pronouncement that 'Only on the ground of wonder – the revelation of the nothing – does the "why?" loom before us' (2002d: 109), Rachel's response reflects the conflation of wonder and the epiphanal moment, in that both allow the individual a glimpse of the truth that typically goes unseen in the average everyday mode of Being-in-the-world.

The numinous

In her 1919 essay, 'Reading', Woolf describes the insatiable sense of wonder and imagination possessed by the author and physician, Sir Thomas Browne (1605–82):

> Strange beyond belief are the capacities that he detects in himself, profound the meditation into which the commonest sight will plunge him, while the rest of the world passes by and sees nothing to wonder at. The

> tavern music, the Ave Mary Bell, the broken pot that the workman has dug out of the field – at the sight and sound of them he stops dead, as if transfixed by the astonishing vista. (1981f: 160)

Reflecting upon Browne's heightened openness and receptiveness to those moments of revelation that arise when ordinary events and objects are experienced and perceived in the mood of wonder, Woolf proceeds to draw attention to a particular obstacle that inhibits and compromises Browne's abundant capacity to experience such a mode of Being:

> What, one asks, as considerations accumulate, is ever to stop the course of such a mind, unroofed and open to the sky? Unfortunately, there was the Deity. His faith shut in his horizon. Sir Thomas himself resolutely drew that blind. His desire for knowledge, his eager ingenuity, his anticipations of truth, must submit, shut their eyes, and go to sleep. Doubts he calls them. (1981f: 159)

Implicit in Woolf's description of Browne's relationship to God is her sense that such a belief system is fundamentally at odds with the mood of wonder, which is grounded upon inexplicable awe, rather than defined faith. The sense of an inherent tension between faith and wonder is also implied in Thiele's discussion of Heidegger's approach to religious faith, where he writes: 'If Heidegger encourages atheism, it is not to promote a disbelief in God . . . but as a means of remaining oriented in awe to that which is unknown, escapes comprehension, and marks our horizon' (1995: 207).[18]

Such a sense of the incommensurable relationship between faith and an openness to that which defies definitive understanding, is reflected in Woolf's *Orlando,* where she equates organised religion with the concealment of revelation and truth. As the promiscuous and recently male-turned-female Orlando lies upon a bed in a coma-like state, the spectral figures of the Ladies of Purity, Chastity and Modesty enter the room. That this trio can be understood as representative of Christian edicts is reflected in the 1815 writings of John Mannock, who warns those of the faith 'to ornament the whole man, both body and soul, with *purity, chastity, modesty*; which may prepare you for the enjoyment of God, and the company of his angels, pure spirits' (1815: 300 – my emphasis). In contrast with the 'austere Gods' of 'Truth, Candour, and Honesty' in *Orlando,* who call for 'The Truth and nothing but the truth!'

(O: 95) in terms of the clarification of Orlando's unconventional and ambiguous condition, the Ladies of Purity, Chastity and Modesty hysterically demand

> 'Truth come not out from your horrid den. Hide deeper, fearful Truth. For you flaunt in the brutal gaze of the sun things that were better unknown and undone; you unveil the shameful; the dark you make clear, Hide! Hide! Hide!' (O: 96)

As 'Truth' finally triumphs over the dictates of Purity, Chastity and Modesty, the three Ladies protest and wail as they take their leave, desperate to seek out the faithful in the form of

> those who honour us . . . those who prohibit; those who deny; those who reverence without knowing why; those who praise without understanding . . . who prefer to see not; desire to know not; love the darkness; those who still worship us. (O: 97)

As such proclamations emphasise, those who possess such faith are defined as blind, unquestioning and unknowing. Such a stance is indicative of Woolf's own perspective as an agnostic, in that, throughout both her non-fiction and fictional writings, she repeatedly calls into question the structures, implications and effects of organised religion.

Despite Woolf's personal and textual critiques of religion, Woolf's moments of Being are nevertheless frequently fundamentally spiritual in nature. In *The Singing of the Real World*, Hussey provides a sustained discussion of Woolf's understanding and treatment of 'reality', suggesting that it is characterised by a numinous quality. Hussey asserts that Woolf's sense of the numinous manifests itself in her writings through 'an abstract "gap" in actual life that cannot be directly referred to in language, but is certainly a potential experience of human being' (1986: 96).[19] The notion of the numinous has its origin in the work of the German theologian Rudolph Otto (1869–1937).[20] As Todd A. Gooch explains, Otto's understanding of the numinous is one that negates the typical association between holiness and morality (2000: 107). Otto characterises the holy as 'a mystery that inspires dread and fascination simultaneously' (Gooch 2000: 2): understood as a mystery, the numinous ultimately defies definition. As Gooch observes, Heidegger was familiar with Otto's work (2000: 107).

Beja notes that while Woolf frequently asks, 'What is meant by "reality"?' (1971: 115), she never reaches a conclusion that satisfies her own questioning, reflecting the intangible and ineffable nature of this notion. Hussey draws attention to a 1928 diary entry that goes some way towards illuminating the meaning of Woolf's 'reality' (1986: 34); recording her impressions during a stay at Monk's House in Rodmell, Woolf writes:

> Often down here I have entered into a sanctuary; a nunnery; had a religious retreat; of great agony once; & always some terror: so afraid one is of loneliness: of seeing to the bottom of the vessel. That is one of the experiences I have had here in some Augusts; & got then to a consciousness of what I call 'reality': a thing I see before me; something abstract . . . Reality I call it. And I fancy sometimes this is the most necessary thing to me: that which I seek . . . Now perhaps this is my gift; this perhaps is what distinguishes me from other people; I think it may be rare to have so acute a sense of something like that – but again, who knows? (*D3*: 196)

In this passage, Woolf emphasises her awareness of her own heightened perceptiveness, which is unique to the artist. Woolf's approach to Being-in-the-world is consistent with that reflected in her previously cited 1926 diary; in both instances, the act of immersing herself in the solitude of the countryside offers Woolf moments of vision that, while confronting, provide an alternative view of the world and reality. Rather than attempting to define this sense of reality in any absolute fashion, Woolf is satisfied to identify it as 'abstract'; through such an approach, the conventional notion of reality as that which is visible, tangible, explainable and easily accessible, is replaced by the understanding that reality shares those characteristics of the numinous that define it as difficult to grasp or define.

In 'A Sketch of the Past', Woolf writes: 'we are sealed vessels afloat upon what it is convenient to call reality; at some moments, without a reason, without an effort, the sealing matter cracks; in floods reality' ('Sketch': 145). For Woolf, numinous reality provides a showing-forth that challenges the surface impressions that are encountered in our everyday experiences. As Woolf's statement suggests, reality is not something that is created through moments of Being; rather, reality is always already present as it awaits discovery. Woolf's particular understanding of reality is explicitly addressed in *A Room of One's Own*, where she emphasises that it is through the seemingly unexceptional experiences of the everyday that the individual comes to be provided with the opportunity to uncover and glimpse the extraordinary:

> What is meant by 'reality'? It would seem to be something very erratic, very undependable – now to be found in a dusty road, now in a scrap of newspaper in the street, now a daffodil in the sun . . . It overwhelms one walking home beneath the stars and makes the silent world more real than the world of speech – and then there it is again in an omnibus in the uproar of Piccadilly . . . Now the writer, as I think, has the chance to live more than other people in the presence of this reality. It is his business to find it and collect it and communicate it to the rest of us. So at least I infer from reading *Lear* or *Emma* or *A la recherche du temps perdu*. For the reading of these books seems to perform a curious couching operation on the senses; one sees more intensely afterwards; the world seems bared of its covering and given an intenser life. (*RO*: 143–4)

Central to Woolf's description of reality in this passage is her emphasis once again upon the unique position of the writer as a conduit through which the underlying reality of Being-in-the-world might be both revealed and communicated.

Conclusion – writing the reality of Being-in-the-world

Neither Woolf's view that the writer is somehow more attuned to the underlying reality of Being, nor Heidegger's understanding in his later philosophy that '"truth happens awesomely" in great art' (Young 2001: 44), is new. As Julian Young attests, art has traditionally been considered a site through which the holy or numinous; that is, that which is ordinarily unintelligible and 'not part of visual experience' is revealed. The world, 'experienced in and through great art . . . becomes translucent', so that, 'Experienced as the self-disclosure of an unfathomable "mystery" it acquires radiance, becomes, as one might also say, numinous' (2001: 45).

Such a perspective is foregrounded in *To the Lighthouse*, where, as the novel draws towards its close, the artist, Lily Briscoe, raises her brush to her canvas and, in so doing, is

> drawn out of gossip, out of living, out of community with people into the presence of this formidable ancient enemy of hers – this other thing, this truth, this reality, which suddenly laid hands on her, emerged stark at the back of appearances and commanded her attention. (*TL*: 151)

In this passage, Woolf provides a compelling example of all that defines the moment of Being: in order to achieve such a state, the individual must transcend everyday preoccupations and prescriptions, so that the reality that ordinarily remains concealed might be revealed and encountered. For Woolf, great art is not only inspired and created through such moments, such art creates a force, however transient, which fractures one's average everyday inauthentic mode of Being-in-the-world. For Heidegger, such a sense of unveiling may be equated with the notion of *Ereignis*, which is understood as a site of unconcealed truth. Julian Young explains that, from Heidegger's perspective, 'to share in the poet's "epiphany" . . . his ecstatic experience of the holiness of the world . . . *is* the *Ereignis* experience' (2001: 107). Theodore Koulouris refers to the Heideggerian notion of '"Being", as an ontological trope which, for Woolf, can only be realizable in the act of "writing"' (2011: 205).[21] Arguably, through her position as a writer, Woolf is more readily able to convey to the 'common reader' her sense of reality than Heidegger as esoteric philosopher. Such a perspective is emphasised in David Cecil's letter to the editor of the *Times Literary Supplement*, which was written in response to Woolf's death on 28 March 1941:

> It is true that she presents life as an unsolved mystery: but no writer has ever shown a more vivid appreciation of its beauty and fascination. The accepted beauties of nature and art – moonlit skies, gardens, the pageantry of the past – she illuminated with a new delicacy of discrimination. But equally she discovered beauty in things hitherto looked on as ugly and prosaic. Seen through the shimmering element of her prose – in itself, surely, as exquisite as anything in English letters – aeroplanes and buses, suburban tea-tables and dusty London streets, reveal themselves as rich in colour and poetry. Most writers need picturesque incidents to evoke romance: Virginia Woolf does it in a description of an uneventful train journey or a casual walk in the park. Indeed, she does more than open the reader's eyes to the beauties which, but for her, would have passed him by. She makes him realize that the mere process of living can be inexhaustibly absorbing and enchanting. (Cecil 1941: 191)

In 'A Sketch of the Past', Woolf attempts to explain and define her experience of what she terms 'moments of being':

> I feel that I have had a blow; but it is not, as I thought as a child, simply a blow from an enemy hidden behind the cotton wool of daily

life; it is or will become a revelation of some order; it is a token of some real thing behind appearances; and I make it real by putting it into words. It is only by putting it into words that I make it whole ... From this I reach what I might call a philosophy; at any rate it is a constant idea of mine; that behind the cotton wool is hidden a pattern; that we – I mean all human beings – are connected with this. ('Sketch': 85)

Affirming that it is the writer, as artist, who is particularly susceptible and ready to absorb, admit, record and inspire this reality, Woolf describes a state of mind that is defined by an openness to Being-in-the-world, thereby allowing for the possibility that the extraordinary nature of the ordinary might show forth in the midst of average everydayness.

Throughout her writings – fictional, non-fictional, personal and public – Woolf describes and represents those moments of Being that define and reveal the individual's inextricable connection to the world. Nevertheless, as emphasised, a defining quality of such moments is that they are inevitably elusive and fleeting; as Heidegger asserts in *Being and Time*: 'In the moment of vision, indeed, and often just "for that moment", existence can even gain the mastery over the "everyday"; but it can never extinguish it' (*BT*: 422). Reflecting Woolf's own approach to Being-in-the-world, Heidegger's sentiments are given fictional representation through the musings of the artist, Lily Briscoe:

> What is the meaning of life? That was all – a simple question; one that tended to close in on one with years. The great revelation had never come. The great revelation perhaps never did come. Instead there were little daily miracles, illuminations, matches struck unexpectedly in the dark. (*TL*: 153–4)

Notes

1. Robert Langbaum asserts that: 'With very few exceptions the epiphanic mode does not appear in fiction until the turn of the century with James, Conrad, Proust and with the development of the modern short story by Chekhov, Joyce, Lawrence' (1983: 340).
2. Wordsworth is also understood to have had a profound influence upon Hardy's writings; as Dennis Taylor suggests, 'Hardy was

thoroughly immersed in Wordsworth and the Wordsworthian tradition' (1986: 441).
3. Ellen Tremper provides a sustained discussion of the influence of Wordsworth upon Woolf's writings, emphasising the 'continuity between the Romantics and the moderns in the significance of the arrested moment' (1998: 18).
4. This extract is taken from the First Part of the Two-Part *Prelude* of 1799: lines 288–96.
5. In 1929, while engaged in the writing of *The Waves*, Woolf's interest in Wordsworth's work is evident as she notes in her diary a number of lines from the seventh book of *The Prelude* that she wishes 'to remember' (*D3*: 247).
6. Sim provides a sustained reading of Woolf's treatment of ecstasy in 'A Sketch of the Past', suggesting that:

> Her positive moments of being present images of the external world flooding into the subject, or a change in the boundary between inner and outer, self and world . . . Her feeling of 'ecstasy' seems, then, connected to her sense of physical encapsulation and unity with the world. (2010: 145)

7. Under the heading, 'Negative Moments of Being: Beneath an Avalanche of Meaning', Sim provides an extensive discussion of negative moments of Being in Woolf's writings, placing particular emphasis upon the significance of the body's response to such moments (2010: 150–5).
8. In *Heidegger's Philosophy of Art*, Julian Young provides two chapters concerning Heidegger's connection with Hölderlin.
9. See Hermione Lee's chapter on Woolf's 'Madness' in *Virginia Woolf* for an extensive and well-considered discussion of the writer's life-long experience of mental illnesses (1996: 175–200).
10. A reference to synaesthesia can also be found in *Jacob's Room*; through her research, the marginal character, Miss Marchmont, wishes to 'confirm her philosophy that colour is sound – or, perhaps, it has something to do with music' (*JR*: 143).
11. Fredrik Svenaeus states that:

> Although a whole chapter in the second division of *Sein und Zeit* is devoted to an analysis of the meaning of death, Heidegger never links the ontological interpretation of death as the finitude of human existence to an analysis of the meaning of illness and health. He makes clear that the existential interpretation of death is prior to any biology or ontology of life, but he also mentions that the medical and biological inquiry into life and dying could be of importance in the analysis of the meaning-structure of human existence . . . The relation between biology and phenomenology is not further discussed, however, nor is a phenomenology of health and illness developed. (2000a: 127)

12. Such a sense of nothingness as a presence is also apparent in *The Years* as a young Eleanor Pargiter awaits the approaching death of her mother:

    > As she passed the doors and went downstairs a weight seemed to descend on her. She paused, looking down into the hall. A blankness came over her. Where am I? she asked herself, staring at a heavy frame. What is that? She seemed to be alone in the midst of nothingness; yet must descend, must carry her burden. (*TY*: 31)

13. Tony E. Jackson draws attention to Bernard's Heideggerian experience of nothingness in the final chapter of *The Waves*:

    > 'For one day,' he begins, 'as I leant over a gate that led into a field, the rhythm stopped' ... The lulling rhythm of the going-on of life suddenly ceases, bringing on a moment of Heideggerian vision ... At first, as if in a replay of the appearance of naturalism, a 'heavy despondency' falls upon him. But he then goes beyond his despair, for the nothingness turns out also to be a fullness, in fact, a 'new world' ... in which the 'old cloak' of his egoic self-representation drops away. (1995: 157)

14. In his discussion of *The Waves*, Ruotolo observes that

    > Only after Percival falls does the fin appear, first in the sixth interlude ... and then as part of Bernard's speculations ... Recalling images in T.S. Eliot as well as in Heidegger, the emptiness of land and water becomes a dimension of being itself. (1986: 154)

15. In 'The Time Being: On Woolf and Boredom', Sara Crangle provides a discussion of both Woolf and Heidegger's treatment of the state of boredom. Crangle draws attention to connections between Heidegger's notion of boredom and the 'tiny yawn[s]' of Clarissa Dalloway in Woolf's *The Voyage Out* (2008: 218).

16. In his discussion of Woolf's treatment of wonder throughout her writings, Hussey observes that: 'This is a style of thought that places her in the company of such thinkers as Pascal, Kierkegaard, and Heidegger, tempered though it is by an English dryness' (1986: xv).

17. Rachel's perspective in this passage is echoed in Heidegger's 1929 lecture, 'What is Metaphysics?', where he claims that the 'truly philosophical mood is "wonder" that there is something rather than nothing' (Young 2001: 109).

18. George Steiner asserts that, in terms of Heidegger's wish to avoid the '"onto-theological" bias in Western thinking', the philospher 'declares tirelessly that his propositions on "Being" entail absolutely nothing as to the existence or nonexistence of God'; nevertheless, Heidegger's philosophy has 'a marked theological edge' (Steiner 63, 62), a characteristic

that is unsurprising considering Heidegger's Catholic upbringing and formal theological training.

19. Referring to 'what Mark Hussey terms an "abstract" or numinous reality', Sim states that such a sense of reality

> is intimately related to the material world. That on many occasions the Woolfian moment not only affirms but emphasizes and celebrates the reality and particularity of the physical world distinguishes it from traditional accounts of the mystical experience which involve a disengagement from, or disavowal of, the empirical world and the senses in favour of a spiritual reality. (2010: 148)

20. Rudolph Otto's book *Das Heilige* was published in 1917, and was highly influential not only in Germany, but also in other parts of Europe, particularly England (Gooch 2000: 134). It was translated into English as *The Idea of the Holy* by John W. Harvey (2nd edition, 1958).

21. Further to this, Koulouris states that:

> Although Woolf does not refer to Heidegger directly, her link between the 'state of being' and 'writing' complicates his notion of *Dasein* as the indivisible designation of 'being' and its resoluteness before history and death. Woolf's linking of 'being' with the act of writing on the one hand calls attention to the importance of history and mortality, whilst on the other, by invoking a certain permanence in writing, she imbues 'being' with a sense of transcendence. (2011: 205, n149)

Confluences, Divergences and Future Directions

In her essay, 'Reading Simone de Beauvoir with Martin Heidegger', Eva Gothlin states that

> Reading Beauvoir with Heidegger can deepen our understanding of Beauvoir's view of human beings and their relation to the world and to others. This approach might be called hermeneutical in the Heideggerian sense: it reveals new meanings without assuming that a final comprehension is ever possible. (2003: 45)

Arguably, this study of the relationship between Woolf's writings and Heidegger's philosophy in *Being and Time* leads to a similar outcome, insofar as Woolf's textual representations of the connections between self, world and the Other are afforded a perspective that has been largely unexamined in previous Woolfian studies. Nevertheless, just as Gothlin advises that her reading of Beauvoir from a Heideggerian perspective does not in itself provide definitive conclusions, no claim is made to any absolute or final reading of Woolf's work in this book; to do so would contradict Woolf's own intention throughout her writings to disrupt Western metaphysical dualisms and the concomitant desire for a grounding of fixed meanings and truth. In a similar vein, attempts to apply a univocal meaning to Heidegger's text runs counter to its author's intention, as reflected in the density and opacity of the form and style of *Being and Time*. Just as truth is a process rather than an endpoint of meaning for both Woolf and Heidegger, so too might this book be understood as one among a number of ways of approaching Woolf's writings.

In the Introduction it was proposed that, despite significant differences in their approaches, the respective writings of Woolf and Heidegger reflect a shared fundamental concern with, and sense of, the relationship between self and world. The individual's connection to the world is defined by an involvement and engagement that is always already situated within a particular social and cultural context; one that is defined by its customs, norms, expectations and prescriptions. In terms of Woolf and Heidegger's textual representations of Being-in-the-world, the central concern for both is the question of how each of us responds, both consciously and unconsciously, to what Woolf describes in 'A Sketch of the Past' as the 'stream' ('Sketch': 92); that is, those influences and forces that direct members of a society to order their lives in a particular manner. As the preceding chapters illustrate, any attempt to live outside the prevailing social order can only ever be temporary. As such, the question for each of us is not how we might permanently evade these forces; rather, as Woolf and Heidegger both attest, each individual's mode of Being-in-the-world is ultimately measured by the balance that he or she finds between the inevitable sway of societal requirements and restrictions, and the pursuit of his or her personal aspirations and convictions.

It is at this point of marked and significant confluence between Woolf and Heidegger's understandings of the relationship between self and world that their respective literary and philosophical approaches diverge, as each proceeds to investigate this defining characteristic of Being-in-the-world from a singular perspective. Heidegger's existential-ontological analysis of Dasein's response to the surrounding social forces – understood as the 'they' – relies upon the notions of inauthentic and authentic modes of Being-in-the-world, where inauthenticity refers to 'a quite distinctive kind of Being-in-the-world – the kind which is completely fascinated by the "world" and by the Dasein-with of Others in the "they"'; in contrast, authenticity as resoluteness can be attained 'only if Dasein specifically brings itself back to itself from its lostness in the "they"' (*BT*: 220, 312). Emphasising the understanding that each individual must find a means of negotiating, rather than denying, the unavoidable discord between the tranquilising dictates of theyness that leads to the forgetting of Being, and the questioning self-awareness that characterises authenticity, Heidegger explains that:

> Even resolutions remain dependent upon the 'they' and its world. The understanding of this is one of the things that a resolution discloses, inasmuch as resoluteness is what first gives authentic transparency to Dasein. In resoluteness the issue for Dasein is its ownmost potentiality-for-Being, which, as something thrown, can project itself only upon definite factical possibilities. Resolution does not withdraw itself from 'actuality', but discovers first what is factically possible; and it does so by seizing upon

it in whatever way is possible for it as its ownmost potentiality-for-Being in the 'they'. (*BT*: 345–6)

In *Virginia Woolf and the Real World*, Zwerdling remarks that:

> One of the most important connections between Woolf's fictional and nonfictional writing is her persistent interest in how people – real and imagined – have negotiated the conflict between what they want and what is expected of them. Her characters are not free agents but must respond to the demands of the world around them. (1986: 5)

As this study has emphasised, throughout the various forms of Woolf's writings, many of 'the demands of the world' that each individual inevitably encounters throughout his or her life are founded upon the political and ideological tenets of the dominant social order. Woolf's preoccupation with the impact of the social and cultural context upon the life of the individual is reflected in Zwerdling's observation that 'Virtually every character in her novels is "placed" socially with unusual exactness' (1986: 89). While Zwerdling's reference to such 'placements' concerns Woolf's representations of the class structures of English society, such a reading can be extended to include Woolf's approaches to a variety of other social issues and concerns, including patriarchal hegemony; gender; education; the divide between the public and the private; and nationalism, imperialism, and war. As discussed in the Introduction, such a view of Woolf's focus of concern lies in sharp contrast to critical accounts of the writer's work as largely apolitical. Indeed, one of the broader implications of this book is a greater understanding of the emphasis that Woolf accords to the effects of political and ideological frameworks upon each individual's average everyday mode of Being-in-the-world.

As argued in the preceding chapters, Woolf's writings reveal her sustained preoccupation with the ways in which individual members of English society in the first half of the twentieth century respond to the expectations and prescriptions of the prevailing social order. Zwerdling remarks that Woolf's

> sense of the subject is deepened by her understanding of the interrelationship of the social forces at work – familial, institutional, ideological, historical – and by her awareness of the range of individual human response – internalization, compliance, rebellion, withdrawal, and all the combinations and contradictions such different reactions can produce. (1986: 5)

As Woolf's writings attest, more often than not, as a result of the individual's immersion in the present demands and circumstances of everyday life, his or her reaction to such forces consists of unthinking adherence as the influence of the social order goes largely unconsidered. In sharp contrast, characters such as Septimus Smith in *Mrs Dalloway*, and Rhoda in *The Waves*, illustrate the perilous, and ultimately intolerable situation of the individual whose rejection of the social order becomes absolute. Located between these extremes are those characters and individuals found throughout Woolf's writings, who seek to uncover and critique the machinations of the status quo, all the while acknowledging their inevitable participation in the social order.

While new approaches to Woolf's writings have been foregrounded in this book through a reading of Heidegger's *Being and Time*, a further implication of this study is the greater accessibility accorded to Heidegger's notoriously complex text, when viewed from the perspective of Woolf's fictional and non-fictional representations of Being-in-the-world. Throughout her writings, Woolf's depictions of the responses of individuals, both real and imagined, to average everyday routines and obligations, the Other, and particular settings and contexts, both demonstrate and illuminate various areas of concern that are evident in Heidegger's text. In her 2008 essay, 'Heidegger in Woolf's Clothing', Storl forwards a similar perspective when, upon referring to *Being and Time*, she writes: 'In order to unpack this dense text, we turn now to Woolf's rich imagery' (2008: 306). Particularly in his later work, Heidegger emphasises the unique role of art and the artist as both site and source for the disclosure of the truth of Being, an understanding that is arguably reflected through Woolf's capacity to convey her particular vision of the relationship between self and world to her readers.

A key element of Being-in-the-world that is given particular emphasis in Woolf's writings, but remains largely unexamined in *Being and Time*, is the significance of certain 'culturally defined' (Dreyfus 1991: 25) factical aspects of the individual's everyday mode of Being-in-the-world, such as gender, embodiment, class and social-historical situatedness. While Heidegger recognises the relevance of these elements, towards which the individual must relate or define his or herself in one way or another, facticity is not a definitive ontological feature of the individual's existence, in that it does not have a determining role concerning the way in which one exists as a particular individual. As such, within the context of Heidegger's analysis of Being-in-the-world, facticity in its particular concrete detail is granted, at best, limited attention. In contrast, for Woolf, the role that such characteristics play in positioning each individual within the societal and ideological context provides the basis for her textual representations of the relationship between self and world. Arguably, Woolf's representations of such factors not only extend Heidegger's analysis in new directions; such an emphasis also addresses concerns raised by various critics regarding the absence of any critical analysis of such factical features within the context of Dasein's average everyday mode of Being-in-the-world.

Despite the prodigious and ever-expanding volume of Heidegger's published works, for reasons outlined in the Introduction, the study of Heidegger's philosophy in relation to Woolf's writings has been largely confined to his 1927 text, *Being and Time*. As a consequence, it is acknowledged that valuable areas of research relating to the connections between Woolf's writings and Heidegger's philosophy remain to be considered. To begin, an area given particular emphasis throughout the works of both Woolf and Heidegger is that of 'language'. In his 1947 essay, 'Letter on Humanism', Heidegger proclaims that: 'Language is the house of Being. In its home man dwells' (2002a: 217). However, as Heidegger also asserts, within the context of 'a technologically structured world', the prevailing emphasis upon language as fundamentally instrumental in nature means that 'words become sheer signs, ciphers that no longer evoke a historic worldliness' (Thiele 1995: 116). Elements of such a critique can be seen in Woolf's 1937 essay, 'Craftsmanship', which deals exclusively with the writer's observations concerning language. Providing her own view of instrumental understandings of language, Woolf refutes the notion that words can be defined as essentially representative and univocal. Referring to 'words', Woolf writes that

> it is their nature not to express one simple statement but a thousand possibilities . . . We pin them down to one meaning, their useful meaning, the meaning which makes us catch the train, the meaning which makes us pass the examination. And when words are pinned down they fold their wings and die. (1942b: 127, 132)

While acknowledging the profound differences in the approaches of each to the issue of language, the study of Woolf and Heidegger's shared sense that the individual's view of reality and the surrounding world is fundamentally influenced and manipulated through language, has the potential to provide a valuable contribution to understandings of the works of both.

The influence of ancient Greek literature and philosophy upon the writings of both Woolf and Heidegger is a further area of study that is situated outside the parameters of this book. Heidegger's significant engagement with Greek thought has been extensively documented; as John Panteleimon Manoussakis suggests: 'As more and more of Martin Heidegger's work become available . . . it is increasingly evident how important to his thinking was Heidegger's encounter with the Greeks – with the Presocratics, with Plato, with Aristotle' (2006: 3).[1] Numerous studies have also drawn attention to Woolf's knowledge of, and interest in, Greek literature and language.[2] In her discussion of Woolf, Emily Dalgarno asserts that 'a biography that focused on her intellectual development would give priority to her study of the Greek language and literature' (2001: 40). Dalgarno draws attention to Woolf's early journals, observing that they 'show her at work on a series of projects translating Plato, Aristotle, Thucydides, and Sophocles', as well as 'Aeschylus, in whose work her own is most deeply grounded' (2001: 42). Such a focus might be compared with Julian Young's claim that 'Heidegger's most fundamental paradigm of great art is . . . Greek tragedy' (2001: 61).

A final area of interest is that of Woolf and Heidegger's textual approaches to the question of technology, in particular, its effects upon the average everyday lives of individuals. In Heidegger's 1953 lecture, 'The Question Concerning Technology' (2002c), the philosopher provides a detailed account of his understanding of, and responses to, the issue of technology. Discussing Heidegger's complex approach to this matter, Hubert L. Dreyfus explains that although 'Heidegger does not oppose technology', he nevertheless 'attempts to point out to us the peculiar and dangerous aspects of our technological understanding of being' (2006: 359). In her edited collection, *Virginia Woolf in the Age of Mechanical Reproduction* (2000), Pamela L. Caughie provides a comprehensive insight into Woolf's responses to a variety of technological changes and developments. Nevertheless, reflecting the sparsity of critical attention directed towards the explication of Woolf's writings from a Heideggerian perspective, throughout this collection there is only one fleeting reference to the philosopher's work.[3] While there have been a limited number of published studies that include responses to Woolf and Heidegger's shared concern with the issue of technology, as yet, an in-depth study has yet to be undertaken.[4]

* * *

To conclude this book, it is useful to draw attention to its relevance in terms of present-day global concerns, particularly in relation to the post-9/11 milieu. Within such a context, the dualisms of self and world, self and Other, and insider and outsider have acquired a new and urgent significance, as have literal and theoretical understandings of home, homelessness and place. The notion of the 'outsider-within' society has come to be defined by the contemporary 'scapegoat', whose faith, ethnicity or appearance are contrary to the ascribed 'norms' of the dominant social order. Sharing marked affinities with Woolf's preoccupations close to a century earlier, issues of nationalism, imperialism and neo-colonialism have come to be foregrounded; while the inherent connection between the past, and the present and future destiny of the collective, has acquired ever-increasing relevance. Just as Woolf questioned the legitimacy and viability of war as a national response to suspected foreign threat during a period that included two World Wars, today's citizens of the world are faced with the same questions in light of the overarching 'war on terror'.

What becomes clear in light of such marked parallels is that, despite the fact that the formations of Woolf and Heidegger's understandings of Being-in-the-world were influenced by a shared historical context that differs in a variety of respects from dominant present-day concerns and preoccupations, the fundamental issues that define this notion are, in a sense, timeless. The individual trying to make his or her way in the world will always be faced with the need to find a balance between the expectations and prescriptions of the social order, and his or her personal aspirations; Being-in-the-world will always be defined by our relations with Others, both known and distant; the past will always impact upon present and future possibilities; and each of us will continue to endeavour to acquire a sense of Being-at-home in the world, despite our fundamental state of existential homelessness.

Notes

1. See, for instance, Julian Young's *Heidegger's Philosophy of Art* (2001), and the edited collection by Drew A. Hyland and John Panteleimon Manoussakis, *Heidegger and the Greeks: Interpretive Essays* (2006).

2. Such studies include, but are certainly not limited to, Jane de Gay's *Virginia Woolf's Novels and the Literary Past* (2007b: 67–95); Jean Wyatt's 'The Celebration of Eros: Greek Concepts of Love and Beauty in *To the Lighthouse*' (1978); Angeliki Spiropoulou's *Virginia Woolf, Modernity and History: Constellations with Walter Benjamin* (2010: 60–74); and 'Virginia Woolf and Reading Greek' (2002) by Rebecca Nagel.
3. This reference is made by Mark Hussey in his chapter entitled 'How Should One Read a Screen?' (2000: 258–9).
4. Emily Dalgarno's *Virginia Woolf and the Visible World* provides an extended discussion of the confluences between Heidegger's 1938 essay, 'The Age of the World Picture', and Woolf's *The Waves* (2001: 101–28); along similar lines, in her 1996 conference paper entitled, 'Nebulous Networks: Woolf's Rethinking of Jeans's Analogy of the Scientist as Artist' (1997: 273), and her monograph *Virginia Woolf and the Discourse of Science: The Aesthetics of Astronomy,* Holly Henry discusses the affinities between Woolf's 1931 novel and Heidegger's essay (2003: 105).

References

Adamczewski, Zygmunt (1970), 'Commentary on Calvin O. Schrag's "Heidegger on Repetition and Historical Understanding"', *Philosophy East and West*, 20:3, 297–301.
Adams, Paul C. (2001), *Textures of Place: Exploring Humanist Geographies*, Minneapolis: University of Minnesota Press.
Aho, Kevin A. (2005), 'The Missing Dialogue Between Heidegger and Merleau-Ponty: On the Importance of the *Zollikon Seminars*', *Body and Society*, 11:2, 1–23.
Ainsworth, Claire (2015), 'Sex Redefined', *Nature: National Weekly Journal of Science*, 518, 288–91.
Alfandary, Isabelle (2013), 'Virginia Woolf/ Friedrich Nietzsche: Life or the Innocence of Becoming in *Mrs Dalloway*', *Le Tour Critique*, 2, 61–72.
Althusser, Louis (2011), 'Ideology and Ideological State Apparatuses (Notes Towards an Investigation)', in I. Szeman and T. Kaposy (eds), *Cultural Theory: An Anthology*, Chichester: Wiley-Blackwell, pp. 204–22.
Anonymous [Orlo Williams] (1941), 'Epitaph on Virginia Woolf: Interpreter of the Age Between the Wars, the Vision and the Pursuit', *Times Literary Supplement*, 12 April 1941, 175.
Bachelard, Gaston (1994), *The Poetics of Space*, trans. M. Jolas, Boston: Beacon.
Bambach, Charles R. (1995), *Heidegger, Dilthey, and the Crisis of Historicism*, Ithaca, NY: Cornell University Press.
Banfield, Ann (2013), 'Art as a Place (or Time) for the Delight in What There Is', *Le Tour Critique*, 2, 165–84.
— (2000a), *The Phantom Table: Woolf, Fry, Russell, and the Epistemology of Modernism*, Cambridge: Cambridge University Press.
— (2000b), 'Tragic Time: The Problem of the Future in Cambridge Philosophy and *To the Lighthouse*', *Modernism/Modernity*, 7:1, 43–75.
— (2003), 'Time Passes: Virginia Woolf, Post-Impressionism, and Cambridge Time', *Poetics Today*, 24:3, 471–516.
Barash, Jeffrey Andrew (1988), *Martin Heidegger and the Problem of Historical Meaning*, Dordrecht, Netherlands: Martinus Nijhoff.
Bauman, Zygmunt (1991), *Modernity and Ambivalence*, Cambridge: Polity Press.
Beer, Gillian (1996), *Virginia Woolf: The Common Ground*, Ann Arbor: University of Michigan Press.
— (2000), 'Introduction' in V. Woolf, *Between the Acts*, London: Penguin, pp. ix–xxxv.

Beja, Morris (1971), *Epiphany in the Modern Novel*, London: Peter Owen.
Bennett, Andrew and Royle, Nicholas (1999), *An Introduction to Literature, Criticism and Theory*, 2nd edn, Harlow: Pearson.
Blair, Emily (2007), *Virginia Woolf and the Nineteenth-Century Domestic Novel*, New York: State University of New York Press.
Boss, Matthew (2009), 'Metaphysics and the Mood of Deep Boredom: Heidegger's Phenomenology of Mood', in B. Dalle Pezze and C. Salzani (eds), *Essays on Boredom and Modernity*, Amsterdam: Rodopi, pp. 85–107.
Bourne-Taylor, Carole and Mildenberg, Ariane (eds) (2010), *Phenomenology, Modernism and Beyond*, Bern, Switzerland: Peter Lang.
Bowlby, Rachel (1997), *Feminist Destinations and Further Essays on Virginia Woolf*, Edinburgh: Edinburgh University Press.
— (2013), 'An Ordinary Mind on an Ordinary Day', *Le Tour Critique*, 2, 251–62.
Bradbury, Malcolm (1976a), 'The Cities of Modernism', in M. Bradbury and J. McFarlane (eds), *Modernism: A Guide to European Literature 1890–1930*, London: Penguin, pp. 96–104.
— (1976b), 'London 1890–1920', in M. Bradbury and J. McFarlane (eds), *Modernism: A Guide to European Literature 1890–1930*, London: Penguin, pp. 172–90.
Bradshaw, David (2006), 'The Socio-Political Vision of the Novels', in S. Roe and S. Sellers (eds), *The Cambridge Companion to Virginia Woolf*, Cambridge: Cambridge University Press, pp. 191–208.
Briggs, Julia (2001), *'This Moment I Stand On': Woolf and the Spaces in Time*, Southport: Virginia Woolf Society of Great Britain.
— (2005), *Virginia Woolf: An Inner Life*, Orlando: Harcourt.
Burns, Christy L. (2002), 'Re-Thinking Modernism after the 1990s', *Modern Fiction Studies*, 48:2, 470–9.
Caputo, John D. (1987), *Radical Hermeneutics: Repetition, Deconstruction, and the Hermeneutic Project*, Bloomington: Indiana University Press.
Carroll, Berenice A. (1978), '"To Crush Him in Our Own Country": The Political Thought of Virginia Woolf', *Feminist Studies*, 4:1, 99–132.
Casey, Edward S. (1993), *Getting Back into Place: Towards a Renewed Understanding of the Place-World*, Bloomington: Indiana University Press.
— (1997), *The Fate of Place: A Philosophical History*, Berkeley: University of California Press.
— (2001), 'Between Geography and Philosophy: What Does It Mean to Be in the Place-World?', *Annals of the Association of American Geographers*, 91:4, 683–93.
Caughie, Pamela L. (ed.) (2000), *Virginia Woolf in the Age of Mechanical Reproduction*, New York: Garland.
Cecil, David (1941), Letter, *Times Literary Supplement*, 19 April 1941, 191.

Cerbone, David R. (2000), 'Heidegger and Dasein's "Bodily Nature": What is the Hidden Problematic?', *International Journal of Philosophical Studies*, 8:2, 209–30.

Chanter, Tina (2001), 'The Problematic Normative Assumptions of Heidegger's Ontology', in N. J. Holland and P. Huntington (eds), *Feminist Interpretations of Martin Heidegger*, Philadelphia: Pennsylvania State University Press, pp. 73–108.

Cixous, Hélène (1980), 'The Laugh of the Medusa', in E. Marks and I. de Courtivron (eds), *New French Feminisms: An Anthology*, Amherst: University of Massachusetts Press, pp. 245–64.

Coleman, Lisa L. (2012), 'Woolf and Feminist Theory: Woolf's Feminism Comes in Waves' in B. Randall and J. Goldman (eds), *Virginia Woolf in Context*, Cambridge: Cambridge University Press, pp. 79–91.

Concilio, Carmen (1999), 'Things that Do Speak in Elizabeth Bowen's *The Last September*', in W. Tigges (ed.), *Moments of Moment: Aspects of the Literary Epiphany*, Amsterdam: Rodopi, pp. 279–92.

Conrad, Joseph (2008), *Lord Jim*, New York: Oxford University Press.

Corngold, Stanley (1994), *The Fate of the Self: German Writers and French Theory*, Durham, NC: Duke University Press.

Covey, Neil (1995), 'Notes Toward an Investigation of the Marginality of Poetry and the Sympathetic Imagination', *South Atlantic Review*, 60:2, 137–51.

Crangle, Sara (2008), 'The Time Being: On Woolf and Boredom', *Modern Fiction Studies*, 54:2, 209–32.

Cuddy-Keane, Melba (1997), 'Virginia Woolf and the Varieties of Historicist Experience', in B. Carole Rosenberg and J. Dubino (eds), *Virginia Woolf and the Essay*, New York: St Martin's, pp. 59–77.

— (2010a), 'Mr Bennett and Mrs Brown: Virginia Woolf on Character in the Novel', *The Book Show*, Radio National, ABC, Australia. Available at: http://www.abc.net.au/radionational/programs/bookshow/mr-bennett-and-mrs-brown-virginia-woolf-on/2962164 (accessed 27 October 2016).

— (2010b), 'Virginia Woolf and the Public Sphere', in S. Sellers (ed.), *Cambridge Companion to Virginia Woolf*, 2nd edn, Cambridge: Cambridge University Press, pp. 231–49.

Dalgarno, Emily (2001), *Virginia Woolf and the Visible World*, Cambridge: Cambridge University Press.

de Gay, Jane (2007a), 'Virginia Woolf's Feminist Historiography in *Orlando*', *Critical Survey*, 19:1, 62–72.

— (2007b), *Virginia Woolf's Novels and the Literary Past*, Edinburgh: Edinburgh University Press.

— (2009), *Virginia Woolf and the Clergy*, Southport: Virginia Woolf Society of Great Britain.

Delourme, Chantal (2013), 'Virginia Woolf among the philosophers', *Le Tour Critique*, 2, I–IX.

Derrida, Jacques (1992), 'This Strange Institution Called Literature: An Interview with Jacques Derrida', in D. Attridge (ed.), *Acts of Literature*, New York: Routledge, pp. 33–75.
— (2000), *Of Hospitality: Anne Dufourmantelle Invites Jacques Derrida to Respond*, trans. R. Bowlby, Redwood City: Stanford University Press.
— (2001), 'Geschlecht: Sexual Difference, Ontological Difference', in N. J. Holland and P. Huntington (eds), *Feminist Interpretations of Martin Heidegger*, Philadelphia: Pennsylvania State University Press, pp. 53–72.
— (2004), *Dissemination*, trans. B. Johnson, London: Continuum.
DeSalvo, Louise A. (2009), *On Moving: A Writer's Meditation on New Houses, Old Haunts, and Finding Home Again*, New York: Bloomsbury.
DeSalvo, Louise A., Fox, Alice and Hill, Katherine C. (1982), 'Virginia Woolf and Leslie Stephen', *PMLA*, 97:1, 103–6.
Detloff, Madelyn (2009), *The Persistence of Modernism: Loss and Mourning in the Twentieth Century*, Cambridge: Cambridge University Press.
Doyle, Laura (1994), *Bordering on the Body: The Racial Matrix of Modern Fiction and Culture*, Oxford: Oxford University Press.
— (2001), 'The Body Unbound: A Phenomenological Reading of the Political in *A Room of One's Own*', in J. Berman and J. Goldman (eds), *Virginia Woolf Out of Bounds: Selected Papers from the Tenth Annual Conference on Virginia Woolf*, New York: Pace University Press, pp. 129–40.
Dreyfus, Hubert L. (1991), *Being-in-the-World: A Commentary on Heidegger's Being and Time, Division 1*, Cambridge, MA: MIT Press.
— (2006), 'Heidegger on the Connection between Nihilism, Art, Technology, and Politics', in C. B. Guignon (ed.), The Cambridge Companion to Heidegger. 2nd edn, Cambridge: Cambridge University Press, pp. 345–72.
Eagleton, Terry (1991), *Ideology: An Introduction*, London: Verso.
— (2002), *Literary Theory: An Introduction*, 2nd edn, Oxford: Blackwell.
Elden, Stuart (2001), *Mapping the Present: Heidegger, Foucault, and the Project of a Spatial History*, London: Continuum.
Eliade, Mircea (1987), *The Sacred and the Profane: the Nature of Religion*, Orlando: Harcourt.
Engels, Friedrich (2009), *The Condition of the Working Class in England*, Oxford: Oxford University Press.
Frank, A. O. (2001), *The Philosophy of Virginia Woolf: A Philosophical Reading of the Mature Novels*, Budapest: Akadémiai Kiadó.
— (1998), *Mappings: Feminism and the Cultural Geographies of Encounter*, Princeton: Princeton University Press.
Froula, Christine (2013), 'Virginia Woolf and the Art of Doubt: Modern Fiction between Moore and Montaigne', *Le Tour Critique*, 2, 209–27.
Garnier, Marie-Dominique (2013), 'Following Suit(e): Woolf, Carlyle, Deleuze', *Le Tour Critique*, 2, 503–14.

Gibbs, Paul (2011), 'The Concept of Profound Boredom: Learning from Moments of Vision', *Studies in Philosophy and Education*, 30:6, 601–13.

Goldman, Jane (1998), *The Feminist Aesthetics of Virginia Woolf: Modernism, Post-Impressionism and the Politics of the Visual*, Cambridge: Cambridge University Press.

— (2006), *The Cambridge Introduction to Virginia Woolf*, Cambridge: Cambridge University Press.

— (2013), 'Crusoe's Dog(s): Woolf and Derrida (Between Beast and Sovereign)', *Le Tour Critique*, 2, 475–87.

Gooch, Todd A. (2000), *The Numinous and Modernity: An Interpretation of Rudolph Otto's Philosophy of Religion*, Berlin: de Gruyter.

Goodstein, Elizabeth S. (2005), *Experience without Qualities: Boredom and Modernity*, Redwood City: Stanford University Press.

Gordon, Lyndall (2001), *Virginia Woolf, a Writer's Life*, New York: Norton.

Gosetti-Ferencei, Jennifer Anna (2007), *The Ecstatic Quotidian: Phenomenological Sightings in Modern Art and Literature*, Philadelphia: Pennsylvania State University Press.

Gothlin, Eva (2003), 'Reading Simone de Beauvoir with Martin Heidegger', in C. Card (ed.), The Cambridge Companion to Simone de Beauvoir, Cambridge: Cambridge University Press, pp. 45–65.

Grosz, Elizabeth (1995), *Space, Time and Perversion: Essays on the Politics of Bodies*, St Leonards, East Sussex: Allen and Unwin.

Hafley, James (1963), *The Glass Roof: Virginia Woolf as Novelist*, New York: Russell & Russell.

Hanaway, Cleo (2011), Review of *Phenomenology, Modernism and Beyond*, ed. Carole Bourne-Taylor and Ariane Mildenberg, *Modernist Cultures*, 6:2, 338–42.

Hancock, Nuala (2012), *Charleston and Monk's House: The Intimate House Museums of Virginia Woolf and Vanessa Bell*, Edinburgh: Edinburgh University Press.

Hankins, Leslie Kathleen (2000), 'Virginia Woolf and Walter Benjamin Selling Out(Siders)', in P. L. Caughie (ed.), *Virginia Woolf in the Age of Mechanical Reproduction*, New York: Garland, pp. 3–35.

Harrison, John and Baron-Cohen, Simon (1994), 'Synaesthesia: An Account of Coloured Hearing', *Leonardo*, 27:4, 343–6.

Heidegger, Martin (1982), *The Basic Problems of Phenomenology*, rev. edn, trans. A. Hofstadter, Bloomington: Indiana University Press.

— (1994), *Basic Questions of Philosophy: Selected 'Problems' of 'Logic'*, trans. R. Rojcewicz and A. Schuwer, Bloomington: Indiana University Press.

— (1995), *The Fundamental Concepts of Metaphysics: World, Finitude, Solitude*, trans. W. McNeill and N. Walker, Bloomington: Indiana University Press.

— (1999), *Ontology: The Hermeneutics of Facticity*, trans. J. van Buren, Bloomington: Indiana University Press.

— (2001a), 'Building Dwelling Thinking', in M. Heidegger, *Poetry, Language, Thought*, trans. A. Hofstadter, New York: Perennial Classics, pp. 141–59.
— (2001b), *Zollikon Seminars: Protocols, Conversations, Letters*, ed. M. Boss, Evanston: Northwestern University Press.
— (2002a), 'Letter on Humanism', in D. F. Krell (ed.), *Basic Writings*, rev. edn, Great Britain: Routledge, pp. 217–65.
— (2002b), 'The Origin of the Work of Art', in D.F. Krell (ed.), *Basic Writings*, rev. edn, London: Routledge, pp. 143–212.
— (2002c), 'The Question Concerning Technology', in D. F. Krell (ed.), *Basic Writings*, rev. edn, London: Routledge, pp. 311–41.
— (2002d), 'What is Metaphysics?', in D. F. Krell (ed.), *Basic Writings*, rev. edn, London: Routledge, pp. 93–110.
— (2004), *Being and Time*, trans. John Macquarrie and Edward Robinson, Malden, MA: Blackwell.
— (2010), 'Why Do I Stay in The Provinces?', in T. Sheehan (ed.), *Heidegger: The Man and the Thinker*, New Brunswick, NJ: Transaction, pp. 27–30.
Henke, Suzette (1989), 'Virginia Woolf's *The Waves*: A Phenomenological Reading', *Neophilologus*, 73:3, 461–72.
— (1999), 'Virginia Woolf's *To the Lighthouse*: (En)Gendering Epiphany', in W. Tigges (ed.), *Moments of Moment: Aspects of the Literary Epiphany*, Amsterdam: Rodopi, pp. 261–78.
Henry, Holly (1997), 'Nebulous Networks: Woolf's Rethinking of Jeans's Analogy of the Scientist as Artist', in D. F. Gillespie and L. K. Hankins (eds), *Virginia Woolf and the Arts: Selected Papers from the Sixth Annual Conference on Virginia Woolf*, New York: Pace University Press, pp. 268–76.
— (2003), *Virginia Woolf and the Discourse of Science: The Aesthetics of Astronomy*, Cambridge: Cambridge University Press.
Hepburn, R. W. (1980), 'The Inaugural Address: Wonder', *Proceedings of the Aristotelian Society, Supplementary Volume* 54, pp. 1–23.
Herr, Cheryl (2006), 'Walking in Dublin', in R. B. Kershner (ed.), *A Portrait of the Artist as a Young Man: A Case Study in Contemporary Criticism*, 2nd edn, New York: St Martin's Press, pp. 413–29.
— (2009), 'Being in Joyce's World', in J. McCourt (ed.), *Joyce in Context*, Cambridge: Cambridge University Press, pp. 163–72.
Hill, Katherine C. (1981), 'Virginia Woolf and Leslie Stephen: History and Literary Revolution', *PMLA*, 96:3, 351–62.
Hillis Miller, J. (2013), '*Waves* Theory: An Anachronistic Reading', *Le Tour Critique*, 2, 113–20.
Hintikka, Jaakko (1979), 'Virginia Woolf and Our Knowledge of the External World', *Journal of Aesthetics and Art Criticism*, 38:1, 5–14.
Hoffman, Piotr (2011), 'Death, Time, History: Division II of *Being and Time*', in C. B. Guignon (ed.), *The Cambridge Companion to Heidegger*, 2nd edn, Cambridge: Cambridge University Press, pp. 222–40.

Holland, Nancy J. (2001), '"The Universe is Made of Stories, Not of Atoms": Heidegger and the Feminine They-Self', in N. J. Holland and P. Huntington (eds), *Feminist Interpretations of Martin Heidegger*, Philadelphia: Pennsylvania State University Press, pp. 128–45.

Hotho-Jackson, Sabine (1991), 'Virginia Woolf on History: Between Tradition and Modernity', *Forum for Modern Language Studies*, 27:4, 293–313.

Huntington, Patricia (2001), 'Introduction I – General Background: History of the Feminist Reception of Heidegger and a Guide to Heidegger's Thought', in N. J. Holland and P. Huntington (eds), *Feminist Interpretations of Martin Heidegger*, Philadelphia: Pennsylvania State University Press, pp. 1–42.

Hussey, Mark (1986), *The Singing of the Real World: The Philosophy of Virginia Woolf's Fiction*, Columbus: Ohio State University Press.

— (2000), 'How Should One Read a Screen?', in P. L. Caughie (ed.), *Virginia Woolf in the Age of Mechanical Reproduction*, New York: Garland, pp. 249–65.

— (2001), '"For Nothing Is Simply One Thing": Knowing the World in *To the Lighthouse*', in B. R. Daugherty and M. B. Pringle (eds.), *Approaches to Teaching Woolf's* To the Lighthouse, New York: MLA, pp. 41–6.

— (2013), '"Thoughts without words": Silence, Violence, and Memorial in Woolf's Late Works', *Le Tour Critique*, 2, 87–98.

Hyland, Drew A. and Manoussakis, John Panteleimon (eds) (2006), *Heidegger and the Greeks: Interpretive Essays*, Bloomington: Indiana University Press.

Jackson, Tony E. (1994), *The Subject of Modernism: Narrative Alterations in the Fiction of Eliot, Conrad, Woolf, and Joyce*, Ann Arbor: University of Michigan Press.

Johnson, Pauline (2004), 'From Virginia Woolf to the Postmoderns: Developments in a Feminist Aesthetic', in S. Sayers and P. Osbourne (eds), *Socialism, Feminism and Philosophy: A Radical Philosophy Reader*, New York: Routledge, pp. 100–21.

Jonsson, AnnKatrin (2006), *Relations*, Bern, Switzerland: Peter Lang.

Katz, Tamar (2010), 'Pausing, Waiting, Repeating: Urban Temporality in *Mrs. Dalloway* and *The Years*', in E. F. Evans and S. E. Cornish (eds), *Woolf and the City: Selected Papers from the Nineteenth Annual Conference on Virginia Woolf*, Clemson: Clemson University Digital Press, pp. 2–16.

Korab-Karpowicz, W. J. (2011), 'Martin Heidegger 1889–1976', *Internet Encyclopedia of Philosophy*. Available at: http://www.iep.utm.edu/heidegge (accessed 21 December 2011).

Kostkowska, Justyna (2004), '"Scissors and Silks," "Flowers and Trees," and "Geraniums Ruined by the War": Virginia Woolf's Ecological Critique of Science in *Mrs. Dalloway*', *Women's Studies*, 33:2, 183–98.

Koulouris, Theodore (2011), *Hellenism and Loss in the Work of Virginia Woolf*, Farnham: Ashgate Publishing.
Kristeva, Julia (1982), *Powers of Horror*, trans. L. S. Roudiez, New York: Columbia University Press.
Lackey, Michael (2000), 'Atheism and Sadism: Nietzsche and Woolf on Post-God Discourse', *Philosophy and Literature*, 24:2, 346–63.
Lamont, Elizabeth Clea (2001), 'Moving Tropes: New Modernist Travels with Virginia Woolf', *Alif: Journal of Comparative Poetics*, 21, 161–81.
Langbaum, Robert (1983), 'The Epiphanic Mode in Wordsworth and Modern Literature', *New Literary History*, 14:2, 335–58.
Lee, Hermione (1984), 'A Burning Glass: Reflection in Virginia Woolf', in E. Warner (ed.), *Virginia Woolf, A Centenary Perspective*, London: Macmillan, pp. 12–27.
— (1996), *Virginia Woolf*, London: Vintage.
— (2008), 'Writers' Rooms: Virginia Woolf', guardian.co.uk, 13 June, Available at: https://www.theguardian.com/books/2008/jun/13/writers.rooms.virginia.woolf (accessed 3 August 2010).
Light, Alison (2007), *Mrs Woolf and the Servants*, London: Penguin.
Lloyd, Genevieve (1993), *Being in Time: Selves and Narrators in Philosophy and Literature*, London: Routledge.
Losey, Jay B. (1989), 'Pater's Epiphanies and the Open Form', *South Central Review*, 6:4, 30–50.
Macann, Christopher (1993), *Four Phenomenological Philosophers: Husserl, Heidegger, Sartre, Merleau-Ponty*, New York: Routledge.
McCracken, Scott (2013), 'All Bets are Off: Woolf, Benjamin, and the Problem of the Future in *Jacob's Room*', *Le Tour Critique*, 2, 31–43.
Maggio, Paula (2010), 'Digging for Buried Treasure: Theories about Weather and Fiction in Virginia Woolf's Essays', *Virginia Woolf Miscellany*, 78, 23–6.
Malpas, Jeff (1999), *Place and Experience: A Philosophical Topography*, Cambridge: Cambridge University Press.
— (2008), *Heidegger's Topology: Being, Place, World*, Cambridge, MA: MIT Press.
Manoussakis, John Panteleimon (2006), 'The Sojourn in the Light', Introduction, in D. A. Hyland and J. P. Manoussakis (eds), *Heidegger and the Greeks: Interpretive Essays*, Bloomington: Indiana University Press, pp. 1–8.
Mannock, John (1815), *The Poor Man's Catechism: Or, the Christian Doctrine Explained. With Short Admonitions*, Baltimore: Bernard Dornin.
Martin, Biddy and Mohanty, Chandra Talpade (1986), 'Feminist Politics: What's Home Got to Do With It?', in T. de Lauretis (ed.), *Feminist Studies/Critical Studies*, Bloomington: Indiana University Press, pp. 191–212.
Maude, Ulrika and Feldman, Matthew (eds) (2009), *Beckett and Phenomenology*, London: Continuum.

Moore, Madeline (1980), 'Nature and Community: A Study of Cyclical Reality in *The Waves*', in R. Freedman (ed.), *Virginia Woolf: Revaluation and Continuity*, Berkeley: University of California Press, pp. 219–40.

Mulhall, Stephen (2003), *Routledge Philosophy GuideBook to Heidegger and* Being and Time, London: Routledge.

Nagel, Rebecca (2002), 'Virginia Woolf on Reading Greek', *The Classical World*, 96:1, 61–75.

Nichols, Ashton (1987), *The Poetics of Epiphany: Nineteenth-Century Origins of the Modern Literary Moment*, Tuscaloosa: University of Alabama Press.

Olk, Claudia (2014), *Virginia Woolf and the Aesthetics of Vision*, Berlin: Walter de Gruyter GmbH.

Olson, Liesl (2003), 'Virginia Woolf's "Cotton Wool of Daily Life"', *Journal of Modern Literature*, 26:2, 42–65.

— (2009), *Modernism and the Ordinary*, Oxford: Oxford University Press.

Otto, Rudolph (1958), *The Idea of the Holy: An Inquiry into the Non-rational Factor in the Idea of the Divine and Its Relation to the Rational*, trans. John W. Harvey, 2nd edn, London: Oxford University Press. (Originally published in German as *Das Heilige*, 1917.)

Overgaard, Søren (2004), 'Heidegger on Embodiment', *Journal of the British Society for Phenomenology*, 35:2, 116–31.

Parkes, Graham (1982), 'Imagining Reality in *To the Lighthouse*', *Philosophy and Literature*, 6.1 and 6.2, 33–44.

Patmore, Coventry (2006), *The Angel in the House*, Teddington: The Echo Library.

Peach, Linden (1999), 'No Longer a View: Virginia Woolf in the 1930s and the 1930s in Virginia Woolf', in M. Joannou (ed.), *Women Writers of the 1930s: Gender, Politics, and History*, Edinburgh: Edinburgh University Press, pp. 192–204.

Pease, Allison (2012), *Modernism, Feminism, and the Culture of Boredom*, New York: Cambridge University Press.

Pezze, Barbara Dalle and Salzani, Carlo (2009), 'The Delicate Monster: Modernity and Boredom', Introduction, in B. Dalle Pezze and C. Salzani (eds), *Essays on Boredom and Modernity*, Amsterdam: Rodopi, pp. 5–34.

Pheby, Keith C. (1988), *Interventions: Displacing the Metaphysical Subject*, Washington, DC: Maisonneuve.

Poole, Roger (1991), '"We All Put Up With You Virginia": Irreceivable Wisdom about War', in M. Hussey (ed.), *Virginia Woolf and War: Fiction, Reality, and Myth*, New York: Syracuse University Press.

Prudente, Teresa (2009), *A Specially Tender Piece of Eternity: Virginia Woolf and the Experience of Time*, Lanham: Lexington Books.

Quinones, Ricardo J. (1985), *Mapping Literary Modernisms: Time and Development*, Princeton: Princeton University Press.

Rattigan, Neil (2001), *This is England: British Film and the People's War, 1939–1945*, Plainsboro Township: Associated University Press.
Reese, Judy S. (1996), *Recasting Social Values in the Work of Virginia Woolf*, Selinsgrove: Susquehanna University Press.
Relph, Edward (1976), *Place and Placelessness*, London: Pion.
— (2000), 'Geographical Experiences and Being-in-the-World: The Phenomenological Origins of Geography', in D. Seamon and R. Mugerauer (eds), *Dwelling, Place and Environment: Towards a Phenomenology of Person and World*, Malabar: Kreiger, pp. 15–31.
Reynolds, Jack (2010), 'Jacques Derrida (1930–2004)', *Internet Encyclopedia of Philosophy*. Available at: http://www.iep.utm.edu/derrida/#SH7b (accessed 22 September 2012).
Ricoeur, Paul (1986), *Time and Narrative*, Vol. 2, trans. K. McLaughlin and D. Pellauer, Chicago: University of Chicago Press.
Rosenbaum, S. P. (1971), 'The Philosophical Realism of Virginia Woolf', in S. P. Rosenbaum (ed.), *English Literature and British Philosophy*, Chicago: University of Chicago Press, pp. 316–56.
— (2013), 'Virginia Woolf among the Apostles', *Le Tour Critique*, 2, 131–46.
Rosenthal, Edna (2013), 'Ethos or Mythos? The Implicit History of Woolf's Modern Sublime', *Le Tour Critique*, 2, 277–90.
Rosner, Victoria (2005), *Modernism and the Architecture of Private Life*, New York: Columbia University Press.
Rotberg, Robert I. (2010), 'Biography and Historiography: Mutual Evidentiary and Interdisciplinary Considerations', *Journal of Interdisciplinary History*, 40:3, 305–24.
Rubenstein, Mary-Jane (2006), 'A Certain Disavowal: The Pathos and Politics of Wonder', *Princeton Theological Review*, 35, 11–17.
— (2011), *Strange Wonder: The Closure of Metaphysics and the Opening of Awe*, New York: Columbia University Press.
Ruotolo, Lucio P. (1973), *Six Existential Heroes: The Politics of Faith*, Cambridge, MA: Harvard University Press.
— (1986), *The Interrupted Moment: A View of Virginia Woolf's Novels*, Redwood City: Stanford University Press.
Safranski, Rüdiger (2002), *Martin Heidegger: Between Good and Evil*, trans. E. Osers, Cambridge, MA: Harvard University Press.
Schatzki, Theodore R. (1991), 'Spatial Ontology and Explanation', *Annals of the Association of American Geographers*, 81:4, 650–70.
Schiff, Karen (1997), 'Moments of Reading and Woolf's Literary Criticism', in B. C. Rosenberg and J. Dubino (eds), *Virginia Woolf and the Essay*, New York: St Martin's Press, pp. 177–92.
Sharr, Adam (2006), *Heidegger's Hut*, Cambridge, MA: MIT Press.
Sheringham, Michael (2009), *Everyday Life: Theories and Practices from Surrealism to the Present*, Oxford: Oxford University Press.

Sim, Lorraine (2010), *Virginia Woolf: The Patterns of Ordinary Experience*, Farnham: Ashgate Publishing.

Simpson, Kathryn (2010), '"Street Haunting," Commodity Culture, and the Woman Artist', in E. F. Evan and S. E. Cornish (eds), *Woolf and the City: Selected Papers from the Nineteenth Annual Conference on Virginia Woolf*, Clemson: Clemson University Digital Press, pp. 47–54.

Snaith, Anna (2000), *Virginia Woolf: Public and Private Negotiations*, New York: St Martin's Press.

Snaith, Anna and Michael W. Whitworth (2007), Introduction, in A. Snaith and M. W. Whitworth (eds), *Locating Woolf: The Politics of Space and Place*, Basingstoke: Palgrave Macmillan, pp. 1–28.

Son, Youngjoo (2006), *Here and Now: The Politics of Social Space in D. H. Lawrence and Virginia Woolf*, New York: Routledge.

Spiropoulou, Angeliki (2010), *Virginia Woolf, Modernity and History: Constellations with Walter Benjamin*, Basingstoke: Palgrave Macmillan.

Squier, Susan M. (1983), '"The London Scene": Gender and Class in Virginia Woolf's London', *Twentieth-Century Literature*, 29:4, 488–500.

— (1985), *Virginia Woolf and London*, Chapel Hill: University of North Carolina Press.

— (1991), 'Virginia Woolf's London and the Feminist Revision of Modernism', in M. A. Caws (ed.), *City Images: Perspectives from Literature, Philosophy, and Film*, New York: Gordon and Breach Science, pp. 99–119.

Steinberg, Erwin R., 'G. E. Moore's Table and Chair in *To the Lighthouse*', *Journal of Modern Literature*, 15:1, 161–8.

Steiner, George (1991), *Martin Heidegger: with a New Introduction*, Chicago: University of Chicago Press.

Stone, Brad Elliott (2006), 'Curiosity as the Thief of Wonder: An Essay on Heidegger's Critique of the Ordinary Conception of Time', *KronoScope*, 6:2, 205–29.

Storl, Heidi (2008), 'Heidegger in Woolf's Clothing', *Philosophy and Literature*, 32:2, 303–14.

Svenaeus, Fredrik (2000a), 'The Body Uncanny: Further Steps Towards a Phenomenology of Illness,' *Medicine, Health Care and Philosophy*, 3:2, 125–37.

— (2000b), 'Das Unheimlich: Towards a Phenomenology of Illness', *Medicine, Health Care and Philosophy*, 3:1, 3–16.

— (2011), 'Illness as Unhomelike Being-in-the-world: Heidegger and the Phenomenology of Medicine', *Medicine, Health Care and Philosophy*, 14:3, 333–43.

Taylor, Dennis (1986), 'Hardy and Wordsworth', *Victorian Poetry*, 24:4, 441–54.

Tetsuro, Watsuji (1988), *Climate and Culture: A Philosophical Study*, trans. G. Bownas, New York: Greenwood.

Thiele, Leslie Paul (1995), *Timely Meditations: Martin Heidegger and Postmodern Politics*, Princeton: Princeton University Press.
— (1997), 'Postmodernity and the Routinization of Novelty: Heidegger on Boredom and Technology', *Polity*, 29:4, 489–517.
Toth, Naomi (2013), '"The very jar on the nerves": Reading Lily Briscoe's Painting with Phenomenology', *Le Tour Critique*, 2, 339–52.
Tratner, Michael (1995), *Modernism and Mass Politics: Joyce, Woolf, Eliot, Yeats*, Redwood City: Stanford University Press.
Tremper, Ellen (1998), *Who Lived at Alfoxton?: Virginia Woolf and English Romanticism*, London: Associated University Presses.
Truss, Lynne (2005), *Eats, Shoots & Leaves*, London: Profile Books.
Wakefield, Jason (2013), 'Mrs. Dalloway's Existential Temporality', *Cosmos and History: The Journal of Natural and Social Philosophy*, 9:2, 60–67.
Walsh, Kelly S. (2009), 'The Unbearable Openness of Death: Elegies of Rilke and Woolf', *Journal of Modern Literature*, 32:4, 1–21.
Wenaus, Andrew C. (2013), 'Metaphor and Metanoia: Linguistic Transfer and Cognitive Transformation in British and Irish Modernism,' PhD thesis, University of Western Ontario.
Whitworth, Michael H. (2006), 'Virginia Woolf and Modernism', in S. Roe and S. Sellers (eds), *The Cambridge Companion to Virginia Woolf*, Cambridge: Cambridge University Press, pp. 146–64.
— (2010), 'Virginia Woolf, Modernism and Modernity', in S. Sellers (ed.), *The Cambridge Companion to Virginia Woolf*, 2nd edn, Cambridge: Cambridge University Press, pp. 107–23.
Wirth-Nesher, Hana (1996), *City Codes: Reading the Modern Urban Novel*, Cambridge: Cambridge University Press.
Wolff, Janet (1985), 'The Invisible *Flâneuse*: Women and the Literature of Modernity', *Theory, Culture & Society*, 2:3, 37–46.
Woolf, Leonard (1975), *Downhill All the Way*, Orlando: Harvest/HBJ.
— (1989), *Letters of Leonard Woolf*, ed. F. Spotts, Orlando: Harcourt.
Woolf, Virginia (1917), 'Lord Jim', *Times Literary Supplement*, 26 July, 355.
— (1924), 'Joseph Conrad', *Times Literary Supplement*, 14 August, 493–4.
— (1928), 'Thomas Hardy's Novels', *Times Literary Supplement*, 19 January, 33–4.
— (1937), 'The Historian and "The Gibbon"', *Times Literary Supplement*, 24 April, 297–8.
— (1942a), 'The Art of Biography', in V. Woolf, *The Death of the Moth and Other Essays*, London: Hogarth Press, pp. 119–26.
— (1942b), 'Craftsmanship', in V. Woolf, *The Death of the Moth and Other Essays*, London: Hogarth Press, pp. 126–32.
— (1942d), 'Professions for Women', in V. Woolf, *The Death of the Moth and Other Essays*, London: Hogarth Press, pp. 149–54.
— (1942e), 'Street Haunting: A London Adventure', in V. Woolf, *The Death of the Moth and Other Essays*, London: Hogarth Press, pp. 19–29.

— (1960), 'The Narrow Bridge of Art' in V. Woolf, *Granite and Rainbow*, London: Hogarth Press, pp. 11–23.
— (1962a), 'Jane Austen', in V. Woolf, *The Common Reader*, First Series, London: Hogarth Press, pp. 168–83.
— (1962b), 'Modern Fiction', in V. Woolf, *The Common Reader*, First Series, London: Hogarth Press, pp. 84–95.
— (1965), 'Moments of Vision', in V. Woolf, *Contemporary Writers*, London: Hogarth Press, pp. 74–6.
— (1966a), 'Mr. Bennett and Mrs. Brown', in V. Woolf, *Collected Essays*, Vol. 1, London: Hogarth Press, pp. 319–37.
— (1966b), 'The Novels of George Meredith', in V. Woolf, *Collected Essays*. Vol. 1, London: Hogarth Press, pp. 224–32.
— (1968), 'On Not Knowing Greek', in V. Woolf, *Collected Essays*, Vol. 1, London: Hogarth Press, pp. 1–13.
— (1975–80), *The Letters of Virginia Woolf*, ed. N. Nicolson and J. Trautmann, 6 vols, Orlando: Harvest/Harcourt Brace Jovanovich.
— (1977–84), *The Diary of Virginia Woolf*, ed. A. O. Bell, 5 vols, San Diego: Harcourt Brace & Company.
— (1978), 'The Captain's Death Bed', in V. Woolf, *The Captain's Death Bed and Other Essays*, Orlando: Harcourt, pp. 37–47.
— (1981a), 'The Artist and Politics', in V. Woolf, *The Moment and Other Essays*, London: Hogarth Press, pp. 180–2.
— (1981b), 'Half of Thomas Hardy', in V. Woolf, *The Captain's Death Bed and Other Essays*, London: Hogarth Press, pp. 61–6.
— (1981c), 'The Moment: Summer's Night', in V. Woolf, *The Moment and Other Essays*, London: Hogarth Press, pp. 9–13.
— (1981d), 'Mr. Conrad: A Conversation', in V. Woolf, *The Captain's Death Bed and Other Essays*, London: Hogarth Press, pp. 74–8.
— (1981e), 'On Being Ill', in V. Woolf, *The Moment and Other Essays*, London: Hogarth Press, pp. 14–24.
— (1981f), 'Reading', in V. Woolf, *The Captain's Death Bed and Other Essays*, London: Hogarth Press, pp. 40–65.
— (1986a), 'De Quincey's Autobiography', in V. Woolf, *The Second Common Reader*, ed. A. McNeillie, Orlando: Harcourt, pp. 132–9.
— (1986b), 'Modes and Manners of the Nineteenth Century', in V. Woolf, *The Essays of Virginia Woolf*, ed. A. McNeillie, Vol. 1, London: Hogarth Press, pp. 330–4.
— (1986c), 'The Niece of an Earl', in V. Woolf, *The Second Common Reader*, ed. A. McNeillie. Orlando: Harcourt, pp. 214–19.
— (1986d), 'Two Parsons', in V. Woolf, *The Second Common Reader*, ed. A. McNeillie, Orlando: Harcourt, pp. 93–107.
— (1987), 'Romance', in V. Woolf, *The Essays of Virginia Woolf*, ed. A. McNeillie, Vol. 2, San Diego: Harcourt, pp. 73–5.
— (1989a), 'The Journal of Mistress Joan Martyn', in V. Woolf, *The Complete Shorter Fiction of Virginia Woolf*, 2nd edn, ed. S. Dick, San Diego: Harcourt, pp. 33–62.

— (1989b), 'Phyllis and Rosamond', in V. Woolf, *The Complete Shorter Fiction of Virginia Woolf*, 2nd edn, ed. S. Dick, San Diego: Harcourt, pp. 17–29.
— (1989c), 'Solid Objects', in V. Woolf, *The Complete Shorter Fiction of Virginia Woolf*, 2nd edn, ed. S. Dick, San Diego: Harcourt, pp. 102–7.
— (1990), *A Passionate Apprentice: The Early Journals, 1897–1909*, ed. M. A. Leaska, San Diego: Harcourt Brace Jovanovich.
— (1992a [1919]), *Night and Day*, London: Vintage.
— (1992b [1927]), *To the Lighthouse*, London: Vintage.
— (1994), 'The New Biography', in V. Woolf, *The Essays of Virginia Woolf*, Vol. 4, ed. A. McNeillie, London: Hogarth Press, pp. 473–80.
— (1996 [1925]), *Mrs Dalloway*, Camberwell, Melbourne, Australia: Penguin.
— (1998 [1933]), *Flush*, ed. K. Flint, Oxford: Oxford University Press.
— (2000a [1941]), *Between the Acts*, ed. S. McNichol, London: Penguin.
— (2000b [1922]), *Jacob's Room*, ed. K. Flint, Oxford: Oxford University Press.
— (2000c [1928]), *Orlando*, ed. B. Lyons, London: Penguin.
— (2000d [1929/1938]), *A Room of One's Own; Three Guineas*, ed. M. Schiach, Oxford: Oxford University Press.
— (2000e [1931]), *The Waves*, ed. K. Flint, London: Penguin.
— (2001 [1915]), *The Voyage Out*, ed. L. Sage, Oxford: Oxford University Press.
— (2002a), 'Am I a Snob?', in V. Woolf, *Moments of Being*, new edn, ed. J. Schulkind, London: Pimlico, pp. 62–77.
— (2002b), 'Old Bloomsbury', in V. Woolf, *Moments of Being*, new edn, ed. J. Schulkind. London: Pimlico, pp. 43–61.
— (2002c), 'Reminiscences', in V. Woolf, *Moments of Being*, new edn, ed. J. Schulkind. London: Pimlico, pp. 1–30.
— (2002d), 'A Sketch of the Past', in V. Woolf, *Moments of Being*, new edn, ed. J. Schulkind, London: Pimlico, pp. 78–160.
— (2002e), *The Years*, ed. J. Johnson, London: Penguin.
— (2003a), 'The Mark on the Wall', in V. Woolf, *Monday or Tuesday*, London: Hesperus, pp. 59–68.
— (2003b), 'Monday or Tuesday', in V. Woolf, *Monday or Tuesday*, London: Hesperus, pp. 25–6.
— (2006a), 'Abbeys and Cathedrals,' in V. Woolf, *The London Scene: Six Essays on London Life*, New York: HarperCollins, pp. 41–51.
— (2006b), 'Great Men's Houses', in V. Woolf, *The London Scene: Six Essays on London Life*, New York: HarperCollins, pp. 29–39.
— (2006c), 'Oxford Street Tide', in V. Woolf, *The London Scene: Six Essays on London Life*, New York: HarperCollins, pp. 17–27.
— (2006d), 'Portrait of a Londoner', in V. Woolf, *The London Scene: Six Essays on London Life*, New York: HarperCollins, pp. 67–77.

Wordsworth, William (1995), *The Prelude: The Four Texts (1798, 1799, 1805, 1850)*, ed. J. Wordsworth. London: Penguin.
Wyatt, Jean (1978), 'The Celebration of Eros: Greek Concepts of Love and Beauty in *To the Lighthouse*', *Philosophy and Literature*, 2:2, 160–75.
Young, Iris Marion (1980), 'Throwing Like a Girl: A Phenomenology of Feminine Body Comportment Motility and Spatiality', *Human Studies*, 3:2, 137–56.
— (1997), *Intersecting Voices: Dilemmas of Gender, Political Philosophy, and Policy*, Princeton: Princeton University Press.
— (2002), 'Lived Body Vs Gender: Reflections on Social Structure and Subjectivity', *Ratio* ns, 15:4, 410–28.
Young, Julian (2001), *Heidegger's Philosophy of Art*, Cambridge: Cambridge University Press.
Zimmerman, Michael E. (1990), *Heidegger's Confrontation with Modernity: Technology, Politics, and Art*, Bloomington: Indiana University Press.
Zwerdling, Alex (1977), '*Mrs. Dalloway* and the Social System', *PMLA*, 92:1, 69–82.
— (1986), *Virginia Woolf and the Real World*, Berkeley: University of California Press.

Index

ambiguity, 28, 54–5, 61, 91, 95, 101n, 113, 221
angst *see* anxiety
anxiety, 17, 23, 107–11, 115, 137, 185, 200–8, 210, 217; *see also* nothingness; uncanny
architecture *see* buildings
art, 9, 23, 34, 48, 133, 185, 194–5, 219, 223–4, 232, 234; *see also* writing
artist, 29, 32, 42, 60, 133, 185, 186, 194–5, 196–7, 219, 222–3, 225, 232
atmosphere, 6–7, 27, 32–8, 202; *see also* weather
attunement, 182, 194, 196, 198, 210, 214, 223
authentic appropriation, 103, 137, 149, 155–7, 163, 177; *see also* thrownness
authenticity, 10, 17, 19, 21, 46–7, 50–8, 60, 77, 103–4, 108, 110, 137, 141, 143, 146, 148–9, 151–2, 154–5, 157, 161, 163–4, 177–8, 179n, 185–6, 194, 196, 200–1, 205, 211, 214, 217–18, 224, 230; *see also* inauthenticity; resoluteness
authority, 29, 45, 55, 59–60, 74, 88–9, 144–5
autobiography, 22, 79, 102, 134, 138n, 189, 191, 192, 215; *see also* biography
average everydayness, 1, 26–7, 47–51, 55, 64, 65, 66, 68, 70–1, 79, 80, 91, 93, 99, 102, 103, 107, 115–17, 121–2, 128, 133, 135, 136, 144, 145–6, 148–9, 170–3, 175–6, 182, 184–5, 187–8, 189, 194, 197, 199, 200, 202, 204–5, 207–9, 211, 213–15, 217, 219, 224–5, 231–2, 233; *see also* concealment; quotidian

Being, 2, 11, 17, 18, 26, 28–9, 30, 31, 40, 48, 54–5, 60, 62, 77, 103, 115, 116, 138n, 144, 149, 151, 172, 224, 227n, 228n, 230, 232
  Woolf definition, 148–9, 184, 228n
  see also Being-in-the-world; non-Being
Being-at-home, 10, 20, 102–39, 196, 235; *see also* homelessness
Being-in-the-world, 25–63
  definition, 1–2, 28, 31

Being-towards-death, 17, 19, 56, 57, 141, 153–6, 200–8, 226n; *see also* death; nothingness
Being-with-Others, 1, 27, 36–47, 62n, 66, 68, 71, 79–84, 87–8, 93, 99, 105, 134, 136, 158, 204, 235; *see also* distance; intersubjectivity
belonging, 46, 59, 93, 96, 102, 111–12, 120, 131, 164–5; *see also* Being-at-home
binary oppositions, 1, 22, 29–31, 62, 92, 94, 165, 229, 235
  gender, 92, 94–5, 166
  inside and outside, 66, 112–13, 125, 226n
  insider and outsider, 22, 93–7, 99, 111–14, 235
  mind and body, 31, 41, 118, 196
  public and private, 22, 125–7, 134, 161–2, 231
  self and Other, 1, 21, 28, 31, 235
  self and world, 27–34, 226n, 235
  subject and object, 1, 19, 21, 28–31, 35
  see also Descartes, René
biography, 12, 20, 34–5, 66, 73–4, 131–2, 140–1, 147, 155, 164, 167, 169–75, 177, 178n, 179n, 180n, 234; *see also* autobiography
Bloomsbury, 89, 100n, 104–9, 137n
Bloomsbury group, 8, 14, 168
body, 8, 31, 41, 114, 116, 118, 123, 137n–8n, 196, 200, 220, 226n
  embodiment, 24, 116–17, 119–20, 137n–8n, 200, 232
  inscription, 121–2
  lived body, 20, 103, 114–21, 122
  see also homelessness; illness
boredom, 13, 19, 185, 208–15, 217, 227n
boundaries, 38, 90, 96, 125, 226n
buildings, 37, 77–8, 80–2, 89, 102, 123–4, 129, 130, 138n
  public, 88–92
  universities, 92, 93, 124, 163
  see also home; religion; walls

capitalism, 36–7, 72, 75
care, 19, 133–4; *see also* solicitude

childhood, 33, 39, 80, 83, 110–12, 132, 189–93, 215–16
  Woolf, 67, 69, 84, 98, 106, 121, 165, 185, 189, 191–2, 193, 215, 224
class, 7, 9, 11, 22, 23, 34, 36, 37, 47, 55, 65, 71, 72–6, 89, 100n, 101n, 108, 113–14, 122–4, 169, 171, 177, 231, 232; *see also* socio-economic
climate *see* weather
collective, 41, 56, 68, 137, 141, 151–2, 158–60, 235
  history, 10, 23, 150, 152–3, 158–9, 162–3, 173, 177, 235
  see also destiny
concealment, 23, 36, 44, 47, 53, 55, 57, 60–2, 107, 130, 142, 146, 148–51, 155–6, 163–4, 172, 175, 184–5, 195, 203–5, 208–9, 211, 213–15, 220, 224; *see also* unconcealment
conformity, 22, 46, 48, 51–3, 57, 59, 88, 91, 107, 109–11, 145, 163, 186; *see also* theyness
Conrad, Joseph, 23, 186–9, 225n
contingency *see* thrownness
Cornwall *see* Talland House
cotton wool *see* non-Being
curiosity, 19, 28, 54–5, 58, 61, 105, 217–18

Dasein, 2, 77, 91, 94, 104, 107–8, 115, 117, 134, 144, 149, 151–2, 154, 158, 182, 203, 230
de-severance, 40, 66, 83–8; *see also* nearness
death, 3, 19, 34, 42–3, 53, 57, 69–70, 80, 83, 105, 118, 130, 133–4, 141, 152–3, 155, 156, 158, 159, 176, 180n, 197, 203, 205–7, 224, 226n, 227n, 228n; *see also* Being-towards-death
Descartes, René, 1, 19, 21, 27, 28–31
destiny, 10, 158–9, 235; *see also* collective
disclosure *see* unconcealment
disconnection, 27, 40–6, 56, 83, 85, 111–12, 135; *see also* distance
dispersal, 53–5, 61, 106, 188
distance, 43, 46, 54, 57, 84–5, 113, 135, 197, 204, 214
  between self and Other, 46, 83–8, 112, 235
  physical, 66, 74, 83, 85–7
  see also de-severance; disconnection; nearness
domestic workers, 39, 70, 73, 118, 122–3, 169–70
doors, 22, 40, 50, 72, 102, 113, 121, 124–7, 130, 168, 197
dualisms *see* binary oppositions
dwelling, 31, 102, 124, 130, 137, 138n, 233

ecstases, 142–5, 219, 224, 226n; *see also* fallenness; projection; thrownness

education, 7, 28, 57, 166
  exclusion of women, 13–14, 57, 92, 93, 96, 124, 135, 160–1, 162–3
  see also buildings
Edwardians, 39, 60
empathy, 40, 94
engagement, 25, 27, 28, 30, 31, 45, 47, 53, 62, 65, 98, 114, 137n, 228n, 230; *see also* involvement
English society, 6, 22, 28, 48–9, 57, 60, 62, 63n, 64–5, 71, 73–4, 75–6, 90–1, 93, 96–7, 99, 106, 108, 110, 125, 127, 159, 162, 164–5, 201, 231
epiphany, 185–9, 194, 224
  epiphanal moments, 184–6, 190–1, 198, 201, 216
  literary, 23, 185, 186–7, 189, 225n
  see also moments of Being; moments of vision
equipment, 27, 77, 82
everyday *see* average everydayness
exceptional moments *see* moments of Being
exclusion, 11, 13, 23, 64, 66, 89, 93, 95–7, 98, 118, 126, 141, 161, 163, 165–70, 176
exile, 67, 96–7, 110
existential-ontological, 11, 32, 102, 108, 151, 230
existential-phenomenology, 1, 17, 114–15
existentialism, 1, 11, 17–18, 22, 32, 46, 66, 68–71, 84, 86, 94, 99, 102, 107–8, 112, 114–15, 117, 136, 151, 172, 182, 185, 188, 226n, 230, 235; *see also* involvement
extraordinary, 23, 184, 185, 188, 194, 199, 210, 217, 218–19, 223, 224–5; *see also* ordinary

facticity, 24, 45, 114–15, 136, 144, 230, 232–3
fallenness, 19, 49–50, 107–8, 111, 142, 149, 161, 187; *see also* ecstases
fate, 84, 97, 115, 153–6, 158, 160, 177; *see also* thrownness
feminism, 7, 8, 11, 14, 53, 92, 100n, 180n

gender, 11, 22, 24, 37, 71, 75, 94–6, 114–17, 122, 137n, 160, 171, 231
Georgians, 39–40, 60, 123
Germany, 4, 10, 142, 159
  post-WWI, 10, 21, 142, 179n
  Weimar, 10–11
gossip, 54–6, 60, 223
Greek literature, 14, 32–3, 96, 162, 180n, 234, 236n
Greek philosophy, 14, 17, 96, 217, 234
guest, 93–8; *see also* host; outsider-within

Hardy, Thomas, 23, 184, 186, 187–9, 225n
Heidegger, Martin
    critical responses, 21
    influence of war, 2–4, 10, 21, 142, 179n
    modernity, 4
    Nazism, 11–12
    politics, 5, 10–12, 48, 104, 163–4
    texts, 13
Heidegger and Woolf see Woolf and Heidegger
heritage, 154, 163
hierarchies, 11, 25, 28, 64, 75–6, 99, 136, 180n
historical discourse, 20, 21, 23, 140–2, 165–70, 172–7, 178n, 179n
historiography, 142, 166, 170, 180n
historicism see historical discourse
historicity, 147, 150–1, 177–8, 179n
history, 40, 140–82, 228n
    marginalised, 141, 166, 169, 172, 174, 175–7
    see also collective: history
home, 22, 61, 64, 95, 99, 102–39, 235
    built form, 41, 69–70, 74, 76–9, 102, 104–5, 121–7
    domestic space, 92, 117–18, 125, 127–8, 131, 134–5, 161–2
    Woolf, 57, 69, 137n, 138n, 208
    see also Being-at home; homelessness-at-home
homelessness, 10, 22, 92, 99, 102–39, 196, 207, 235
    -at-home, 22, 103, 110, 118, 131–2, 135–6
    unembodiment, 119–20
    see also outsider; thrownness; uncanny
homogeneity, 55, 97
    time, 23, 141–3, 148, 177
    truth, 61–2
homosexuality, 59
host, 95–6
hotel, 82–3, 113
Hyde Park Gate see Kensington

ideology, 5–6, 8, 11, 27, 35, 39, 48, 57, 58, 62, 64, 89, 141, 160, 173, 189, 230, 233
idle talk, 19, 28, 54–7, 60–1, 63n, 204, 205, 214
illness, 8, 185, 195–200, 226n; see also mental illness
imperialism, 9, 10, 14, 23, 31, 66, 153, 158–9, 231, 235
inauthentic appropriation, 141, 155
inauthenticity, 21, 23, 27, 45–8, 50–5, 94, 103–4, 108–10, 115, 136, 141, 142, 144, 146, 148–9, 151–2, 154–5, 157–8, 160–5, 172, 179n, 184–5, 189, 206, 214, 217, 224, 230; see also fallenness; inauthentic appropriation; stream
inclusion, 64, 89, 93, 96, 124, 161, 170
industrialisation, 10, 36–7, 68, 210
insider, 22, 95–6, 97, 111–13, 126, 235; see also binary oppositions
intersubjectivity, 1, 18, 27, 38–47, 81, 85, 105; see also Being-with-Others
involvement, 1, 22, 24, 25, 27, 29–32, 53, 65–6, 68–71, 83–8, 91, 99, 102, 112, 116–17, 122, 128, 138n, 149, 155, 185, 197, 208, 230; see also existentialism
isolation, 45, 64, 86, 97–8, 107, 128, 191

Kensington, 59, 69, 104–9, 123

language, 233–4
literature, 32, 34, 39, 48, 60, 100n, 145, 170, 194, 219, 223
London, 20, 22, 30, 31, 35–7, 42, 44, 48, 52, 54, 65–8, 71, 72–3, 75, 80–1, 85, 87–90, 96, 99–100n, 101n, 104–7, 113, 129, 132, 156, 159, 208, 216, 224

marginalisation, 23, 101n, 141, 165–7, 169–77; see also exclusion; history
media, 7, 40–1, 51, 55, 63n, 161–2, 176
medical profession, 28, 31, 58, 97, 109–10, 144, 160–1
memories, 64, 79, 80–1, 88, 98, 130–2, 133, 150–1, 163, 176, 182, 188, 191
mental illness, 58, 67–8, 97, 109, 185, 195–200, 208, 226n; see also illness
metaphysics, 29–31, 61–2, 210, 229
    time, 23, 142–4, 146, 148, 166, 177, 210
    see also time: linear
milieu, 3–5, 7–8, 25, 142, 235; see also social: context
modernism, 3–4, 15, 16, 17, 99n, 100n, 141, 179n, 180n, 186, 203
modernity, 2–5, 10, 28–9, 62, 209–10, 217
moments of Being, 20, 23, 184, 185–6, 189, 191–3, 195, 201, 217, 222, 224–5, 226n
moments of vision, 177–8, 184, 186–9, 193–5, 197–8, 201, 207, 211, 222, 225, 227n
Monk's House, 67, 79, 99n, 129, 208, 211, 222
moods, 13, 17, 23, 26, 99n, 107, 182–4, 198, 199, 201–2, 208; see also anxiety; boredom; wonder
Moore, G. E., 14–16

nationalism, 7, 9, 66, 93, 96, 99, 158, 162, 182, 231, 235
nature, 77
Nazism, 11–12, 159

nearness, 83–8, 101n; *see also* de-severance; distance
newspapers *see* media
non-Being, 47, 148, 172, 184, 189, 191
  cotton wool, 148, 184, 191–2, 194, 197, 224–5
  see also Being
not-Being-at-home *see* homelessness; uncanny
nothingness, 17, 18–19, 23, 109, 185, 200–8, 211, 219, 227n; *see also* Being-towards-death
numinous, 185, 219–23, 228n

objects, 22, 25, 30, 31, 34, 98, 102, 119, 131–6, 138n–9n, 190, 198, 216, 220; *see also* tables
obscure, 123, 166–9, 172–3, 184–5, 205
ontic, 91, 102, 151, 198
ontological, 2, 5, 11, 18, 30, 48, 114, 117, 134, 137, 172, 182, 198, 207, 224, 226n, 232; *see also* existential-ontological
openness, 32, 143, 146, 149, 182, 185, 190, 194, 218, 220, 225
ordinary, 23, 184, 185, 187, 188, 198–9, 201, 210, 216–20, 224–5; *see also* extraordinary; quotidian
Other, 1, 21–2, 27, 28, 29, 38–47, 51, 54, 56, 62n, 64, 66, 71, 75, 79–83, 84–8, 91, 94, 97, 98, 102, 134, 146, 184, 229, 235; *see also* Being-with-Others
outsider, 22, 45, 49, 59–60, 93, 95, 100n, 103, 110–14, 120, 124, 126–7, 164–5, 199–200, 235
  -within, 22, 93–8, 235
  see also binary oppositions; homelessness

patriarchy, 3, 7, 9, 22, 23, 31, 57, 66, 89, 90, 92, 103, 119, 125, 132, 136, 144, 160–2, 166, 177, 180n, 182, 231
performativity, 53, 117, 120, 169, 170, 176
phenomenology, 11, 13, 15–16, 26, 116–17, 138n, 144, 196, 203, 226n
place, 21–2, 64–101, 102–39, 194, 235
  private, 22, 70, 72, 103, 125–6, 127–31, 134–5, 144, 231
  public, 22, 66, 72, 88–90, 92, 96, 125, 127, 134, 231
  temporality, 75–9, 130–1
  see also home
political, 35, 48, 62, 99, 158, 160, 173, 180n, 188–9, 230
politics, 27, 34, 174–5
  definition, 5–6
possibilities, 10, 23, 27, 44, 46, 54, 78, 80, 86, 94, 98, 103–4, 107, 115, 124–5, 137, 141, 150–65, 177, 198, 200, 209, 225, 230, 233, 235; *see also* repetition; thrownness
present *see* time
professions, 135, 171, 175
  women, 57, 96, 106, 125, 126, 127, 135, 137n, 160–3, 164, 168
  see also medical profession
projection, 137, 141–2, 152, 157–60, 163–4, 230; *see also* ecstases
public places *see* place
public transport, 7, 31, 36, 38, 41, 46, 49, 51, 67, 91, 101n, 119, 151, 212–13, 223, 224, 233

quotidian, 26, 68, 70, 102, 185, 190, 197; *see also* ordinary

radio *see* media
reality, 16, 29, 51, 60–2, 174, 184, 193, 198–9, 207–8, 211, 221–5, 228n, 233
religion, 20, 28, 31, 34, 39, 58–9, 63n, 89–90, 125, 167, 169, 182, 220–2, 227n
  places of worship, 35, 36, 59, 89–90, 101n
repetition, 10, 141, 157–8, 160–5, 177–8; *see also* possibilities
resoluteness, 154, 177, 185, 228n, 230; *see also* authenticity
Richmond, 67–8, 79, 106
Rilke, Rainer Maria, 69
Rodmell *see* Monk's House
Romanticism, 185, 189–95, 216, 226n; *see also* Hardy, Thomas; Wordsworth, William
rooms, 22, 69–70, 78–80, 82, 102, 122–4, 126–32, 135
Russell, Bertrand, 14–16

St Ives *see* Talland House
scapegoat, 96–7, 101n, 235; *see also* outsider-within
sensations, 54, 58, 132, 182, 183–4, 191, 195, 198, 202, 212; *see also* moods
servants *see* domestic workers
social
  context, 7–8, 35, 57, 142, 160, 165, 230, 235
  order, 4, 5, 6, 8, 11, 22, 25, 28, 31, 36, 47, 49, 52–3, 55, 58–9, 66, 72, 76, 91–3, 98, 99, 103–4, 107, 109–10, 115, 119–20, 124, 127, 132, 134, 141, 160–1, 163, 165, 171, 173, 177, 182, 189, 230–2, 235
  prescriptions, 22, 23, 25, 39, 47–53, 55, 58, 59, 91, 97, 103–4, 108–9, 119–20, 122, 124, 126, 145, 146, 148, 165, 171, 172, 182, 211, 224, 230–1, 235
societal machine, 25, 28, 57–60, 207

society, 9, 25, 39, 45, 47, 49–50, 89, 91, 93, 103, 115, 142, 145, 173, 204; *see also* English society; social
socio-economic, 7, 8, 65, 72–5, 101n, 108, 181n, 210; *see also* class
solicitude, 40, 134; *see also* care; disconnection
solitude, 45, 64, 67, 82, 102, 129, 134, 208, 222
somnolence, 187, 188, 199
spatiality, 22, 64–5, 70, 79, 81–2, 83–4, 87, 91–4, 115, 116–17, 122, 124, 138n
Stephen, Leslie, 86, 140, 147, 167, 170, 178n, 179n, 180n
stranger, 93–5, 101n; *see also* outsider-within
stream, 47, 49–50, 55, 59, 148, 199, 203, 230; *see also* theyness
streets, 30–1, 37, 40, 44–5, 46, 52, 54, 64, 65, 70–5, 81, 85, 88, 90, 96, 100n, 113, 127, 144, 145, 152, 156, 159, 160, 197, 207, 214, 223, 224
subject and object *see* binary oppositions
suicide, 46–7, 51, 98, 138n, 192, 197, 205
synaesthesia, 198, 226n

tables, 26, 29–30, 43, 56, 70, 75, 79–80, 84, 110, 131–2, 134–6, 138n, 190, 205, 209, 212, 213, 219, 224
Talland House, 69, 98, 121, 191–2
technology, 10, 234
temporality, 20, 23, 65–6, 77, 137, 140–3, 146–7, 160, 210–11
  Dasein, 1, 19–20, 23, 77–8, 143, 147, 149, 151–2, 154, 157, 177–8, 179n, 190–1, 205, 212–13, 217
  see also historicity; homogeneity; place
theyness, 17, 19, 22, 27–8, 47–53, 55, 58–61, 94, 103, 107–10, 115, 117, 172, 184–6, 205, 230–1; *see also* Being-at-home; Being-with-Others; conformity; stream
thrownness, 19, 22, 103–4, 108–9, 114–15, 117, 120, 136–7, 141, 142, 150–3, 157, 159–60, 163–4, 180n, 200, 203, 207, 230; *see also* authentic appropriation; ecstases; fate; inauthentic appropriation; possibilities
time, 179n
  clock, 141, 144–6, 150–1, 179n, 212
  linear, 23, 77, 141–4, 146–7, 165–6, 180n,
  monumental, 144–5
  present, 23, 28, 77, 79, 131, 142–3, 144, 146–51, 153, 156, 172, 177–8, 186, 211, 213–14, 217, 232
  see also homogeneity; metaphysics; temporality

tradition, 7, 10, 13, 81, 102, 141, 161–5, 177, 180n
truth, 18, 56, 60–2, 133, 139n, 143, 175, 198, 204, 208–9, 219–21, 223–4, 229, 232

uncanny, 107–11, 196; *see also* anxiety; homelessness
unconcealment, 23, 50, 51–2, 55, 60–2, 81, 107–8, 114, 139n, 149, 172, 175, 183–6, 188, 192–5, 199, 201–6, 210–12, 214–16, 222–4, 230; *see also* concealment
understanding, 40, 55, 94, 149, 151
uniformity, 51, 57, 74, 91

Victorians, 9, 107, 123, 132, 134, 165, 170–1

walls, 26, 40, 43, 45, 69, 82, 90, 92, 102, 105, 130, 164
war, 2–5, 9, 23, 62n, 76, 81, 84, 139n, 141, 142, 151, 158–60, 161–2, 164, 167, 169, 174–5, 176, 179n, 180n, 181n, 201, 235
weather, 27, 32–8, 62n, 74, 98, 133, 159
wonder, 17, 18–19, 23, 44, 185, 190, 207, 215–20, 227n
Woolf, Virginia
  critical reception, 8–9, 16, 231
  influence of war, 2–4, 6, 7, 8, 62n, 66, 100n, 129, 142
  philosophy, 13–16
  politics, 5–9, 62, 98–9, 104, 231
Woolf and Heidegger, 24
  affinities, 1, 2, 4, 5, 16–20, 21–2, 29, 98–9, 104, 128–9, 133–4, 136, 138n, 148–9, 151–2, 157, 163–4, 172–3, 177–8, 183–4, 186, 196, 203, 204, 206, 211, 227n, 229–30, 233–4, 236n
  contemporaneity, 2–5
  critical responses, 17–20
  disanalogies, 1, 2, 4, 5, 10, 11, 27, 48, 99, 104, 117, 121–2, 138n, 158–9, 163, 183, 224, 228n, 230, 232–3
Wordsworth, William, 23, 82, 185, 189–90, 193–5, 225n, 226n
work, unpaid domestic, 118, 122, 125, 127, 132, 135, 162, 168; *see also* domestic workers; professions; work-world
work-world, 64, 82, 91, 128–30, 133; *see also* work
world, 1, 25–6, 61; *see also* Being-in-the-world
writing, 6, 9, 19, 32, 38, 47, 62, 92, 118, 163, 167, 168–9, 186, 193–5, 196–7, 223–5, 228n

EU representative:
Easy Access System Europe
Mustamäe tee 50, 10621 Tallinn, Estonia
Gpsr.requests@easproject.com